JOURNAL FOR THE STUDY OF THE OLD TESTAMENT SUPPLEMENT SERIES

91

Editors
David J.A. Clines
Philip R. Davies

JSOT Press
Sheffield

THE
IDEOLOGY
OF
RITUAL

Space, Time and Status
in the Priestly Theology

Frank H. Gorman, Jr.

Journal for the Study of the Old Testament
Supplement Series 91

In memory of
George and Laura Shepherd

Copyright © 1990 Sheffield Academic Press

Published by JSOT Press
JSOT Press is an imprint of
Sheffield Academic Press Ltd
The University of Sheffield
343 Fulwood Road
Sheffield S10 3BP
England

Typeset by Sheffield Academic Press
and
Printed in Great Britain
by Billing & Sons Ltd
Worcester

British Library Cataloguing in Publication Data
Gorman, Frank
  The ideology of ritual: space, time and status in the
  priestly theology
  1. Theology
  I. Title   II. Series
  230

ISSN 0309-0787
ISBN 1-85075-231-1

CONTENTS

Acknowledgments   3
Abbreviations   4
Introduction   7

Chapter 1
RITUAL: A METHODOLOGICAL FRAMEWORK   13

Chapter 2
PRIESTLY WORLD VIEW AND PRIESTLY RITUAL   39

Chapter 3
LEVITICUS 16   61

Chapter 4
LEVITICUS 8   103

Excursus I
EXODUS 34.29-35: MOSES THE EXALTED
   INAUGURATOR OF THE CULT   149

Chapter 5
LEVITICUS 14.1-20   151

Excursus II
THE ROLE OF BLOOD IN THE *KIPPER*-ACT
   BLOOD AS A SYMBOL OF LIFE AND DEATH   181

Chapter 6
NUMBERS 19   191

Chapter 7
NUMBERS 28–29   215

Conclusion   229
Bibliography   235
Index of Biblical References   249
Index of Authors   257

ACKNOWLEDGMENTS

The present work is a revision of my doctoral dissertation, written at Emory University under the supervision of Professor John Hayes. I want to express my deepest thanks to John for his encouragement and support in both academic matters and matters of life. In addition, a word of appreciation goes to Professors Martin Buss and Robert Paul, both at Emory University, for their contribution to my thinking on matters concerning ritual and culture.

I also want to say thank you to Professor Jacob Milgrom who read the dissertation and made extremely valuable comments and suggestions for the revision process. My debt to his work is clear from the beginning to the end of this work. I have also profited greatly during the revision process from conversation with Leo Perdue and Mary Knutsen. Each one of them helped me to clarify issues and push my work beyond its original scope. Of course, not all of the suggestions of these persons have been followed so that I must take full responsibility for the present argument. Three students at Bethany College, Bethany, West Virginia, have helped me in various ways with the preparation of the manuscript. David Warwick, Peter Jessic, and Ella Belling all deserve thanks for their help with the not so glamorous sides of publishing a book.

Finally, I want to thank my Mom and Dad for their continued encouragement and support, both financial and emotional, through the long years of education and on into the present.

ABBREVIATIONS

AA	*American Anthropologist*
AARSR	American Academy of Religion Studies in Religion
AJSoc	*American Journal of Sociology*
AmerSch	*American Scholar*
ASR	*American Sociological Review*
ASTI	*Annual of the Swedish Theological Institute*
ATR	*Anglican Theological Review*
BAR	*Biblical Archaeologist Reader*
BBB	Bonner biblische Beiträge
BES	Biblical Encounter Series
Bib	*Biblica*
BibT	*The Bible Today*
BSHT	Breslauer Studien zur historischen Theologie
BSR	Bibliothèque des Sciences religieuses
BTB	*Biblical Theology Bulletin*
BTFT	*Bijdragen. Tijdschrift voor filosophie en theologie*
BWANT	Beiträge zur Wissenschaft vom Alten und Neuen Testament
BZ	*Biblische Zeitschrift*
BZAW	Beihefte zur *ZAW*
CB	Coniectanea Biblica
CBQ	*Catholic Biblical Quarterly*
CurAnt	*Current Anthropology*
DBSup	*Dictionnaire de la Bible, Supplément*
EC	Études et Commentaires
EncJud	*Encyclopaedia Judaica*

FRLANT	Forschungen zur Religion und Literatur des Alten und Neuen Testaments
HAT	Handbuch zum Alten Testament
HR	*History of Religions*
HTR	*Harvard Theological Review*
HUCA	*Hebrew Union College Annual*
ICC	International Critical Commentary
IDBSup	*Interpreter's Dictionary of the Bible,* Supplementary Volume
IESS	*International Encyclopedia of the Social Sciences*
Int	*Interpretation*
JAAR	*Journal of the American Academy of Religion*
JAOS	*Journal of the American Oriental Society*
JBL	*Journal of Biblical Literature*
JHNES	Johns Hopkins Near Eastern Studies
JQR	*Jewish Quarterly Review*
JR	*Journal of Religion*
JRAI	*Journal of the Royal Anthropological Institute*
JSOT	*Journal for the Study of the Old Testament*
JSOTSup	Supplements to *JSOT*
JSS	*Journal of Semitic Studies*
LJLE	The Library of Jewish Law and Ethics
LTQ	*Lexington Theological Quarterly*
NCB	New Century Bible
NICOT	New International Commentary on the Old Testament
OTL	Old Testament Library
OTS	*Oudtestamentische Studiën*
PEQ	*Palestine Exploration Quarterly*
RAS	Ranchi Anthropology Series
RB	*Revue biblique*
RevExp	*Review and Expositor*
RP	*Recherches philosophiques*
SBLASP	Society of Biblical Literature Abstracts and Seminar Papers
SBT	Studies in Biblical Theology
SEAJT	*South East Asia Journal of Theology*
SH	*Scripta Hierosolymitana*
SJLA	Studies in Judaism in Late Antiquity
SJT	*Scottish Journal of Theology*

SMRit	Symbol, Myth and Ritual Studies
SR	*Studies in Religion / Sciences religieuses*
StANT	Studien zum Alten und Neuen Testament
TD	*Theology Digest*
TDNT	*Theological Dictionary of the New Testament*, ed. G. Kittel and G. Friedrich
THAT	*Theologisches Handwörterbuch zum Alten Testament*, ed. E. Jenni and C. Westermann. Munich: Kaiser Verlag, 1971/1976.
ThZ	*Theologische Zeitschrift*
VT	*Vetus Testamentum*
VTSup	*Vetus Testamentum*, Supplements
WBC	Word Biblical Commentary
WMANT	Wissenschaftliche Monographien zum Alten und Neuen Testament
ZAW	*Zeitschrift für die alttestamentliche Wissenschaft*
ZDPV	*Zeitschrift des deutschen Palästinavereins*
ZThK	*Zeitschrift für Theologie und Kirche*

INTRODUCTION

While the Priestly ritual texts of the Pentateuch have received a great deal of attention over the years, there have been very few attempts to analyze and understand the conceptual, ideological, or theological framework of the Priestly cult embodied in these texts. Employing methods of analysis developed in the general study of the Pentateuch, studies have focused on literary-critical, form-critical,[1] and traditio-historical questions. The emphasis has been on the analysis of texts rather than ritual. It is true that there have been studies of Israelite sacrifice, but these have normally focused on the mechanics and meaning of the individual sacrifices and have not given attention to the Priestly ritual system.

There are three primary reasons for this neglect of the Priestly ritual system. First, as already indicated, Old Testament scholarship has been guided on the whole by a specific set of methodological tools and goals. The concern has been primarily text-oriented. The neglect, then, is, in part, dictated by the methods and concerns of the discipline.

---

1 This would seem to be a case of scholarship not learning from itself. If literary genres are distinct, calling for the interpreter to understand their distinctiveness, it follows that distinct genres would call for distinct methods of analysis. So, it might well be asked, are methods of interpretation used in the study of narrative texts equally useful in the study of ritual texts? More important is the methodological issue of whether the analysis of ritual texts should focus on *texts* or the ritual depicted in the texts.

8 The Ideology of Ritual

Second, there has been a general bias in Old Testament scholarship, particularly among its Protestant practitioners, against Priestly ritual.[1] Wellhausen gave voice to this perspective and, in many ways, established the direction that study of Priestly ritual texts would take. From this perspective, the Priestly ritual texts represent a view of religion and worship that by its very nature takes away the life of true religion and worship. In Judaism, at the heart of which lies the Priestly Code, 'the law thrusts itself in everywhere; it commands and blocks up the access to heaven; it regulates and sets up limits to the understanding of the divine working on earth. As far as it can, it takes the soul out of religion and spoils morality'.[2] Such judgments, value-laden as they are, are not stimulants to the study of the ideological and theological framework of ritual.

A third problem that has diverted attention from the study of the Priestly ritual system has been a basic assumption that narrative was the primary form of Israel's theological reflection. This belief diverted attention away from Priestly ritual in theological discussions. Once the literary-critical division between Pg, constituted primarily by narratives, and Ps, constituted primarily by rituals, was made,[3] scholarship directed its attention to the theology of P by examining the Priestly narratives (= Pg).

Recent years have seen a shift away from this earlier perspective. J. Milgrom,[4] B. Levine,[5] M. Haran,[6] and G.J.

1 J.H. Hayes and F. Prussner, *Old Testament Theology: Its History and Development* (Atlanta: John Knox, 1985), pp. 274-75.
2 'Israel', in *Prolegomena to the History of Israel* (Gloucester, Mass.: Peter Smith, 1973), p. 509, and see pp. 361, 402-403. Wellhausen was certainly not alone in this perspective.
3 M. Noth, *Überlieferungsgeschichtliche Studien I* (Tübingen: Max Niemeyer, 1943), pp. 182-85; K. Elliger, 'Sinn und Ursprung der priesterlichen Geschichtserzählung', *ZThK* 49 (1952), pp. 121-43.
4 The basic features of Milgrom's work may be found in his *Studies in Levitical Terminology*, I (Berkeley: University of California, 1970); *Cult and Conscience* (Leiden: Brill, 1976); *Studies in Cultic Theology and Terminology* (SJLA 36; Leiden: Brill, 1983). See also his articles in *IDBSup*: 'Atonement in the OT', pp. 78-82; 'Leviticus', pp. 541-45; 'Sacrifices and Offerings, OT', pp. 763-71.
5 'The Descriptive Tabernacle Texts of the Pentateuch', *JAOS* 85 (1965), pp. 307-18; 'On the Presence of God in Biblical Religion', in *Religions in*

Wenham[1] have all, in various ways, sought to uncover and explicate a larger conceptual framework for understanding Priestly ritual. These scholars have attempted to address the question not only of the operation of the Priestly rituals, but also the *meaning* of those rituals. They have examined specific rituals in the context of the larger Priestly ritual system in an effort to understand the larger structure of meaning that informs the various rituals.

The present study takes these works as its starting point and seeks to develop more fully the precise nature of the conceptual, ideological, and theological framework that informs specific Priestly rituals and which is, in turn, constructed, in part, by those rituals. It is argued that the Priestly ritual system is best understood as the meaningful enactment of world in the context of Priestly creation theology. The argument requires the following: (1) theoretical precision and clarity in understanding the nature of ritual; (2) precision and clarity in explicating the nature of Priestly creation theology; and (3) explication of specific Priestly rituals in the context of Priestly creation theology.

The theoretical and methodological framework for the study has been drawn primarily from cultural anthropology. Drawing particularly on the works of C. Geertz,[2] V. Turner,[3] M. Douglas,[4] and R. Rappaport,[5] the work seeks to understand

Antiquity (ed. J. Neusner; Leiden: Brill, 1968), pp. 71-87; *In the Presence of the Lord* (SJLA 5; Leiden: Brill, 1974).

6 The major results of his work are found in his *Temples and Temple-Service in Ancient Israel* (Oxford: Clarendon, 1978).

1 *The Book of Leviticus* (NICOT; Grand Rapids: Eerdmans, 1979).

2 *The Interpretation of Cultures* (New York: Basic Books/Harper Colophon Books, 1973).

3 *The Forest of Symbols: Aspects of Ndembu Ritual* (Ithaca: Cornell University Press, 1967); *The Ritual Process: Structure and Anti-Structure* (SMRit. 1969; rpt Ithaca: Cornell University Press, 1979); *Dramas, Fields, and Metaphors* (SMRit; Ithaca: Cornell University Press, 1974); *From Ritual to Theatre: The Human Seriousness of Play* (New York: Performing Arts Journal Publications, 1982).

4 *Purity and Danger: An Analysis of the Concepts of Pollution and Taboo* (1966; rpt. London: Routledge & Kegan Paul, 1979); *Natural Symbols: Explorations in Cosmology* (2nd edn; London: Barrie & Jenkins, 1973); *Implicit Meanings: Essays in Anthropology* (London: Routledge & Kegan Paul, 1975).

Priestly creation theology and Priestly ritual in terms of the thick webs of meaning and significance that constitute culture. In particular, the concern is to bring some precision to our understanding of the relationship between cosmos, society, and cult.

More specifically, the analysis will focus on the way in which the conceptual categories of space, time, and status function in specific Priestly rituals (Lev. 16; 8; 14.1-20; Num. 19; 28–29) in the context of Priestly creation theology. It has long been recognized that spatial and temporal categories play an important and meaningful role in sacred rituals. It is equally clear that the way a particular culture views and 'interprets' space and time is an important part of its world view and, hence, of its cosmology. Spatial and temporal categories thus provide a significant intersection of cult and cosmos.

Status, as used here, moves in two directions. First, it refers to a person's standing within society. This may be understood in institutional terms, e.g., the priesthood, but may also be understood, in the Priestly traditions, in terms of the categories of purity and pollution. Indeed, the achievement and maintenance of purity may be said to form one of the dominant unifying concerns of the Priestly ritual system. Ideas concerning purity and pollution play a role not only in the cult, however, but also in the structure, organization, and operation of the larger social body.[1] The conceptual categories of purity and pollution form one means by which the status of persons is classified and located with reference both to the cult and society. In this way, the categories of purity and pollution offer one more example of the way in which the Priestly traditionists perceive and interpret the world.

Secondly, however, the priests are concerned with the status of objects and space. At the center of this concern is the taber-

5 *Ecology, Meaning, and Religion* (Richmond, CA: North Atlantic Books, 1979).
1 See M. Douglas, 'Pollution', *IESS* 12 (1968), pp. 336-42; P. Rigby, 'Some Gogo Rituals of 'Purification': An Essay on Social and Moral Categories', in *Dialectic in Practical Religion* (ed. E. Leach; Cambridge: Cambridge University Press, 1968), pp. 153-78; S.S. Bean, 'Toward a Semiotics of 'Purity' and 'Pollution' in India', *AA* 8 (1981), pp. 575-95.

nacle structure and the holy of holies. The state of this holy area, set apart from all other areas, must be carefully maintained. Thus, rituals must be undertaken which will preserve the status of the holy and, when necessary, restore it. In that the holy tabernacle structure is understood by the priests to be the dwelling place of Yahweh, it is clear that this concern for the status of holiness forms yet another part of Priestly cosmology. It is also clear that in this instance spatial categories and categories of status intersect.

The study begins in Chapter 1 with a discussion of the relationship of culture and world view. The chapter then attempts to being some theoretical and methodological precision to the study of ritual. Chapter 2 analyzes the world view of the Priestly traditionists and presents a general context for understanding Priestly rituals. Chapters 3–7 examine specific Priestly ritual texts in light of the discussion of the first two chapters, in each case asking the question: How does this ritual function in the context of the Priestly world view?

Chapter 1

RITUAL: A METHODOLOGICAL FRAMEWORK

Introduction

The analysis of Priestly rituals has all too often been under-taken without sufficient and intentional concern for the role of ritual in its socio-cultural context. This is a problem based in large part on the fact that the Priestly rituals come to us in texts without an observable social context. Thus, research has focused primarily on textual analysis without great concern for the social nature of ritual. Rituals must be understood in terms of their socio-cultural context. This demands a methodological shift in the study of Priestly rituals from a text oriented analysis to a socio-cultural analysis. The following questions must be asked: What is the nature and function of ritual? What is the goal of the interpretation of rituals? What elements of the ritual need to be analyzed if the ritual is to be understood? What are the ways in which ritual may be interpreted?

Drawing on cultural anthropology and theoretical dis-cussions of ritual, this opening chapter explores the nature of ritual and the way it functions in a socio-cultural context as a meaningful enactment of world view. The discussion begins by defining the nature of socio-cultural context in terms of meaning. A model for understanding the structure of world view is then presented. The chapter concludes with a working definition of ritual and a discussion of the major elements that need analysis in the study of ritual.

Ritual and its Socio-Cultural Context

The beginning point for the study of ritual must be the recognition that ritual is a social act which takes place in a specific socio-cultural context.[1] This is true of all ritual acts, whether 'secular' or 'sacred',[2] private or communal. As such, rituals must be seen as specific processes of a society[3] which are embedded in, integrally related to, supported by, and which give support to specific socio-cultural situations. Thus, rituals must be interpreted and understood in terms of the social and cultural contexts of which they are a part.

In arguing that Priestly rituals must be located, interpreted, and understood in a socio-cultural context, it must be recognized that such a context cannot be limited to questions of the historical, social world in which the ritual took place or was constructed. Indeed, a precise historical and social setting for

---

1   R. Rappaport (*Ecology, Meaning, and Religion*, p. 174) states that ritual is *the* basic social act. A similar position is taken by R. Wuthnow, *Meaning and Moral Order: Explorations in Cultural Analysis* (Berkeley: University of California Press, 1987), pp. 97-144. For a review of anthropological and sociological analyses of ritual which have proceeded along this line, see E.R. Leach, 'Ritual', *IESS* 13 (1968), pp. 520-26.

2   For an extremely important and insightful essay on the similarities and differences between 'secular' and 'sacred' ritual, see S.F. Moore and B.G. Myerhoff, 'Introduction: Secular Ritual: Forms and Meanings', in *Secular Ritual* (ed. *idem* [Amsterdam/Assen: Van Gorcum, 1977], pp. 3-24. They argue that a dichotomy between 'secular' ritual and 'sacred' ritual is too simplistic and is in need of further refinement. This simple distinction received classic formulation by E. Durkheim, *The Elementary Forms of the Religious Life* (1915; rpt New York/London: The Free Press/ Collier Macmillan, 1965). See also Rappaport, *Ecology, Meaning, and Religion*, p. 209.

3   This is a key emphasis of V. Turner. See his *The Ritual Process*, p. vii; *Dramas, Fields, and Metaphors*, pp. 23-59; *From Ritual to Theatre*, pp. 61-88. A similar position is taken by S.F. Moore ('Epilogue: Uncertainties in Situations, Indeterminacies in Culture', in *Symbol and Politics in Communal Ideology* [ed. S.F. Moore and B.G. Myerhoff; Ithaca: Cornell University Press, 1975], p. 219). Such analysis of ritual and social processes is extremely helpful in classifying the purposes and structures of Priestly ritual as this work will show.

Priestly rituals is most difficult to specify because of the conservative nature of ritual and also because of the lack of agreement on the precise historical location of the priests. Furthermore, our knowledge of the specific social structure of Israel at any given time is, at best, fragmentary.

As used here, socio-cultural context refers primarily to the context of meaning which gives rise to and is embedded in the rituals.[1] It is a world of meaning that gives shape to and is shaped by the rituals. Thus, Priestly rituals must be understood in the context of the world of meaning operative in and through the rituals. The interpreter must seek to discover the world view that stands behind the rituals, that gives rise to the rituals, that is enacted and made real in the rituals. The 'world' of ritual is a world of meaning, a world of symbols; it is the world of meaning and significance within which the ritual is conceptualized, constructed, and enacted.[2]

World View and Ritual: A Dynamic Structure

An important element of the socio-cultural context within which ritual operates is its world view. It is clear that the way in which one views the structure and operation of the world has intricate connections with religious beliefs and rituals. A

---

1 For similar views, see Turner, *The Ritual Process*, pp. 1-43; C. Geertz, *The Interpretation of Cultures*, pp. 3-32; Turner, *Dramas, Fields, and Metaphors*, pp. 23-59; H.P. Sullivan, 'Ritual: Attending to the World', *ATR* 57 (1975), pp. 9-32; E.M. Zuesse, 'Meditation on Ritual', *JAAR* 43 (1975), pp. 517-30; Rappaport, *Ecology, Meaning, and Religion*, pp. 173-217; T. W. Jennings, 'On Ritual Knowledge', *JR* 62 (1982), pp. 111-27; Turner, *From Ritual to Theatre*, pp. 20-60; T.W. Wheelock, 'The Problem of Ritual Language: From Interpretation to Situation', *JAAR* 50 (1982), pp. 49-71; L.E. Sullivan, 'Sound and Senses: Toward a Hermeneutics of Performance', *HR* 26 (1986), pp. 1-33.

2 This idea is adapted from literary criticism which speaks of the 'narrative world' that is created and operative in narrative texts. In the same way, it is appropriate to speak of the 'ritual world' that is created and enacted in and through ritual. On 'narrative world', see S. Crites, 'The Narrative Quality of Experience', *JAAR* 39 (1971), pp. 291-311 and P. Ricoeur, 'The Narrative Function', *Semeia* 13 (1978), pp. 177-202. For similar views of ritual, see Wheelock, 'The Problem of Ritual Language', pp. 63-66; Sullivan, 'Ritual', pp. 9-17; Zuesse, 'Meditation on Ritual', pp. 517-27; L. Kliever, 'Fictive Religion: Rhetoric and Play', *JAAR* 49 (1981), p. 658.

world view is one means by which a society attempts to structure the world and human existence within that world.[1] It attempts to bring order into existence. It is the contention of this study that a central feature of the Priestly world view is a concern for order.

World view as used here[2] is a dynamic notion and is made up of three interrelated elements.[3] First, there is a body of knowledge which serves to identify and categorize the world 'out there' or the 'real' world. This cognitive and linguistic side of world view is primarily an attempt to identify the elements of the cosmos and organize these elements into a systematic view of the structure of the world.[4] Second, there is a set of meanings related to the structure of the world that serves to locate human existence in the cosmos and give meaning to

1 The precise meaning of 'world view' as used here will become clear in the following discussion. For discussions of the meaning of world view, see the following: S.C. Pepper, *World Hypotheses: A Study in Evidence* (Berkeley: University of California Press, 1961); T. Luckmann, *The Invisible Religion: The Problem of Religion in Modern Society* (London: Collier-Macmillan, 1967), p. 53. He defines world view as 'an encompassing system of meaning in which socially relevant categories of time, space, causality and purpose are superordinated to more specific interpretive schemes in which reality is segmented and the segments related to one another' (p. 53). See also Geertz, *The Interpretation of Cultures*, pp. 89-123. O.E. Klapp (*Models of Social Order: An Introduction to Sociological Theory* [Palo Alto, CA: National Press Books, 1973], pp. 1-26) offers important insights into the issue in his discussion of 'social order'.

2 The use of 'world view' adopted here follows closely V. Turner's discussion of *Weltanschauung* in 'The Anthropology of Performance', in *Process, Performance, and Pilgrimage: A Study in Comparative Symbology* (RAS 1; New Delhi: Concept, 1979), pp. 76-85. Turner bases his own discussion on the work of W. Dilthey. See W. Dilthey, *Dilthey's Philosophy of Existence: Introduction to Weltanschauungslehre* (London: Vision Press, 1957), pp. 21-51.

3 Turner, 'The Anthropology of Performance', p. 76. See also Luckmann, *The Invisible Religion*, pp. 57-58.

4 This is the focal point of analysis in cognitive anthropology. For important discussions of cognitive and symbolic anthropology, see J.W.D. Dougherty and J.W. Fernandez, 'Introduction', *AA* 8 (1981), pp. 413-21; B.N. Colby, J.W. Fernandez, and D.B. Kornfeld, 'Toward a Convergence of Cognitive and Symbolic Anthropology', *AA* 8 (1981), pp. 422-50; E. Ohnuki-Tierney, 'Phases in Human Perception/Conception/Symbolization Processes: Cognitive Anthropology and Symbolic Classification', *AA* 8 (1981), pp. 451-67.

that human existence. This system of meaning attempts to establish what it means to be human within a particular cosmic structure. Finally, there is a system of conduct, a system of praxis, which gives direction to proper and appropriate actions within a particular world of meaning. Ritual action, as a major element of the system of praxis, serves as an important means by which the individual locates the self in the world and thereby participates in, realizes, and enacts the world order. By so participating in the order of the world the individual, and also the community in communal rituals, helps to maintain and sustain that order.[1]

Praxis, related to the more common ethos, is not always included as an element of world view. Geertz, for example, distinguishes 'ethos', the moral and evaluative elements of culture, from 'world view', the cognitive and existential aspects of culture.[2] He sees them as intimately connected, however, in religious belief and ritual. He states:

> The ethos is made intellectually reasonable by being shown to represent a way of life implied by the actual state of affairs which the world view describes, and the world view is made emotionally acceptable by being presented as an image of an actual state of affairs of which such a way of life is an authentic expression.[3]

In that the Priestly world view is decidedly religious, it is clear that ethos, or praxis, may be seen as one of the elements comprising that world view. A religious world view is not only concerned with the structure of the world, but also with the appropriate way to live in that world.[4]

1 See Rappaport, *Ecology, Meaning, and Religion*, pp. 93-97.
2 *The Interpretation of Cultures*, pp. 126-27.
3 *Ibid.*, p. 127. See also P. Rigby, 'Some Gogo Rituals of "Purification"', pp. 153-78.
4 Geertz (*The Interpretation of Cultures*, p. 112) states: 'In a ritual, the world as lived and the world as imagined, fused under the agency of symbolic forms, turn out to be the same world ...' Rappaport (*Ecology, Meaning, and Religion*, pp. 116-21) presents a hierarchical structure of liturgical orders, consisting of five levels, that shows the relationship of different types of beliefs and ritual actions. Moore and Myerhoff (*Secular Ritual*, p. 4) state, 'Ritual not only belongs to the more structured side of social behavior, it also can be construed as an attempt to structure the way people *think* about social life'.

18 *The Ideology of Ritual*

A particular view of the world order will give rise to a particular system of conduct that is congruent with that way of seeing the world. Indeed, certain forms of action will be seen as necessary for the continuation of that world order.[1] This means that inappropriate actions or actions that are prohibited will be viewed as disruptions of the order of the world. When such a breakdown in the world order occurs, rituals serve as one means to effect restoration.[2] If this is so, then it may be said that appropriate or prescribed actions serve to maintain and sustain the world order. Rituals become one means by which individuals and communities uphold and continue the order of the world as they perceive it. Thus, as Turner states, Weltanschauungen must be performed.[3] World view, seen as a means by which a culture defines the world and itself, entails not only a cognitive aspect but also a performative aspect. Both of these elements are important means of defining and bringing into being order and meaning in human existence.

Ritual

The word 'ritual' has a number of different definitions and usages in the literature. One may use ritual to refer to a general class of social actions that covers a broad range of behavior.[4] Such a usage emphasizes that ritual behavior is

---

1 Moore and Myerhoff (*Secular Ritual*, p. 17) state, 'Through order, formality, and repetition it [ritual] seeks to state that the cosmos and social world, or some particular small part of them are orderly and explicable and for the moment fixed'.
2 Turner ('The Anthropology of Performance', pp. 63-64) suggests four main phases for social dramas—breach, crisis, redressive action, reintegration —and emphasizes their ability to restore social order. See further his *From Ritual to Theatre*, pp. 75-85. See also Moore, 'Epilogue', p. 219.
3 'The Anthropology of Performance', p. 77.
4 See, as examples, Moore and Myerhoff, *Secular Ritual*, pp. 3-24; J. Goody, 'Against Ritual', *Secular Ritual*, pp. 25-35; Turner, 'The Anthropology of Performance', pp. 60-93; Rappaport, *Ecology, Meaning, and Religion*, pp. 173-221; R.L. Grimes, *Beginnings in Ritual Studies* (Lanham/New York/London: University Press of America, 1982), pp. 53-69.

social behavior and does not distinguish, for example, between sacred ritual and profane ritual in its broad and general definition of ritual. Any action that partakes of all the characteristics of ritual, as characterized by the interpreter, is ritual action. Second, one may use ritual to refer to a specific act or process, that is, a 'rite'. The second use is distinguished from the first in that the specific ritual has a distinct purpose (or purposes) and constitutes one specific example of actions that are in general called 'ritual'. Thus, one can speak of a ritual to be performed in a specified situation, to be performed at a specified time, or to be performed at a specified place. Finally, one may speak of 'ritual' as a ritual system.[1] A ritual system is made up of a number of distinct rituals that are related by similar forms, symbols, conceptual categories, and/or purposes. Thus, one can speak of the Priestly ritual system which is made up of the many distinct Priestly rituals. The Priestly ritual system is only one ritual system in the broader socio-cultural system of ancient Israel.

'Ritual' as used here refers to a complex performance of symbolic acts, characterized by its formality, order, and sequence, which tends to take place in specific situations, and has as one of its central goals the regulation of the social order.[2]

---

1   See P. Smith ('Aspects of the Organization of Rites', in *Between Belief and Transgression: Structuralist Essays in Religion, History, and Myth* [ed. M. Izard and P. Smith; Chicago/London: University of Chicago, 1982], pp. 103-12) for a discussion of the relationship between individual rites and ritual systems. He also points out that a given society may have multiple ritual systems operative within it. See also Rappaport, *Ecology, Meaning, and Religion*, p. 176.

2   This characterization is not presented as an original formulation. The following were influential: Moore and Myerhoff, *Secular Ritual*, pp. 3-24; Turner, 'The Anthropology of Performance', pp. 60-93; Grimes, *Beginnings*, pp. 53-69; Geertz, *The Interpretation of Cultures*, pp. 89-123; D. Schneider, 'Notes Toward a Theory of Culture', in *Meaning in Anthropology* (ed. K.H. Basso and H.A. Selby; Albuquerque: University of New Mexico, 1976), pp. 197-220; Turner, *From Ritual to Theatre*, pp. 61-88.

20 *The Ideology of Ritual*

A Complex Performance

Ritual always involves action—something is done or enacted.[1] Although performance has always played some role in the discussion of ritual, it has received a great deal of attention recently by anthropologists. Turner, in particular, has analyzed ritual as 'social drama'.[2] In discussing ritual in this fashion, he characterizes it with such terms as 'conscious acting', 'stylized performance', 'evocative', 'a presentational style of staging', and similar theatrical terms.[3] More and more society is coming to be seen as the stage on which rituals are dramatically performed.[4]

Performance here refers not only to the manifestation of form, but to 'the processual sense of "bringing to completion" or "accomplishing"'.[5] In the context of 'social drama' it refers to the enactment of a process by which the drama is brought to some resolution. For Turner, the process begins when there is a breach or break in the established social order that demands resolution.[6] To this restorative aspect of rituals, understood as social dramas, however, should be added those rituals that arise from the possibility of social breach, of a breakdown in order, and seek to prevent the breach. These are preventative

---

1 Rappaport (*Ecology, Meaning, and Religion*, p. 176) sees 'formality' and 'performance' as the two basic and necessary characteristics of ritual. See also Grimes, *Beginnings*, pp. 59-63; Turner, *From Ritual to Theatre*, p. 79; E.M. Zuesse, 'Meditation on Ritual', pp. 517-18; W.R. Comstock, 'A Behavioral Approach to the Sacred: Category Formation in Religious Studies', *JAAR* 49 (1981), pp. 631-39.

2 *Dramas, Fields, and Metaphors*, pp. 23-59; *From Ritual to Theatre*, pp. 61-88.

3 'The Anthropology of Performance', p. 87.

4 See, for example, R. Schechner, *Essays on Performance Theory, 1970-1976* (New York: Drama Books, 1977); Grimes, 'Ritual and Theater', *Beginnings*, pp. 162-66; Turner, 'Dramatic Ritual/Ritual Drama: Performative and Reflexive Anthropology' (pp. 89-101), and 'Acting in Everyday Life and Everyday Life in Acting' (pp. 102-23), in *From Ritual to Theatre*. R.E. Park ('Behind Our Masks', *Survey* 56 [1926], pp. 135-39) speaks of the roles that humans play as actors in society. See also Wuthnow, *Meaning and Moral Order*, pp. 97-123; B. Kapferer, 'Performance and the Structuring of Meaning and Experience', in *The Anthropology of Experience* (ed. V. Turner and E.M. Bruner, Chicago: University of Illinois, 1986), pp. 188-203.

5 Turner, *From Ritual to Theatre*, p. 91.

6 'The Anthropology of Performance', pp. 75-85.

rituals, no less the dramas of society than those concerned with breach, and may be understood as rituals of maintenance. They seek to preserve the established order and must be taken with all seriousness in light of the possibility of the inbreaking of chaos which they are designed to prevent.

The idea of ritual as performance, however, raises the issue of ritual as a form of communication. Ritual, so understood, implies transmitters and receivers—those who perform the ritual and those for whom it is performed.[1] One peculiarity of ritual communication is that the transmitters and receivers are often one and the same. One simple distinction that can be made is between the participants of a ritual and the social body within which the ritual is performed. It is a simple step to say that the ritual is performed primarily for the social body so that the message encoded in the ritual is transmitted to the larger social body. The situation is more complex than this, however, because many rituals are performed in which the social body is involved in the ritual. For example, the ritual of Leviticus 8, which is primarily a ritual of ordination for the priesthood, is set in the context of the whole community, gathered at the door of the tent of meeting (vv. 3, 4). While this note plays a minor role in the text, it serves to place the ritual in the context of the social body and, indeed, the social body by its prescribed presence is a participant in the ritual.

This suggests that the communicative aspect of ritual as performance has as one of its major elements reflexivity. It is concerned with 'the ways in which a group tries to scrutinize,

---

1 Rappaport (*Ecology, Meaning, and Religion*, p. 192) states, 'The notion of communication implies, minimally, transmitters, receivers, messages, and channels through which messages are carried from the transmitters to receivers'. R. Grainger (*The Language of the Rite* [London: Darton, Longman & Todd, 1974], pp. 1-22) stresses that ritual is to be understood as a form of communication. For a discussion of the relationship of form, communication, and understanding, particularly as related to texts but with helpful insights for the study of ritual as a form of communication, see M.J. Buss, 'Understanding Communication', in *Encounter with the Text: Form and History in the Hebrew Bible* (ed. M.J. Buss; *Semeia Sup*; Philadelphia/Missoula: Fortress/Scholars Press, 1979), pp. 3-24.

portray, understand, and then act on itself'.[1] Ritual is a means by which the individual and society enter into a self-awareness and then act upon that awareness. Ritual serves to make public the multiple and complex relationships embodied in society and to comment on the value, meaning, and condition of those relationships.[2] Ritual is thus performed for the self and for society, but always with the understanding that both the self and society occupy the stage on which the performance takes place.

These performances are always complex. This is not to deny that some of society's rituals are simple in execution—a greeting, a gesture, a meal. Rather, it draws attention to the fact that these 'simple' acts of ritual are always part of a larger socio-cultural situation and receive their significance and meaning only in conjunction with that complex cultural system. As such they form one part of a larger system and must be understood in terms of their relationship to the other parts of that system.[3] Thus, ritual performances are complex not in terms of the precise actions required for their execution, but in terms of their place in the larger social system.

Symbolic Acts

The basic building blocks of ritual performance are symbols, so that ritual action is always symbolic action.[4] Symbol here refers to any object, activity, movement, relation, event, gesture, spatial unit, or temporal unit which serves as a vehicle for a conception and/or conveys a socially meaningful mes-

---

1 Turner, *From Ritual to Theatre*, p. 75. See also Grainger, *The Language of the Rite*, pp. 82-85; Rappaport, *Ecology, Meaning, and Religion*, pp. 191-201.
2 See Grainger, *The Language of the Rite*, p. 107.
3 On systems as complex structures, see J.E. Gedo and A. Goldberg, *Models of the Mind: A Psychoanalytic Theory* (Chicago: University of Chicago, 1973), pp. 3-10. This view also follows that of the structuralist Lévi-Strauss. Structuralism seeks to examine systems and the relations between systems and the way in which they are organized. See C. Lévi-Strauss, *Structural Anthropology* (New York: Basic Books, 1963), p. 33.
4 Turner, *The Ritual Process*, p. 14; Sullivan, 'Ritual', pp. 12-17; Geertz, *The Interpretation of Cultures*, pp. 89-123; Wuthnow, *Meaning and Moral Order*, pp. 97-109.

sage.[1] The symbolics of ritual derive their meaning from the
cultural system within which human beings live their lives.
Culture is here seen as a system of meaningful symbols which
provides a framework within which people perceive and
understand themselves, others, and the world. Geertz, a
leading exponent of such a viewpoint, defines culture as 'an
historically transmitted pattern of meanings embodied in
symbols, a system of inherited conceptions, expressed in symbolic forms by means of which men communicate, perpetuate,
and develop their knowledge about and attitudes toward life'.[2]
Ritual actions, then, are meaningful actions—the structured
interactions of human beings with themselves and the world
—which derive their meaning from the cultural system
within which they are enacted. Symbolic actions are actions
whose performance involves meanings that go beyond the
simple description of the mechanics needed to perform the
action. The meanings which are found in ritual actions are
derived from and, in turn, help support the cultural system
that informs human existence with order, structure, and
meaning.

An insightful framework for the interpretation of ritual
symbols, from the work of an anthropologist, is proposed by

---

1 Geertz, *The Interpretation of Cultures*, p. 91; Schneider, 'Notes Toward a
   Theory of Culture', p. 206. A similar view is taken by T. Parsons and
   E. Shils, *Toward a General Theory of Action* (Cambridge, Mass.: Harvard
   University, 1961) and A.L. Kroeber and T. Parsons, 'The Concepts of
   Culture and of Social System', *ASR* 23 (1958), pp. 582-83. The following
   works are also helpful in understanding the idea of cultural and ritual
   symbols as used here: R. Firth (*Symbols: Public and Private* [SMRit;
   Ithaca: Cornell University, 1973], pp. 15-206) reviews the various uses of
   symbols in anthropology; S.K. Langer, *Philosophy in a New Key: A Study
   in the Symbolism of Reason, Rite, and Art* (3rd edn; Cambridge, Mass.:
   Harvard University, 1980); P. Ricoeur ('Metaphor and Symbol', *Interpretation Theory: Discourse and the Surplus of Meaning* [Fort Worth:
   Texas Christian University, 1976], pp. 45-69) offers an interesting discussion of symbol from a hermeneutical concern with texts that can be
   helpful in 'reading' culture as well. See also J. Skorupski, *Symbol and
   Theory: A Philosophical Study of Theories of Religion in Social
   Anthropology* (Cambridge: Cambridge University Press, 1976).
2 *The Interpretation of Cultures*, p. 89.

Victor Turner.[1] Turner distinguishes between dominant ritual symbols and instrumental ritual symbols. Dominant symbols are those that are ends in themselves and have value in and of themselves. Such symbols may appear in a wide range of distinct rituals and will have a fairly constant meaning throughout these rituals. Dominant symbols may be said to be organizing symbols. Instrumental symbols are symbols that achieve their meaning only in the execution of a particular ritual. They serve as means to attain a desired effect and must be analyzed for their meaning within the context of the specific ritual in which they are found.

Dominant ritual symbols, according to Turner, have three major characteristics: condensation; unification of disparate referents; and polarization of meaning. By condensation Turner means the ability of a single symbol to contain a great deal of meaning. Such symbols are thus multivocal and not univocal. In this way, a symbol is able to carry a great freight of meaning. At the same time, symbols are capable of unifying a number of different ideas and referents. Through the analogy of similar qualities or by conventional association, a symbol can draw together a wide range of distinct ideas and phenomena. It gives an interconnectedness to seemingly divergent things. Finally, dominant symbols operate to draw together two distinct fields of meaning. One is biologically and physiologically based in the human organism. This sensory pole brings feelings, desires, and basic human longings to the symbol. The other pole is based in social organization and the norms and values that are operative in the social world. This ideological pole serves to give social constraint and convention to the symbol. Thus, a dominant ritual symbol draws together the sensory and ideological poles of meaning and 'causes an exchange between these poles in which the biological referents are ennobled and the normative referents are charged with emotional significance'.[2]

Ritual is an enactment; something is done. Indeed, it is only as rituals are enacted that they are realized. At the same time,

---

1 The discussion is drawn from his *The Forest of Symbols*, pp. 19-47; *The Ritual Process*, pp. 1-43; *Dramas, Fields, and Metaphors*, pp. 23-59.
2 *Dramas, Fields, and Metaphors*, p. 55.

however, rituals say something about the participants in the ritual and the world in which they live. Symbols are the vehicles for communication in ritual. It is only by analyzing these symbols in their socio-cultural setting and in light of the world view they presuppose, that the communicative aspects of rituals may be understood.

It must be granted that the ideal situation for the interpretation of rituals and their symbols is an actual social field. Even then, however, the analysis will only be partial. In examining biblical texts as here suggested, the social field of action is obviously not available for direct study.[1] If, however, there is indeed a close relationship existing between ritual and its socio-cultural context, then it should be possible to gain clues to the shape of the socio-cultural context through the rituals. In this case, close attention to the language used to depict the ritual situation must be a focal point of attention. Language is the means for opening up the possibilities of what the social field of the Priestly ritual might have been. At the same time, however, it can also act as a constraint on what the social field was not.

Formality, Order, and Sequence

Ritual actions are characterized by formality, order, and sequence.[2] Ritual actions, as a general class of actions, reflect a normative pattern. Indeed, the enactment of patterned behavior is at the heart of ritual. Such patterned behavior is formalized behavior, or action that effects the realization of a form. Form, as used here, means more than sequence; it refers also to the quality of the actions undertaken and the style in which those actions are performed.[3] In this regard, ritual action has

---

1   See Geertz ('Blurred Genres: The Refiguration of Social Thought', *AmerSch* 49 [1980], pp. 165-79) for a discussion of the changes of style in recent anthropological discourse and analysis. He notes the text analogy as one way in which anthropologists interpret culture by 'reading' it (pp. 175-77).

2   See Rappaport, *Ecology, Meaning, and Religion*, pp. 175-84; Moore and Myerhoff, *Secular Ritual*, pp. 7-10; T.S. Turner, 'Transformation, Hierarchy and Transcendence: A Reformulation of van Gennep's Model of the Structure of Rites de Passage', in *Secular Ritual*, pp. 55-69.

3   Grimes, *Beginnings*, pp. 36-39.

a certain traditional nature about it which is passed on and presented as a possible pattern which other and subsequent members of society may enact.[1] Thus, the formal nature of ritual is the normative and patterned style in and by which the ritual is enacted.

A second characteristic of ritual action is 'order'.[2] Order, as used here, has three aspects. First, it suggests that ritual is a structured event that reflects a set of established relations between certain patterns of behavior and states or situations. By undertaking the performance of a given pattern of behavior, it is possible to bring into being a desired state or situation. In this way, ritual order reflects the prescribed relationships between actions and effects. Second, order suggests predictability. Ritual actions are actions that may be repeated and consistently produce the same effects and consistently communicate the same message. For example, the ritual for the recovered leper (Lev. 14.1-20) will consistently bring about the leper's cleansing and will communicate that the leper has been cleansed and, therefore, brought back into a proper standing within society. It is the repeatable and predictable aspects of ritual order that contribute to the durability of ritual acts, and thereby provide a sense of continuity within culture. Finally, order suggests control and manageability. Because rituals reflect an established structure of relations, and are repeatable and predictable, they may be used to control and manage life situations. Ritual is, thus, a means of imposing order on the indeterminancy of the socio-cultural situation.

> Every ceremony is par excellence a dramatic statement against indeterminancy in some field of human affairs. Through order, formality, and repetition it seeks to state that the cosmos and social world, or some particular small part

---

1   It must be emphasized, however, that ritual only occurs when the form is realized by its performance. As Rappaport states (*Ecology, Meaning, and Religion*, p. 192), 'A liturgical order is an ordering of *acts* or *utterances*, and as such it is enlivened, realized, or established *only when* those acts are performed and those utterances voiced'.
2   See Moore and Myerhoff, *Secular Ritual*, pp. 17-19; I. Jenkins, *Social Order and the Limits of Law* (Princeton: Princeton University, 1980), pp. 20-29.

of them are orderly and explicable and for the moment fixed.[1]

Sequence refers to the relatively invariant pattern of actions which occurs in a given ritual.[2] The first act is followed by the second act, and the second act is followed by the third act, and so on. Such sequencing should not be thought of as mere repetition of acts, but as meaningful elements of a form of communication. The sequence offers the possibility of standard and repeatable actions. It should also be noted that the sequence of ritual often has built into its structure the possibility for free or spontaneous moments.[3]

Performed in Specific Situations

To say that ritual performances take place in specific situations is to recognize the integral relationship between context and action.[4] Ritual, as a class of action, is understood to be action that is called forth or elicited by specific cultural situations. Two of the most fundamental elements of cultural situations are time and place.[5] Generally, rituals are appro-

---

1 Moore and Myerhoff, *Secular Ritual*, p. 17. They write further that ritual 'veils the ultimate disorder, the non-order, which is the unconceptualized, unformed chaos underlying culture' (p. 17). See also Sullivan, 'Ritual', 9; T. Turner, 'Transformation, Hierarchy and Transcendence', pp. 60-63.

2 Rappaport (*Ecology, Meaning, and Religion*, p. 175) takes 'the more or less invariant sequences of formal acts and utterances' as central elements of his definition of ritual. V. Turner (*From Ritual to Theatre*, p. 80) states that 'performative *sequencing* is intrinsic and should be taken into account in any definition of ritual'. See also M. Douglas, *Purity and Danger*, p. 64.

3 See Moore, 'Epilogue', pp. 220-24; T.W. Jennings, 'On Ritual Knowledge', p. 113.

4 Grimes, *Beginnings*, pp. 64-67; Zuesse, 'Meditation on Ritual', pp. 521-24; K. Lynch, *What Time is This Place?* (Cambridge, Mass./London: MIT, 1972), pp. 40-43; P.A. Sorokin, *Sociocultural Causality, Space, Time: A Study of Referential Principles of Sociology and Social Science* (New York: Russell & Russell, 1964); Smith, 'Aspects of the Organization of Rites', p. 108.

5 In addition to the works cited in the preceding note, see W.E. Moore, *Man, Time, and Society* (New York/London: John Wiley & Sons, 1963), pp. 7-9; P.A. Sorokin and R.K. Merton, 'Social Time: A Methodological and Functional Analysis', *AJSoc* 42 (1937), pp. 615-29; G. van der Leeuw, *Religion in Essence and Manifestation: A Study in Phenomenology*, 2, (1938; rpt New York: Harper & Row, 1963), pp. 384-402; W.B. Kristensen,

priate in, and only effective in, specified times and places. Quite often there is a convergence of time and place that produces a matrix calling for specified ritual action. A certain type of behavior that is appropriate at one place may not be appropriate at another place. The same is true of time. The reason for this is that space and time are both creations of culture and, thereby, receive symbolic meanings. Both space and time are 'interpreted' and 'conventionalized'.[1] Thus, culture supplies 'meanings' to space and time, which then converge to create situations for ritual.

The Regulation of Societal Order
Ritual is a means of regulating, or controlling, the structures, processes, and relations of society. It does this in two ways. First, ritual provides a means for maintaining an already existing socio-cultural system. In this sense ritual acts are themselves part of the regular operation of society. Societal order is, to a great extent, characterized by the normative and regularly recurring rituals that take place within and as a part of it.[2] A second way in which ritual serves to regulate society arises when the normative order has been broken or ruptured. In this situation, ritual provides a means for restoring societal order. Thus, ritual serves as a means of maintaining and, when necessary, restoring societal order.

    This raises the question of the meaning of 'societal order'. As used here, 'culture' refers to the socially constructed world of meanings, embodied in symbols, which informs and gives

---

The Meaning of Religion (The Hague: Martinus Nijhoff, 1960), pp. 357-88. The nature of time in the Priestly material will be discussed in Chapter 6.

1   Sorokin, *Sociocultural Causality*, p. 124.

2   T. Turner ('Transformation, Hierarchy and Transcendence', p. 63) states that 'the effectiveness of ritual and ceremony as means of bringing about the reordering, or preventing the disordering, of a set of relations is a function of the ritual's or ceremony's character as an iconic model of that set of relations and its relation to the higher-level, transformational operations that control or have power over it'. See also Rappaport, *Ecology, Meaning, and Religion*, pp. 193-97.

meaning to human communication, actions and values.[1] Order, in this sense, is primarily an order of meaning in which human beings live.[2] The difference between 'culture' and 'social structure', then, can be viewed with Geertz as follows: 'Culture is the fabric of meaning in terms of which human beings interpret their experience and guide their action; social structure is the form that action takes, the actually existing network of social relations'.[3] It may be further stated that 'culture' is the human attempt to impose an order of meanings, or a meaningful order, on the world and reality.

Rituals are the performances of the members of a society and may be seen as their attempt to enact a meaningful order in human life. The social situation is the stage on which these performances take place and reflects in its own structure the cultural order—the system of meanings and the symbols that serve as carriers of those meanings. Rituals are thus means of holding back social confusion, indeterminacy, and chaos because they provide patterns for enacting an ordered existence. In this way, rituals regulate societal order by giving normative patterns for maintaining order and constructive patterns for restoring that order when it has been lost. As such, ritual is a performed and enacted system of meaning.

It is possible to see this system of meaning in 'static' or 'fixed' terms. As understood here, however, society and the cultural system within which society operates are never 'in pause', but are constantly evolving and changing in the diachronic unfolding of social processes, social dramas, and history.[4] Processual and dramatic analysis of ritual suggests that the socio-cultural order be viewed in terms of dynamic processes. While

---

1 It is recognized that other models, such as the structural-functional model or the conflict model, are also available for interpretation. The present model, which views culture as an ordered system of meaningful symbols in process, is used because it is most helpful in analyzing the Priestly ritual system, a system concerned with cultural order.

2 This is in line with Geertz's contention (*The Interpretation of Cultures*, p. 5) that analysis of culture is 'not an experimental science in search of law but an independent one in search of meaning'. See also V. Turner, *From Ritual to Theatre*, p. 76.

3 *The Interpretation of Cultures*, p. 145.

4 *Ibid.*, pp. 17-20; V. Turner, *From Ritual to Theatre*, pp. 20-23; 'The Anthropology of Performance', pp. 62-70.

it must be recognized that there are stable features in cultural organization—roles, statuses, institutions, relations—there are also elements of change and movement. Thus, this analysis views the cultural order as a system of dynamic processes which are made up of meaningful symbols. The societal order spoken of here is primarily an order of meaning. It is possible to isolate moments in the unfolding of a culture, but it must be understood that such arresting of the processes is a moment frozen from a larger and on-going process.

Problems and Pragmatics

There are certain problems and questions that arise in the application of social scientific models to biblical texts that need to be addressed. The answers to these questions will give rise to a discussion of some pragmatic questions relating to this study.

One question that arises is whether, and if so to what extent, one can interpret texts using models and methods of analysis developed in conjunction with the analysis of societies. If these are methods of analysis that have been developed and applied 'in the field', is it possible to apply them to texts which offer no opportunity for the actual observation of the social processes being analyzed? Will the data allow an adequate analysis when the primary sources of information are texts?

As Malina points out, the models for interpreting biblical texts provided by the social sciences are theoretical models.[1] In applying a sociological or anthropological model of interpretation to a text, there is obviously no naive belief that sociology or anthropology, in the sense of statistical analysis or field work, is being accomplished. Models provide a framework for interpretation. This means that they supply the interpreter with a set of questions to ask of the material to be interpreted (= data) and a way of integrating the answers derived from

---

1   B.J. Malina, 'The Social Sciences and Biblical Interpretation', *Int* 36 (1982), pp. 237-40. On the use of models in interpretation, see I.G. Barbour, *Myths, Models, and Paradigms: A Comparative Study in Science and Religion* (New York: Harper & Row, 1974), pp. 6-8. For a discussion of different types of models that may be used in the interpretation of ancient cultures, see T.F. Carney, *The Shape of the Past: Models and Antiquity* (Lawrence, KS: Coronado, 1975), pp. 7-11.

those questions into a larger interpretive framework. In applying to biblical texts a socio-cultural viewpoint that emphasizes the symbolic nature of human life, the goal is to see if a 'reading' or an interpretation of the material may be presented that is both helpful in illuminating the material and also consistent.

It must be recognized that there will be gaps in the data.[1] There will be information needed which is simply not available. While this is lamentable, it is a fact.[2] It is a fact, however, that is equally true of all methods that are concerned with the life or history of ancient Israel. The key issue is whether the material that is available can be interpreted through a social or cultural model and yield a consistent interpretation that helps clarify the material?

The present analysis is concerned with the interpretation of texts which spell out in some detail the performance of specific rituals. The texts will be used to deduce what the rituals might have looked like if actually enacted, and it is the meaning and significance of that enactment that will be the focus of study.

Elements of Ritual

There are several basic elements of ritual that are subject to analysis and need to be studied in order to understand the rituals being examined.[3] The analysis of these elements will figure prominently in the discussion of the Priestly rituals in this study. An adequate analysis of Priestly rituals must become self-consciously aware of these elements, even when the texts may not supply all the necessary information to make definitive statements about them. It is through these elements of ritual that rituals receive their specific structural make-up and their particular style.

---

1 J.W. Rogerson, 'Sacrifice in the Old Testament: Problems of Method and Approach', in *Sacrifice* (ed. M.F.C. Bourdillon and M. Fortes; New York: Academic Press, 1980), pp. 45-47.
2 This is also true, to a degree, for those 'in the field'. There will always be gaps in the data. See Geertz, *The Interpretation of Cultures*, pp. 5-10.
3 This discussion follows to a degree that of Grimes, *Beginnings*, pp. 19-33.

Ritual Space

It has long been recognized that space plays a key role in the organization of ritual.[1] Ritual actions are generally effective and meaningful only when performed in an appropriate spatial setting. Ritual space is a definite and distinct type of social space.[2] As such it is always interpreted and socially constructed space and must be understood in the context of the larger social construction of meaning concerned with space. Where the ritual is performed, and the movement from one space to another within a complete ritual process, can provide important clues to the purpose and meaning of a ritual because the spatial categories themselves are socially meaningful elements of the ritual process.

The key spatial category of Priestly ritual is the tabernacle. Indeed, Priestly ritual may be characterized, in large part, by its orientation with reference to the tabernacle. At the same time, however, as in the ritual for the recovered leper (Lev. 14.1-20), the camp boundary may play a crucial role in the performance of the ritual and will, thereby, provide important clues for a proper understanding of the ritual. Thus, one important spatial distinction in the Priestly texts is that between 'inside the camp' and 'outside the camp'. Further, the Priestly texts may emphasize the difference between 'clean' and 'unclean' space (e.g., Num. 19.9; Lev. 14.40). Such categorical distinctions between types of space are examples of a socially defined order constructed by means of divisions and separations. It is appropriate to speak of the establishing of boundaries, lines of demarcation, between basic categories of space. The tabernacle, reflecting various grades of holiness,[3]

1 In addition to the works cited above (p. 27, note 4), see van der Leeuw, *Religion in Essence and Manifestation*, 2, pp. 393-402; M. Eliade, *The Sacred and the Profane: The Nature of Religion* (New York/London: Harcourt Brace Jovanovich, 1959), pp. 20-65; O.F. Bollnow, 'Lived-Space', in *Readings in Existential Phenomenology* (ed. N. Lawrence and D. O'Connor; Englewood Cliffs: Prentice-Hall, 1967), pp. 178-86; J.Z. Smith, *Map is Not Territory* (SJLA 23; Leiden: Brill, 1978), pp. 88-103.

2 Sorokin, *Sociocultural Causality*, pp. 142-48; Bollnow, 'Lived-Space', pp. 178-86; Berger and Luckmann, *The Social Construction of Reality* (Garden City, New York: Doubleday, 1966), p. 26.

3 See M. Haran, 'The Complex of Ritual Acts Performed Inside the Tabernacle' (*SH* 8; Jerusalem: Magnes, 1961), pp. 272-302; I. Abrahams, 'Tabernacle', *EncJud* 15 (1972), pp. 679-87; J. Milgrom, 'Atonement, Day

forms the basic paradigm for these conceptions. The inner
sanctum, the most holy place, is separated from all other
places by the כפרת. The כפרת functions as an objective and
material witness to the conceptual boundary drawn between
the area behind it and all other areas.[1]

Ritual Time

Time is also a social convention.[2] Time is often viewed in terms
of measurement, but it can also be viewed in terms of its
quality or characteristics.[3] There are distinct kinds of time.
Ritual constructs times which are appropriate for specific
ritual performances.[4] An extension of this is the way in which

---

of', *IDBSup* (1976), pp. 82-83; *idem*, 'The Compass of Biblical Sancta [Lev.
5:15]', *JQR* 65 (1975), pp. 205-16; *idem*, 'The Graduated Hatta't of Lev 5:1-
13', *JAOS* 103 (1983), pp. 249-54; *idem*, 'Israel's Sanctuary: The Priestly
Picture of Dorian Gray', *RB* 83 (1976), pp. 390-99; *idem*, 'Sacrifices and
Offerings, OT', *IDBSup* (1976), pp. 763-71.

1 The spatial categories must always be understood in the context of and in
relation to the larger system of spatial categories operative in the Priestly
ritual system. The inner sanctum is the most holy place and provides the
standard by which other areas are measured. It is possible, however, to
call the area at the outer altar a holy place, but only in relation to the *most*
holy place and other areas that are not holy.

2 Berger and Luckmann (*The Social Construction of Reality*, pp. 26-28)
speak of the various levels at which human beings in society experience
temporality. A.J. Gurevich ('Time as a Problem of Cultural History', in
Cultures and Time [ed. L. Gordet et al.; Paris: Unesco, 1960], p. 229) notes
that time reflects social practice and, at the same time, contributes to the
moulding of social practice. Lynch (*What Time is This Place?*, p. 1) sees a
reciprocal relationship between time and space in the human search for
well-being. S.C. Pepper ('The Order of Time', in *The Problem of Time*
[Berkeley: University of California, 1935], p. 10) argues for a three-fold
stratification of time: (1) calendar; (2) the passage of time; (3) the natural
order of time. See also Moore, *Man Time, and Society*, pp. 7-9; Sorokin and
Merton, 'Social Time', pp. 615-29; G. Gurvitch, 'The Problem of Time', *The
Spectrum of Social Time* (Dordrecht, Holland: Reidel, 1964), pp. 18-38.

3 Sorokin and Merton ('Social Time', p. 623) state that time is qualitative and
not only quantitative and note that the qualitative aspect of time is derived
from the beliefs and customs of the society.

4 For discussions of 'ritual' time, see van der Leeuw, *Religion* 2, pp. 384-87;
M. Eliade, *The Myth of the Eternal Return or, Cosmos and History*
(Princeton: Princeton University, 1954), pp. 51-92; *idem, The Sacred and
the Profane*, pp. 68-113; Grainger, *The Language of the Rite*, pp. 107-43;

a systematic ordering of rituals over the course of time, for example the yearly cycle of ritual occasions, may serve to impose order on the temporal flow of society (e.g., Num. 28–29).[1] Caution must be used at this point, however, to keep distinct two aspects of ritual time. On the one hand, there is the time of the individual rituals. Thus, a given ritual is to be performed at a given time and will take place within a specific time period. On the other hand, ritual time may refer to the larger cycles of rituals which serve to organize a number of different rituals into a network or system.

Ritual Objects

The key questions with reference to objects and materials are: what is specifically used, how is it used, and why is it used?[2] While it is not always possible to answer all of these questions, and this is true even for those doing field work, it is important to become aware of them and address them. In analyzing ritual objects and materials it is necessary to look for meanings in their usage. What is it that these particular objects or materials contribute to the accomplishment of the ritual?

Ritual Roles

It is important in analyzing cultic rituals to ask who is involved in the performance of the ritual and what role or roles they actually play in accomplishing the ritual. In what way does a specific role function in the execution of the ritual? There are three basic categories of ritual roles that need to be distinguished. First, there is the ritual specialist, the priest in the Priestly material, whose presence is necessary for the performance of the ritual. It would be misleading to say that the priest is the performer of the ritual since he is not the only

P. Ricoeur, 'The History of Religions and the Phenomenology of Time Consciousness', in *The History of Religions: Retrospect and Prospect* (ed. J.M. Kitagawa; New York/London: Macmillan/Collier Macmillan, 1985), pp. 13-30.

1 Rappaport, *Ecology, Meaning, and Religion*, p. 187. See ch. 7 below for a discussion of time in Num. 28–29.

2 See Grimes (*Beginnings*, pp. 23-24) for a set of interpretive questions to be applied to ritual objects.

one involved in it.[1] In the Priestly material the priest's involvement is required in two situations: (1) when the ritual prescribes activity to be performed on or around the outer altar or inside the tabernacle proper and (2) when the ritual prescribes some manipulation of the blood of a slaughtered animal. One or both of these elements will be found in all Priestly rituals, so that the priest plays a prominent role in all Priestly rituals.

A second role that must be distinguished is found in the person whose situation has generated the ritual. This refers to the one on whose behalf the ritual is performed. For example, Lev. 14.1-20 details the ritual for a recovered leper. It may thus be said that the ritual is performed on behalf of the recovered leper. Caution, however, must be exercised at this point. Because of the nature of this ritual, with its emphasis on the recovered leper's readmittance to a proper social standing, the ritual may be said to be enacted on behalf of the social body. The social body, however, acts as a passive observer and is not said to be an active participant in the actual performance of the ritual.[2] Ritual roles, as used here, refers to those roles that are actively involved in the actual performance of the ritual and are so designated in the text. The intention, however, is not to undermine the role of society as an observer and, therefore, to some degree, varying from one ritual to another, a participant.

A final category of ritual roles that needs attention concerns the one or ones before whom a ritual is performed. In this regard it is accurate to say that the priest fulfills this role, particularly when the ritual process includes a declaration by the priest concerning the state or status of a person or object (e.g., Lev. 14.44). As already indicated, the social body may be understood to fulfill this role in certain rituals. A distinct situation, in this regard, is found in communal rituals. In such

1 For example, in the ritual of the burnt offering, the offerer slaughters the animal while the priest burns it (Lev. 1.5-9). In Lev. 16.21, the goat designated for Azazel is taken to the wilderness by an unnamed person after the priest has placed the transgressions of the people on its head.

2 It may well be the case that society played an active role in the ritual expulsion of the leper from the social body through psychological as well as physical means, and might then give expression to the validity of the recovered leper's return to the social body.

instances, the ritual of יום הכפרים in Leviticus 16 being one such example, it is the case that the ritual is performed on behalf of, in the sense noted above in the second category, the observers. Thus, the ones on whose behalf the ritual is performed and the ones who observe the ritual are the same.

As this discussion indicates, the question of ritual roles is a complex one. In particular, one must be careful to watch for situations in which two or more roles are fulfilled by the same participant or participants. In the present analysis, attention will be focused on those roles which are actively involved in the performance of the ritual as detailed in the texts.

Ritual Actions
Actions are at the heart of ritual. Ritual produces its effects only in and through the performance and enactment of particular actions. This is a particularly difficult element to see clearly through the texts, and generally the actions that can be deduced from the texts will be actions of a general kind.[1] The style and manner of the ritual actions will not be clearly detailed in texts. Still, the forms of action will constitute a basic unit of study.

Ritual Sound and Language
It is in the area of ritual sounds and utterances that the Priestly texts are most silent. There are very few indications of speech given in the texts, the majority of cases being a declaration, by the priest, of an achieved state of being by a ritual participant. Indeed, on the basis of the Priestly texts, one would have to say that the priests envisioned a silent cult for the lay person.[2] It is doubtful, however, in light of the Psalms, if

---

1 Many of the actions may have had a certain style or nuance associated with them which the texts do not indicate. For example, the movements of the high priest in the ritual of Lev. 16 are noted, but they are not characterized (e.g., he walked slowly or quickly, he walked erect or slightly bent). The texts present the primary actions, but they do not indicate the particular way these actions were performed.

2 Y. Kaufmann, *The Religion of Israel: From its Beginnings to the Babylonian Exile* (trans. M. Greenberg; Chicago: University of Chicago Press, 1960), pp. 302-304. See also N.M. Sarna, 'The Psalm Superscriptions and the Guilds', in *Studies in Jewish Religious and Intellectual History*

such was the case. The texts are simply silent, for the most part, on this question.[1]

What is Communicated?

The discussion of 'what' is communicated by ritual will focus on the Priestly ritual system. It should be remembered in this discussion that the Priestly ritual texts present a system of belief whose parts are interrelated. Thus, while the parts may be separated for purposes of discussion, there are connections and relations between them in the operation of the cult. This means that when a ritual is enacted, it may produce effects in several, interrelated areas.

The Priestly ritual system communicates with reference to four particular areas. In each case, the ritual may generally be understood to bring about a change in the state of being or status of one or more of these areas and/or to make a declaration about the state of being or status in one or more of these areas. First, the Priestly rituals may say something about the state of being or status of an individual. Such rituals may move the individual from one status to another and, at the same time, serve to declare that the new status has been achieved. Rituals of this nature function to indicate that the individual has achieved a particular state within the social body and, at the same time, to declare that an ordered social situation has been effected.

A second area of concern for Priestly rituals is the state of society. Society itself, to a certain degree, becomes the 'performer' of ritual and receives the effects of the ritual. The chief purpose of such rituals is societal well-being. The Priestly ritual system provides the means for society to maintain its well-being and order, but also provides, when necessary, the means to reestablish the societal order when it is broken. In this way, it serves as a safeguard against the breakdown of order and socio-cultural chaos that would result from such a breakdown.

(ed. S. Stein and R. Loewe; Alabama: University of Alabama, 1979), pp. 281-300.
1 See Rogerson, 'Sacrifice in the Old Testament', p. 52.

Third, Priestly rituals show a concern for the state of the cosmos. As indicated, the Priestly ritual system includes in its world view definite ideas about the cosmos and the created order. This created order goes beyond the societal order and includes a concern for the natural world as well. Priestly ritual is a means by which human beings may participate in the maintenance of the divinely created order. Ritual serves to make a declaration about the state of the created order.

Finally, Priestly ritual may serve to communicate something about the community's perception of the state of God in relation to an individual, society, or the cosmos. This is suggested by the concern of the Priestly writers that sacrificial ritual take place 'before Yahweh' or 'at the door of the tent of meeting'. Sacrifice and the ritual processes in which it plays a role were not only performed in the presence of the deity, but were also thought to have some effect or effects in relation to the deity. A central concern of the study of Israelite sacrifice has been an attempt to understand how it relates to and affects the deity. Many different answers have been offered, but the tendency has normally been to try and find one answer. This is too narrow a view of the relations between God and the cult.

Again, it must be emphasized that these four areas are interrelated. To produce a change of status in one of them will normally produce changes in the others. There is no need to relate these in any hierarchy of importance or sequence of effect. Ritual will accomplish its tasks and state its messages simultaneously in multiple areas.

Chapter 2

PRIESTLY WORLD VIEW AND PRIESTLY RITUAL

A central feature of the Priestly world view is the belief that
the world order is a created order, brought into being by
Yahweh.[1] Indeed, at the heart of Priestly theology is the belief
that Yahweh brought into being an ordered world and that at
the heart of that created order is a ritual order. For the
Priestly writers, creation and cult cannot be separated; they
are dynamically interrelated aspects of the Priestly world
view.[2] The element of the Priestly world view that holds
together Priestly creation theology and Priestly ritual is the
desire to bring order to human existence.

The Priestly creation account in Gen. 1.1–2.4a gives clear
expression to this concern for order. It can be characterized as
a process in which God brings into existence or constructs the
order of creation. The Priests present the creative work of God

---

1 H.H. Schmid ('Creation, Righteousness, and Salvation', in *Creation in the
Old Testament* [ed. B.W. Anderson; Philadelphia/London: Fortress/SPCK,
1984], p. 111) states, 'All factors considered, the doctrine of creation, name-
ly the belief that God has created and is sustaining the order of the world
in all its complexities, is not a peripheral theme of biblical theology but is
plainly the fundamental theme'. See also his *Altorientalische Welt in der
alttestamentlichen Theologie* (Zurich: Theologischer Verlag, 1974), pp. 31-
63, 145-64. See also the more general discussion of order and chaos in
J. Levenson, *Creation and the Persistence of Evil* (San Francisco: Harper
& Row, 1988), pp. 3-50.
2 See Levenson (*Creation*, pp. 121-27) for a discussion of the relationship of
cult and chaos in which cult is understood as a means of neutralizing
chaos.

as the establishing of order and they contrast the order of creation with the ever present threat of chaos. Von Rad characterizes the Priestly creation account as a movement from chaos to cosmos and argues that the true concern of the account is 'to give prominence, form, and order to the creation out of chaos'.[1] The very nature of this account, with its seven day temporal framework and its formulaic way of expressing the various creative acts, points to a concern for order.[2]

One way in which this concern for order is expressed is through the use of the word בדל. Creation is depicted, in part, as an act of dividing between various elements and there is present in this characterization a system of classification of the world.[3] The act of separation is explicitly noted in the creative acts of day one and day two—'and God separated the light from the darkness' (v. 4); 'and God separated the waters which were under the firmament from the waters which were above the firmament' (v. 7). The act of separation is also implied for the third day in which the waters under the heavens are gathered together over against the dry land (v. 9).[4] The creative acts of these three days serve to bring into existence and distinguish the basic elements of creation—light and dark, or as Westermann emphasizes, the temporal

1 *Genesis* (rev. edn; Philadelphia: Westminster, 1972), p. 51. If this text does originate in the exilic period, then the relationship of Priestly creation theology, taking shape as it does between the dynamic possibilities of chaos and cosmos, to Israel's reflection on the exile, as a form of historical and national chaos, is of importance for an adequate understanding of Priestly theology. On the relationship of exile and chaos, see J.Z. Smith, 'Earth and Gods', *JR* 49 (1969), pp.103-27; W. Brueggemann, 'Weariness, Exile and Chaos (A Motif in Royal Theology)', *CBQ* 34 (1972), pp. 19-38.

2 This is emphasized by M. Fishbane, *Text and Texture: Close Readings of Selected Biblical Texts* (New York: Schocken, 1979), pp. 7-11 and C. Westermann, *Genesis 1–11: A Commentary* (Minneapolis: Augsburg, 1984), pp. 84-90.

3 For a discussion of the importance of cosmological classification among 'primitive peoples' and the relationship of cosmological classification to the structure of society, see E. Durkheim and M. Mauss, *Primitive Classification* (Chicago: University of Chicago, 1963) and Douglas, *Purity and Danger*.

4 So Westermann, *Genesis*, pp. 120-21. See also E.L. Leach, *Genesis as Myth and Other Essays* (London: Jonathan Cape, 1969), pp. 7-23 and M. Casalis, 'The Dry and the Wet: A Semiological Analysis of Creation and Flood Myths', *Semiotica* 17 (1976), pp. 35-67.

progression of day and night so important for the narrator's temporal framework of seven days,[1] the firmament that separates above and below, and the waters and dry land of the earth. The remaining acts of creation will serve to populate these basic elements with their appropriate objects (e.g., stars, sun, and moon) and life forms (e.g., birds, animals, and humans).[2] The idea of separation is found again in the account of the fourth day in which the lights are placed in the firmament to separate (להבדיל) the day from the night (v. 14) and the light from the darkness (v. 18).[3]

Inherent in such a conceptualization of creation is the idea that the order of creation was brought about through the separation and classification of the basic elements of creation. Order is brought about through divisions, separations, and distinctions between one element and another. It is only as these lines of demarcation, or boundaries,[4] are established that order is realized. If true, it means that these divisions must be recognized and maintained if the created order is to continue to exist and not collapse into confusion and chaos.[5]

---

1 *Genesis*, pp. 89-90.
2 This is noted by Douglas (*Purity and Danger*, pp. 53-56) and J. Soler, 'The Dietary Prohibitions of the Hebrews', *New York Review of Books* 26 (June, 1979), pp. 24-30.
3 For the importance of this conception in the Priestly traditionists' understanding of temporal categories, see below, Chapter 7.
4 The use of the idea of boundaries is drawn from Douglas (*Purity and Danger* and *Implicit Meanings*. 'Boundaries' refer to the conceptual categories of persons, objects, and ideas within the classification system of a culture. Douglas, in both works, addressed Israel's system of classification of 'clean' and 'unclean' animals in terms of the created order. This approach has also been employed by G.J. Wenham, 'Why Does Sexual Intercourse Defile [Lev 15.18]?' *ZAW* 95 (1983), pp. 432-34.
5 A culture's system of world classification and world categorization helps to define the cultural order. If the boundaries that serve to separate the cultural categories are not observed, if they are crossed over or confused, then, it may be said, the cultural order is disrupted, because its structural order has been broken, and cultural chaos takes its place. Rituals and pollution ideas act as protective agents for the categories needed to maintain the cultural order. This is the emphasis of Geertz (*The Interpretation of Cultures*, pp. 92-95) in saying that cultural patterns serve as models *of* and models *for* reality.

This provides an important clue into the way in which the Priestly writers viewed not only creation but all of human existence. The created order, which includes the established order within which human existence takes shape, is understood to exist only insofar as clear lines of distinction between various conceptual categories are maintained. These divisions or boundaries are established in creation, but they are subject to breaks and ruptures for various reasons. In the Priestly writings the two most significant threats to order are sin and defilement. It thus becomes necessary for a means to be established by which the created order may be maintained and, when necessary, restored. The thesis here is that the Priestly cult is the means by which this is accomplished.

It has often been pointed out that the giving of the instructions for and the actual construction of the tabernacle have important literary and conceptual links to the Priestly creation account.[1] These conceptions point to the Priestly belief that God brought into being and established the tabernacle cultic order in the same way that he brought into being and established the cosmic order.[2] Indeed, it points to the belief that the cultic order is established as an integral part of the created order and, as proposed here, is the primary means by which the order of creation is upheld.

The Priestly traditionists see a properly structured cultic order as a central element of cosmic order. This is indicated in Exod. 29.43-46 at the conclusion of Yahweh's instructions for the ordination of the priesthood and the establishment of the tabernacle cult.

---

1   See J. Blenkinsopp, 'The Structure of P', *CBQ* 38 (1976), pp. 278-83; P.J. Kearney, 'Creation and Liturgy: The P Redaction of Ex 25–40', *ZAW* 89 (1977), pp. 375-78; Fishbane, *Text and Texture*, pp. 11-13; N. Lohfink, 'Creation and Salvation in Priestly Theology', *TD* 30 (1982), pp. 4-5; V. Hurowitz, 'The Priestly Account of the Building of the Tabernacle', *JAOS* 105 (1985), pp. 21-30.

2   See Fishbane, *Text and Texture*, p. 13. On the relationship of creation to the giving of the law with important insights on their relationship, see A.S. Kapelrud, 'Die Theologie der Schöpfung im Alten Testament', *ZAW* 91 (1979), pp. 163-65; B.D. Napier, 'Community Under Law: On Hebrew Law and its Theological Presuppositions', *Int* 7 (1953), pp. 413-14; J. Levenson, 'The Theologies of Commandment in Biblical Israel', *HTR* 73 (1980), p. 28.

> There [at the door of the tent of meeting, v. 42] I will make
> myself known to the children of Israel, and it shall be made
> holy by my glory. And I will make holy the tent of meeting
> and the altar and I will make Aaron and his sons holy, to be
> priests to me. And I will dwell in the midst of the children of
> Israel, and I will be their God. Indeed, they will know that I
> am Yahweh their God who brought them out of the land of
> Egypt to dwell in their midst. I am Yahweh their God.

A central element of this theological complex is the idea that
God brings into being and establishes order through speech.
God spoke and brought into being the cosmological order in
Gen. 1.1–2.4a. In a similar way, God spoke and brought into
being the tabernacle cultic order in Exodus 25–31. Having
said this, however, it is necessary to broaden the context of
God's creative activity to include society itself. The tabernacle
rests in the midst of the Israelite tribes, the outer bounds of the
tribal residency forming the camp boundaries, so that the
tabernacle cult is presented in the context of the social organization of the twelve tribes. It is an ordered situation with
definite boundaries established within which the people are to
live. Israelite society is an established order that has, as a
central element of that order, Yahweh dwelling in the midst of
the nation in the holy shrine, and includes, as part of that
order, specific prescriptions for how the people are to live in
order to maintain the order of creation. This order was established by Yahweh in the giving of the laws to Moses. The
prescriptions spoken by Yahweh to Moses provided the
blueprint for the structure of Israelite society and the means
by which the Israelites could effectively live within that structure and thereby maintain it. It is thus appropriate to say that
God brought into being, through the act of speech, the Israelite
societal order.[1] In this way, the Priestly tabernacle cult and

---

1 The argument here is that the created order consists of three distinct
   orders—cosmic, social, and cultic—which are interrelated and interactive. While a separation of social order and cultic order might be ques-
   tionable from a modern sociological perspective, such a modern view must
   not be imposed on the Priestly traditionists. They placed cult in an interactive context with society, but saw these as distinct and 'separate' orders
   of creation.

Israelite society are related to the word first spoken at creation.[1]

The world view of the Priestly writers has as its framework three distinct orders of creation—the cosmological, the societal, and the cultic. All three orders were given shape, brought into being, and established by the speech of God. What must be seen, however, is that these various orders are not independent of one another but are intricately connected. The wilderness tabernacle in the center of the wilderness camp is a reflection of the social order which is in turn a reflection of the cosmological order. The cultic order and the social order are part of—reflecting in their own structure and in turn helping to structure—the cosmological order. At the same time, this tripartite understanding of the divinely created order reflects the structure of a world view discussed earlier: the cosmological order reflects a system of identification, the social order reflects a system of meaning and value, while the cultic order reflects a system of praxis.

The conceptual element that holds these three orders together is that of order through separation. Just as the cosmological order is achieved by acts of separation—the establishing of boundaries between different categories of created things—so also the societal and cultic orders achieve order through categorical distinctions. Indeed, the charge to Aaron as priest is 'to divide [להבדיל] between the holy [הקדש] and the common [החל] and between the unclean [הטמא] and the clean [הטהור]' (Lev. 10.10). The separation of conceptual cate-

---

1 Blenkinsopp ('The Structure of P', pp. 275-92) has presented a similar argument based on the command–execution formulae in the Priestly traditions. He argues that the completion formula plays an important role in three specific places in the Priestly work: the creation of the world (Gen. 1.1, 2); the setting up of the sanctuary cult (Exod. 39.32; 40.33); and the establishment of the cult in the land and the division of the land by Joshua (Josh. 19.51). These three events all take place according to the plan of Yahweh and as a result of Yahweh's speaking. There is a convergence of these three events in the plan of Yahweh concerning the divinely created order. The completion formula, then, serves not only to connect the execution of instructions to the giving of the instructions, but, on a higher level, to mark the accomplishment of Yahweh's plan for the created order. In this way, the Priestly tabernacle cult and Israel living in the land are related to the word first spoken at creation.

gories focuses on three areas in the Priestly ritual material—
space, time, and status—and Priestly ritual functions within
the context of clearly defined and demarcated categories of
space, time, and status. Each of these conceptual categories is
given concrete expression through a foundational image of
separation: space in the separation of the holy of holies from all
other areas; time in the separation of the Sabbath from all
other days; status in the separation of the priests from all other
persons. Each of these is said to be 'set apart' and categorically
distinct by the Priestly traditionists. Thus, the central conceptual element of the Priestly world view that is present in
the cosmological, existential, and praxeological elements of
that world view, and is operative within the framework of the
cosmological, societal, and cultic orders, is the idea that order is
established through the careful observation of categorical
divisions, through the recognition and maintenance of boundaries.

In Israel, the order of creation—cosmic, social, cultic—was
threatened by the sin of the people and the impurity that arises
from that sin and defiles the sanctuary. The sin of the nation
threatened Yahweh's continued presence in the midst of the
community and brought about the possibility that Yahweh
might be driven from their midst. If this were to happen, it
would threaten the security and well-being of the community
because it was Yahweh's dwelling in the sanctuary that
brought about the security and well-being of the community.
The confusion of categories—defilement in the holy place and
camp—brought about a collapse of order. This collapse of
order, brought about by the confusion of categories, was
reflected in the possibility that Yahweh would be driven from
the tabernacle—a clear image of chaos and disorder.

The Priestly Redaction of the Sinai Material
(Exod. 24.15–Lev. 16.34)

Introduction
The Priestly redaction of Exod. 24.15–Lev. 16.34 provides an
important key to a proper understanding of the Priestly world
view as it relates to ritual. It must be assumed that the material could have been shaped differently than it now is struc-

46 *The Ideology of Ritual*

tured. Thus, it is important to give close attention to the way in which the Priests did structure and shape these texts. It will be argued that the redaction of this material reflects a theological concern for sacred space.[1]

    I.   Introduction: Yahweh on Mount Sinai (Exod. 24.15-18)

    II.   Instructions for construction of sacred space (Exod. 25–31)

             JE narrative: Golden calf rebellion[2]

    III.   Construction of sacred space (Exod. 35–40)

    IV.   Instructions for sacrificial activity in sacred space (Lev. 1–7)
          A.   From the viewpoint of the offerer (Lev. 1–5)

               1. עלה (1.3-17)
               2. מנחה (2.1-16)
               3. שלמים (3.1-17)
               4. חטאת (4.1–5.13)
               5. אשם (5.14-26)

          B.   From the viewpoint of the priests[3] (Lev. 6–7)

               1. עלה (6.1-6)
               2. מנחה (6.7-11)
               3. Offering of priesthood on day of anointing (6.12-16)
               4. חטאת (6.17-23)
               5. אשם (7.1-10)
               6. זבח שלמים (7.11-18)
               7. Concluding instructions (7.19-38)

    V.   Ordination of priesthood in sacred space (Lev. 8–9)

    VI.   Narrative: Improper practices in sacred space (Lev. 10)

1 E.G. Newing ('A Rhetorical and Theological Analysis of the Hexateuch', *SEAJT* 22 [1981], pp. 1-15) has argued that the redactional structure of the Hexateuch itself has placed the central focus on God's *presence* in the tent (Exod. 33.1-17), 'mediated through the face to face encounter with Moses and represented realistically in the Covenant Law written on the tablets of stone' (p. 11). In other words, at the heart of the Hexateuch is a concern for divine presence presented in spatial categories.

2 For the purposes of the present argument, it is not necessary to take account of this JE narrative.

3 For this distinction between Lev. 1–5 and Lev. 6–7, see G.J. Wenham, *The Book of Leviticus*, pp. 116-19. Milgrom ('Leviticus', *IDBSup*, p. 541) understands chs. 6–7 to be structured according to the sanctity of the sacrifices and offerings.

VII.   Causes of defilement and purification rituals concerned with
       sacred space (Lev. 11–15)
       A.   Clean and unclean animals: dietary instructions
            (Lev. 11)
       B.   Defilement through birth and purification (Lev. 12)
       C.   Defilement from leprosy (Lev. 13–14)
            1. Determination of leprosy (Lev. 13)
            2. Purification from leprosy defilement (Lev. 14)
       D.   Uncleanness derived from bodily discharge (Lev. 15)

VIII. Annual day of purification and restoration of sacred space
       (Lev. 16)

In Exodus 25–31 Yahweh gives Moses instructions for constructing the tabernacle. Seven times the phrase 'and Yahweh
said to Moses' occurs in these texts (Exod. 25.1; 30.11; 30.17, 22,
34; 31.1; 31.12). The recurrance of this phrase serves to
emphasize the divine origin of the instructions for the tabernacle.[1] Kearney has argued that the seven speeches by
Yahweh in Exodus 25–31 correspond to the seven speeches of
creation in Gen. 1.1–2.4a, the seventh speech in both cases
emphasizing the holiness of the Sabbath.[2] While not all of
Kearney's arguments for correspondence are convincing, the
attempt to relate cosmos and cult is important. Cosmos
provides the necessary context for correct enactment of ritual;
ritual only has meaning within a specific cosmos. Furthermore, these texts indicate that just as cosmos originated with
Yahweh, so also the form of sacred space, of cult, originated
with Yahweh.

The purpose of the tabernacle is stated in three texts: an
introductory statement in Exod. 25.8-9; a passage discussing
the ark in Exod. 25.22; and a summary statement in Exod.
29.38-46. The introductory text is of central importance: 'and
let them make me a sanctuary, that I may dwell in their
midst. According to all that I show you concerning the pattern

---

1 A similar emphasis is made in those texts that state that the *tabnit* of the
   tabernacle complex was *shown* to Moses (Exod. 25.9, 40; 26.30; 27.8). The
   Priestly traditionists have preferred 'speaking' as the dominant form of
   revelation in the final redaction of the material. On the importance of the
   speech formulae in the Pentateuch, see C.J. Labuschagne, 'The Pattern of
   the Divine Speech Formulas in the Pentateuch', *VT* 32 (1982), pp. 268-96.
2 'Creation and Liturgy', pp. 375-87.

of the tabernacle, and of all its furniture, so you shall make it (Exod. 25.8-9)'. A similar idea is reiterated in Exod. 29.45: 'And I will dwell among the people of Israel, and I will be their God'. Of central importance for the Priestly traditionists is the idea that the tabernacle serves as the dwelling place of Yahweh—it is the means by which Yahweh will dwell in the midst of Israel.

In Exodus 35–40 the writers tell of the building and construction of the tabernacle. These chapters emphasize that the work was done in accord with what Yahweh had commanded Moses. No fewer than twenty-one times is this idea found in these chapters. Exod. 40.17-33 is of particular importance. These verses describe the actual construction of the tabernacle by Moses. In this brief text, the phrase that Moses did 'just as Yahweh had commanded' occurs seven times (vv. 19, 21, 23, 25, 27, 29, 32). Thus, the instructions are given in seven speeches of Yahweh and the actual construction of the tabernacle takes place in seven distinct acts. The Priestly traditionists have clearly linked this text to the Priestly creation account by the use of the phrase 'so Moses finished the work' (v. 33), a clear parallel to the phrase 'so God finished his work' in Gen. 2.2.[1]

At the conclusion of the text narrating the construction of the tabernacle, the Priests state that the cloud covered the tent of meeting and the glory of Yahweh filled the tabernacle (Exod. 40.34-38). Yahweh has descended from the mountain and taken up residence in the tabernacle. The tabernacle now reflects the realization of a goal—Yahweh dwelling in the midst of Israel.

It is often argued that the instructions for sacrifice in Leviticus 1–7 interrupt the narrative of the construction of the tabernacle and the ordination of the priesthood (Lev. 8–9). There is a certain 'logic', however, that seems to be at work in this particular shaping of the material. Sacred space has been constructed according to the pattern given by Yahweh; it is now necessary to detail the form of activity that is to take place in sacred space. Just as Yahweh gave instructions for the

---

1 Blenkinsopp ('The Structure of P', p. 278) notes this.

construction of sacred space, Yahweh now gives instruction for the ritual that is to take place in that sacred structure.

Again, the phrase 'and Yahweh said to Moses' plays an important structural role in these texts. Excluding the introductory statement of Lev. 1.1-2 and the concluding statement in Lev. 7.37-38, the phrase occurs seven times in these speeches (5.14; 6.1, 8, 19, 24; 7.22, 28). This series of seven speeches giving instructions for proper activity in sacred space parallel the seven speeches giving the instructions for constructing sacred space, which in turn reflect the seven acts of speech in the construction of cosmos in Gen. 1.1–2.4a. That the priests understood sacrificial activity in the context of sacred space is clearly supported by the repeated emphasis that such activity is to take place 'before Yahweh' (Lev. 1.5; 3.6, 12; 4.4), at the 'door of the tent of meeting' (Lev. 1.3; 3.2; 4.4), or at the altar of the door of the tent of meeting (Lev. 1.5, 11; 4.7). Sacred activity is clearly oriented by its being enacted in relation to sacred space. Thus, the tabernacle structure joins together the two ideas of Yahweh's presence in the midst of Israel and Israel's presence before Yahweh in the sacrificial cult.

Leviticus 8–9 present the ordination of Aaron and his sons into the priesthood and the inauguration and founding of the tabernacle cult. The ritual of ordination is to be enacted in the context of the whole community (Lev. 8.1-4) and is focused spatially on the door of the tent of meeting (Lev. 8.3, 33). Indeed, the entire seven day period of the priests' ordination is a time when Aaron and his sons are to remain at the door of the tent. Conjoined with the ritual of the ordination of the priesthood is the ritual of the anointing of the tabernacle and its utensils in order to consecrate them, to set them apart.

The text of Lev. 8 also reflects the redactional structure of seven speeches already seen repeatedly above. The phrase, 'as Yahweh commanded Moses', indicating that Moses was following the instructions of Yahweh, occurs seven times (vv. 4, 9, 13, 17, 21, 29, 36). The importance of this structuring pattern of seven for the larger context can be seen in the following:

7 acts of speech: construction of the created order (Gen. 1.1–2.4a)

> 7 speeches: instructions for the construction of sacred space
>   (Exod. 25–31)
> 7 acts of Moses: the actual construction of sacred space
>   (Exod. 40.17-33)
> 7 speeches: instructions for sacrificial activity in sacred
>   space (Lev. 1–7)
> 7 acts: the ritual for the ordination of the priesthood (Lev. 8)

The 'logic' of this argument is clear: (1) construction of cosmos; (2) construction of sacred space; (3) instructions for sacrificial activity in sacred space; (4) ordination of the priesthood which will conduct the sacrificial activity in sacred space.

Leviticus 9 narrates the first presentation of sacrifices by the newly ordained priesthood at the door of the tent. These sacrifices are offered so that the glory of Yahweh will appear at the tent (vv. 4, 6). The sacrifices were offered, the people were blessed, 'and the glory of Yahweh appeared to all the people. And fire came forth from before Yahweh and consumed the burnt offering and the fat upon the altar; and when all the people saw it, they shouted, and fell on their faces' (Lev. 9.23-24). The tabernacle cult has become operational. The space has been constructed, the priests have been set apart to that space, and the appropriate activity has been undertaken. All the people see the fire of Yahweh come forth and consume the offering and know that Yahweh dwells in their midst. An ideal has been realized.

No sooner has the tabernacle cult become operative, however, than two of Aaron's sons perform improper activity in the sacred space—they offer unholy fire before Yahweh. Leviticus 10 narrates a problem raised by sacred space and uses as its example two members of the priesthood. A central focus of this chapter is clearly that of sacred space. Nadab and Abihu died *before Yahweh* when fire came forth from the presence of Yahweh. Further, Moses cautions Aaron, Mishael, and Elzaphan: 'Do not go out from the door of the tent of meeting, *lest you die*, for the anointing oil of Yahweh is upon you' (Lev. 10.7).

Finally, Leviticus 10 not only looks back and addresses a problem raised by the construction of sacred space, but also looks forward to problems of defilement of sacred space. In

vv. 8-11, Yahweh speaks to Aaron and says in part: 'You are to separate (להבדיל) the holy from the not-holy and the clean from the unclean; and you are to teach the people of Israel all the statutes which Yahweh has spoken to them by Moses'. A central element of the Priestly duties is to make distinctions, to separate, between the holy and not-holy, the clean and the unclean. Just as cosmic order was established through a series of separations, so social and cultic order, in addition to cosmic order, are realized and maintained by the observation of categorical and conceptual 'separations'. It is to such matters of the distinction between clean and unclean that the Priestly writers now turn.

Leviticus 11–15 present a series of *torot* which are spoken by Yahweh to Moses and Aaron. Yahweh instructs them on causes of defilement of sacred space. The key issue throughout these chapters is the distinction between clean and unclean, and this emphasis clearly grows out of a concern for the integrity of sacred space. In Lev. 15.31, a conclusion of sorts, we read: 'Thus you shall keep the people of Israel separate from their uncleanness, lest they die in their uncleanness by defiling my tabernacle that is in their midst'. Clear statement is given here to the belief that the sin of the people produces defilement of the sanctuary (cf. Lev. 20.3; Num. 19.20).

Defilement of the sanctuary is of such concern to the Priestly writers because it threatens the integrity of sacred space, the dwelling place of Yahweh. Thus defilement of the tabernacle threatens to drive Yahweh from the midst of Israel. It is Yahweh's dwelling in the tabernacle that is of crucial theological importance for the Priestly writers. It is one constitutive element of their notion of order. Thus, sacred space must be protected and cleansed when necessary in order to maintain Yahweh's presence in the holy of holies.

Leviticus 16 serves as a closure to this block of material focused on sacred space. This chapter details the ritual to be enacted once a year in the context of the whole Israelite community; a ritual which serves to purify the tabernacle and eliminate sin from the camp. This view of the ritual is clearly stated in v. 16: 'Thus Aaron shall perform the act of *kipper* for the holy place because of the uncleanesses of the people of Israel, and because of their transgressions, all their sins, so he shall do for the tent of meeting which abides with them in the midst of their uncleannesses'. The summary statement in vv. 29-34 echoes this idea: 'For on this day shall the act of *kipper* be performed for you, to cleanse you; from all your sins you shall be clean *before* Yahweh' (v. 30). The act of *kipper* shall be performed, v. 33 states, for the sanctuary, the tent of meeting and altar, for the priests and for all the people of the assembly. This day recognizes the threat to the holy place posed by uncleanness and provides an annual ritual means to purge defilement from the camp and to eliminate the sin of the people. It is the annual, communal ritual by which sacred space can be restored to a state of purity and holiness so that Yahweh can remain in the midst of Israel.

Conclusion

The conceptual category of sacred space plays a key role in the Priestly understanding of order, of meaning, of blessing, of national identity. The Priestly writers have placed the construction and meaning of sacred space in the context of the construction and meaning of cosmic order. Just as Yahweh constructed the created order in seven acts of speech, so Yahweh gave instructions for the construction of sacred space in seven speeches. So also Yahweh gave instructions for the sacrificial activity to be performed in sacred space in seven speeches. Moses constructs the tabernacle in seven acts and ordains the priesthood in seven acts. Cult is situated in cosmos; they are interrelated. The cultic order is one element of the created order. The Priestly writers have focused on the conceptual category of sacred space to make this clear.

Order and the Types of Rituals

The argument of this study is that Priestly rituals are concerned with the establishment and maintenance of order and that this ritual concern is grounded in Priestly creation theology. It will thus be useful to present a typology of Priestly rituals in order to demonstrate the various ways in which ritual functions in relation to order.

Rites of Passage

The seminal work of A. van Gennep[1] on rites of passage has given basic shape to the study of ritual from a cultural perspective. Van Gennep argued that rites of passage have a basic structure which may be graphically presented as follows:

<u>Status A // Marginal Period // Status B</u>

Rites of passage, as the name suggests, are rites designed to pass a person or community from one social, and therefore conceptual, status to another. Such rites take place in a social context and require a social context with its roles and institutions in order to function. The marginal period of the rite is the crucial segment of the rite. It is in this period that the person or persons undergoing the rite are neither in status A nor status B—they are in a state of passage.

Victor Turner has given specific and careful attention to rites of passage and has clarified the way they work, their structure, and their characteristics.[2] Turner studied rites of passage in terms of his larger understanding of the processual nature of society. His particular focus has been on van Gennep's marginal stage, or, as Turner prefers, the liminal stage of a rite. This is a time when the person undergoing passage is 'betwixt and between'. The person is no longer in status A, but neither has the person arrived in status B. Thus, the person in the liminal stage of the rite stands outside the normal structures of society.

Turner details a number of characteristics of the liminal stage of rites of passage. First, in the liminal stage of a rite of passage the normal structures of society are not operative. Thus, it is a time of disorder, or what might be called chaos. It is a ritual state in which the norms of everyday life cease to function. A second characteristic, which is a reflection of the breakdown of order, is that of status reversal, commonly found in community rituals.[3] Those of high status are brought

---

1 *The Rites of Passage* (trans. M.B. Vizedom and G.L. Caffee; Chicago: University of Chicago, 1960).
2 *The Forest of Symbols*, pp. 93-111; *The Ritual Process*, pp. 94-165; *From Ritual to Theatre*, pp. 20-60.
3 *The Ritual Process*, pp. 166-203.

low and the low are exalted. This produces a leveling effect and a situation of equality. A third characteristic is what Turner calls communitas.[1] People placed in a common ritual state of liminality discover a special bond among themselves. Standing outside normal societal structures and discovering equality in their common 'outsider' status, people are brought together in a unique relationship of mutual respect, concern, and humility. The liminal stage of the ritual breaks down the normal order of society in order to reconstruct at the end of the ritual a new state of societal order. Such rituals ultimately serve to guarantee the normal order of society, but they do this by first producing the experience of social 'chaos'. It is through this experience of the breakdown of order that order is ultimately reestablished and maintained.

It is precisely in terms of this concern for order that Turner's discussion of liminality is insightful for understanding Priestly rituals. As already argued, the Priestly traditionists had as a primary theological concern the establishment of order—cosmic, social, and cultic. Ritual serves as the primary means by which they address the question of order. There are three basic types of rituals in the Priestly ritual system when viewed from the concern for order.

Founding Rituals. Founding rituals are rituals designed to bring into being a certain state, institution, or situation. These rituals present the founding act or origin of something. As such they found some element of the larger order of creation, society, or cult. Two examples from Priestly rituals are the ordination of the priesthood in Leviticus 8 and the inauguration of the tabernacle cult in Leviticus 9. While it is clear that these two rituals are closely interrelated, they both present distinct moments of origin. The official priesthood of the tabernacle is founded in Leviticus 8, and, indeed, comes into being through the enactment of that ritual. The tabernacle cult becomes operative in Leviticus 9 when the newly founded priesthood offers the sacrifices for the first time and fire comes forth from Yahweh and consumes the sacrifice. These rituals reflect the normal structure of rites of passage in

1 *Ibid.*, pp. 94-165.

that they pass, in these cases, persons and space from one status to another.

Maintenance Rituals. Maintenance rituals are rituals designed to maintain the already established order. Such rituals may be seen as protectors of the divinely created order of cosmos, society, and cult. The annual cycle of rituals as detailed in the Priestly ritual code in Numbers 28–29 is a good example of this. The regularly prescribed sacrifices and offerings are clearly distinguished from the occasional sacrifices and offerings called for by sin, defilement, or vows. These regularly prescribed sacrifices and offerings are designed to maintain the divinely created order and demonstrate the ongoing existence of that order.

Restoration Rituals . The dominant type of rituals found in the Priestly ritual system are rituals of restoration. These rituals are designed to restore the order of creation when it has been broken, ruptured, or damaged. The ritual for purification of the leper is a clear example of this type of ritual. The individual is passed from a state of defilement to a state of purity. In a similar way it may be said that the ritual of *yom hakkippurim* passes the tabernacle and camp from a state of impurity to purity.

Space, Time, and Status

Spatial Categories

Spatial categories play a crucial role in the enactment of the Priestly rituals. It will be useful at this point to present graphically the basic map of the tabernacle cult. This map is operative throughout Priestly rituals. It will be clear that space is understood as more than just a series of places, but takes on specific qualities with specific meanings in the Priestly ritual system.

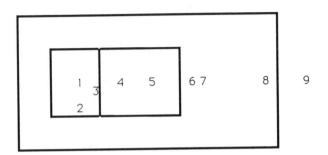

1. This represents the כפרת and the ark on which it rests. It is the place where Yahweh resides and is the place from which Yahweh will speak (Exod. 25.22; Num. 7.89).

2. This represents the inner sanctum of the sacred structure. In Leviticus 16 it is simply called 'the holy place' (הקדש) and further defined as the area behind the veil (מבית לפרכת; v. 2). Elsewhere, this area is referred to as 'the most holy place'. 'The veil shall separate (והבדילה) for you the holy place from the most holy place' (קדש הקדשים; Exod. 26.33; cf. Exod. 26.34; Num. 4.4, 19; 18.9, 10).

3. This represents the פרכת, the veil, that separates the holy area from the most holy area (see Exod. 26.31-33). It marks the key boundary between the spatial area where Yahweh resides and all other areas.

4. This represents the golden altar of incense. This is the altar where the special 'inner' incense was burned (see Exod. 30.7-8).

5. This represents the area inside the tent but separated from the inner sanctum. It is a 'holy place',[1] and thus a place reserved for the priests, but less holy than the inner sanctum, which is barred to all the priests except the high priest who is permitted to enter only once a year.

---

1 On the use of the designations 'holy' and 'most holy', see Haran, *Temples*, p. 172 n. 50 and Milgrom, 'The Compass of Biblical Sancta', *JQR* 65 (1975), pp. 205-16.

6. This represents the area generally designated 'before Yahweh' (לפני יהוה). It is often qualified by the phrase 'at the door of the tent of meeting' (Lev. 16.7; cf. Exod. 4.11, 42; Lev. 1.3; 14.11, 23; 15.14). This is not a precisely defined area. The outer bound seems to be the altar of the burnt offering which is located at the door of the tabernacle (Exod. 40.29; cf. Lev. 4.7, 18) and may serve as the place to which the people come to present their offerings to Yahweh. The area between the altar of the burnt-offering and the opening to the tent was probably limited to the priests. The area just beyond the altar would be the place where the people gave their offerings to the priests.[1]

7. This represents the altar of the burnt offerings which is located at the door of the tent of meeting.

8. This represents the border of the Israelite camp. This boundary is carefully guarded in the ritual of Leviticus 16 against the impurity that might enter the camp through the one who leads the goat to Azazel and the one who takes the refuse of the offerings outside the camp to be burned. Such a careful drawing of the camp boundary suggests that there is a distinction made between the space 'inside' the camp and the space 'outside' the camp.

9. This represents the area termed 'outside the camp'. It is, as noted above, a spatial category that is emphatically distinguished from the area 'inside the camp'.

Temporal Categories

In the same way that space takes on meaning in Priestly ritual, so also ritual time becomes meaningful, interpreted time. Temporal categories provide one of the means by which the Priestly traditionists mapped out and enacted a meaningful experience of the created order. Certain rituals, directed at the concern for order, are called for at specific times and because of specific situations. Just as rituals cannot be per-

---

1 For a discussion of the area of the tabernacle complex specified for the priests, see Haran, *Temples*, pp. 181-87 and the criticisms of Haran in Milgrom 'The Shared Custody of the Tabernacle and a Hittite Analogy', *JAOS* 90 (1970), pp. 207-208, n. 25.

formed at just any place, so they cannot be performed at just any time.

Precision is called for in this context, however, in that temporal categories are operative in several distinct ways in the Priestly ritual system. First, a distinction must be drawn between three distinct 'times' calling for rituals. These three times reflect the three types of rituals in the Priestly ritual system discussed earlier. There is the time of founding rituals. This 'time' is a time in the distant past when the tabernacle, priesthood, and cult were founded. While rituals reflecting similar structure and concerns may have been performed regularly, the time of the founding of cult is placed by the Priestly writers in the time of the wilderness, at Mt Sinai. Secondly, there are the 'times' which call for the regularly prescribed sacrifices and offerings designed to maintain the divinely created order. These regularly prescribed times are times built into the very structure of the created order and serve as one means of maintaining that order. Finally, there are the ritual 'times' called for by a disruption of order— cleansing and purification rituals. These 'times' are generated when a person or the community sins or becomes impure. These rituals are prescribed, but are enacted only as occasion and need demand their enactment.

In addition to these 'times' that call for ritual, there is also the time required to enact a ritual. The primary temporal category in the Priestly ritual system is a seven day period of ritual enactment. Paralleling the seven days of the creation of cosmic order, several Priestly rituals call for a seven day period for the full enactment of the ritual: the recovered leper (Lev. 14.8,9); purification from corpse-contamination (Num. 6.9-10, Num. 19.11, 12, 14, 16; Num. 31.9); at the birth of a male child (Lev. 12.2); cleansing from bodily discharge (Lev. 15.13, 19, 24, 28); the ritual for the ordination of the priesthood (Exod. 29.35; Lev. 8.33-35) and the consecration of the altar (Exod. 29.37). Thus, the analysis of ritual must pay close attention to the way that ritual time functions as meaningful time and how it functions in the enactment and completion of the ritual.

Status

It is clear that the Priestly ritual system is concerned to a great degree with the status of place (the holy place), people (priests, clean and unclean), and objects (the altar). Further than this, the Priestly rituals are concerned with the status of cosmos, society, and cult. Ritual is a means of establishing, changing, and transforming the status of persons and objects within the order of creation.

This concern for status reflects the Priestly understanding that order emerges through the correct separation of categories—of the maintenance of boundaries of existence. The priests are told to separate between the holy and the not-holy, between the clean and the unclean. In a world view so concerned with category distinction, it is not surprising that a major concern of ritual focuses on the issue of status. The holiness of the holy place must be guarded, protected, maintained. If it is not so maintained, the integrity of the holy place is disrupted, is broken, and chaos results. The set apart status of the priesthood is carefully guarded. It would be inappropriate for a non-priest to enter and perform service in the holy place. The camp must be protected from impurity and defilement, lest the whole camp suffer. Thus, it can be seen that the issue of status plays a part in the three types of Priestly rituals: founding of status (the ordination of the priesthood and the consecration of the holy place); maintenance of status (the maintenance of the holiness of the holy place and the purity of the camp); the restoration of status (the passage from defilement to purity).

Priestly Ritual and Priestly Theology

Ritual is one means by which society enacts a world of meaning, acts in and on a world of meaning, positions itself in a world of meaning, and reflects on the nature and meaning of that world. Rituals are not simply a series of formal actions undertaken for the sake of actions. Rituals are one means of world construction.

It is the world in which Priestly rituals take place and the world constructed through these rituals that is sought after in this study. Taking clues from the shape of the Priestly traditions, the study argues that creation theology forms the broad context of meaning for understanding Priestly rituals. The divinely created order—consisting of cosmos, society, and cult—serves as the primary context of meaning for these rituals. The primary question addressed in examining specific parts of the larger Priestly ritual system concerns the way in which the rituals relate to the foundation, maintenance, and restoration of the divinely created order.

Thus, it may be said that for the priests, ritual was one means, and it appears to be the primary means, for theological reflection. In their rituals they interact in various ways with the divinely created order. Such ritual interaction is based on reflection and meaning. Thus, the study will not only look at the mechanics of how the rituals unfold in their enactment, but the way in which the rituals serve as meaningful statements about God, the world, and human existence.

Chapter 3

LEVITICUS 16

Introduction
Leviticus 16 details an annual ritual which is communal in
nature. It is a yearly ritual undertaken to deal with the
problems of sin and defilement in the context of the whole
Israelite community.[1] Its concerns are clearly socio-cultic, but
at the same time it reflects broader categories. The ritual
clearly reflects the structure of a community rite of passage.
More specifically, it reflects community passage to a renewed
and reordered state of existence. Thus, it must be seen
primarily as a ritual of restoration—it serves to restore the
community to its prescribed and founded state. Thus, restoration will include in this context the idea of re-founding—a
return to the founded order of creation.

Within this context, it will be demonstrated that the central
organizing categories operative in the ritual are broader than
defilement and cleansing. The concern of the ritual is a
concern for the reestablishment of order, and the restructuring of the categories of order and chaos. Thus, the ritual
reflects the need for an annual reestablishment of the order of
creation, an order consisting of cosmic, social, and cultic
categories. As such, the ritual reflects characteristics of

---

1 See Milgrom, 'Atonement, day of', *IDBSup* (1976), pp. 82-83; M. Noth,
Leviticus (OTL; rev. edn Philadelphia: Westminster, 1977), p. 122; G.J.
Wenham, *The Book of Leviticus*, pp. 227-28, 236-37.

annual new year festivals.[1] This is an annual ritual concerned
with the reestablishment of the prescribed and founded order
of creation in which the community situates itself in the world,
a world constructed and enacted ritually.

The central interpretive question, then, must be concerned
with discovering how the ritual functions to effect the passage
of cosmos, community, and cult to a renewed and restored
state. This is clearly a question that goes beyond the issue of the
mechanics of the ritual to a question of meaning. How does
this ritual function as a meaningful enactment of world in
Priestly ideology and theology? The present analysis of Leviticus 16 will seek to locate the ritual in the context of the
Priestly world view and will present arguments in support of
the following theses:

1. Leviticus 16 reflects a coherent, intelligible conception
   of ritual action as an enactment of world through the
   ritual breakdown and reestablishment of the categorical distinctions of holy/profane, pure/impure, and
   order/chaos. Each of these sets of relations has one
   element that is a dangerous, destructive, invasive power
   which must be ritually ordered.

2. These sets of categories are given ordered relations
   through a carefully constricted time, place, person, and
   series of actions in which all of the sets of relations are
   undone in a period of ritual liminality and through
   which alone the order and life of cosmos, camp, and cult
   are reordered.

3. The key to this liminal confusion and reestablishment of
   the categories, undertaken on behalf of cosmos, camp
   and cult, is the ritual role of the high priest who, as the
   representative of the people and in the context of a
   liminal state, sets aside the normal separations of the
   categories of holy/profane, pure/impure, and order/
   chaos and, through his ritual actions, restores the
   normal, ordered relations of these categories.

1 See M. Eliade, *The Myth of the Eternal Return*, pp. 51-62.

Textual Framework

Lev. 16.29-34 presents a final summary statement concerning
the ritual and includes a call to be careful to observe the ritual
once a year (vv. 29-30, 34). This summary is generally considered to be a later addition to the text because of the shift in
these verses to second person plural forms.[1] As such, it represents an important level of tradition regarding the ritual and
is to be valued as a synthesizing 'interpretation' of the whole
ritual.

Several distinct ritual elements are addressed in these
verses. Temporal notices are given in v. 29: בחדש השביעי בעשור
לחדש; v. 31: שבת שבתון היא; and v. 34: enact this ritual אחת בשנה.
Those involved in the ritual are noted as follows: v. 29: האזרח והגר
הגר בתוככם (instructed to refrain from work); v. 32: הכהן אשר־ימשח
אתו ואשר־ימלא את־ידו לכהן תחת אביו (the one who performs the
primary act of the ritual, the *kipper*-act); v. 33: עם הקהל; הכהנים;
v. 34: בני ישראל (the ones for whom the *kipper*-act is performed). The objects and materials used in the ritual are noted
as follows: בגדי הבד בגדי הקדש (the clothes worn by the priest
performing the *kipper*-act); המזבח, אהל מועד, מקדש הקדש (the
objects that receive the *kipper*-act). The ritual actions to be
observed and performed are indicated: v. 29: תענו את־נפשתיכם (see
also v. 31) and וכל־מלאכה לא תעשו (observed by the native and the
alien); v. 33: כפר (performed by the priest with reference to the
אהל מועד, מקדש הקדש, and המזבח). Verse 30 states the purpose of
the central ritual act of the priest with regard to the people
involved in the ritual: יכפר עליכם לטהר אתכם (see also vv. 33-34).
Thus, vv. 29-34 state that this is a ritual to be enacted *once* a
year, on the tenth day of the seventh month, that revolves
around two central ritual acts: (1) the ritual humbling of the
people and (2) the *kipper*-act performed by the anointed priest
with reference to the priests, the people, and the holy shrine.

The opening verses (vv. 1-3a) and the context of the ritual
suggested there move in a different direction. Verse 1 relates
the ritual to the context of the death of Aaron's two sons,

---

1 K. Elliger, *Leviticus* (HAT 4; Tübingen: Mohr [Paul Siebeck], 1966), p. 207;
   Noth, *Leviticus*, p. 126. Neither of these writers sees a literary unity in
   these verses.

presumably Nadab and Abihu, as recounted in Lev. 10.1-3.[1] In Lev. 16.1, their death is placed in conjunction with their draw-ing near before Yahweh (בקרבתם לפני־יהוה וימתו). Their death presents the occasion for Yahweh to give instructions on how Aaron, the high priest, can *safely* draw near to Yahweh.[2] Lev. 10.1-3 indicates that they died because they 'offered unholy fire before Yahweh, such as he had not commanded them' (vv. 1-2). The text focuses attention on the *unholy fire* brought *before Yahweh*.[3]

While the precise nature of the 'unholy fire' remains unclear,[4] the problem may be resolved by comparing the instructions given to Aaron on how to enter before Yahweh in Lev. 16.12-13. He is to take fire from the coals of fire (האש מעל) on the altar *before Yahweh*. This is the only fire that may be used for safe entry before Yahweh. Lev. 10.2 emphasizes that Nadab and Abihu died 'before Yahweh', thereby focusing attention on the issue of coming 'before Yahweh'. Thus, the fire of the incense is an important element for safe passage 'before Yahweh', but the incense, according to Lev. 16.12-13, can only achieve its protective ritual function when it is burned by the fire from upon the altar 'before Yahweh'.

---

1 For the literary-critical problems, see Noth (*Leviticus*, pp. 12-13) and Elliger (*Leviticus*, pp. 11-12, 104-39).

2 Literary criticism has often overlooked the significance of the way in which the narrative of P (= Pg) is used as the occasion for specific ritual instructions. This has brought about an undue emphasis on the dichotomy between Pg and its supplements. The very fact that the narrative has brought about explication through ritual instruction should give rise to a concern for this relationship. If one can speak of a Priestly circle that stands behind the Priestly traditions, then the relationships established between the Priestly narratives and the Priestly rituals must be given more weight in the formulation of Priestly theology.

3 The immediate context of this story should not be lost. In Lev. 9.22-24, upon the first offering of sacrifices by the newly ordained priests, the glory of Yahweh appeared to all the people, 'and fire came forth from before Yahweh and consumed the burnt offering and the fat upon the altar' (v. 24). Just as fire came forth from Yahweh and consumed the offerings affirming proper offering, so fire came forth from Yahweh and consumed Nadab and Abihu for offering improper fire.

4 For detailed discussions of the Nadab and Abihu incident, see R. Gradwohl, 'Das "fremde Feuer" von Nadab und Abihu', *ZAW* 75 (1963), pp. 288-96 and J.C.H. Laughlin, 'The "Strange Fire" of Nadab and Abihu', *JBL* 95 (1976), pp. 559-65.

Thus, both Lev. 10.1-3 and Leviticus 16 have as a central concern the way in which the priests may come 'before Yahweh'—Lev. 10.1-3 by demonstrating an instance of 'unsafe' entry and Leviticus 16 by prescribing a means for 'safe' entry. The entry of Nadab and Abihu was improper because they brought in fire that had its origin 'outside' the realm of the sacred, it was 'unholy fire'. They, thus, threatened the integrity of the sacred by bringing in fire that was categorically distinct from the realm of the holy. It was fire distinct from that commanded by Yahweh who resides in the holy of holies. Their sin can thus be interpreted as a confusion of categories:[1] fire from outside the sacred area was brought into the sacred area. [2] This shows the intersection of conceptual categories, the holy and the not-holy, and spatial categories, the holy place 'before Yahweh' and all other places.

The 'drawing near before Yahweh' in Lev. 16.1-2 reflects this same intersection of categories, although it focuses more specifically on spatial categories—Aaron and his sons are not to come at any time into *the holy place* behind the פרכת, to the front of the כפרת which is on the ark. The ritual process that is depicted in Lev. 16 gives the means for accomplishing this. It is made clear, however, that this entry 'before Yahweh' is to happen only *once* a year and is to be for the purpose of performing the *kipper*-act. Thus, there is also the intersection of temporal categories.

Type of Material

Leviticus 16 is presented as instructions of Yahweh, spoken to Moses, to be related by Moses to Aaron. Verse 1 places the passage in the larger narrative context of the death of Aaron's two sons. Throughout vv. 1-28 the instructions are given in the

---

1 On the idea of boundaries and the understanding of 'sin' and 'pollution' as the breaking of boundaries, see Douglas, *Purity and Danger*, pp. 1-28; *idem, Implicit Meanings*, pp. 47-59. On the relation of cultural categories and ritual taboo, see E.M. Zuesse, 'Taboo and the Divine Order', *JAAR* 42 (1974), pp. 482-504; Comstock, 'A Behavioral Approach to the Sacred', pp. 625-43.
2 M. Haran, *Temples*, p. 232.

third person singular form and intended for Aaron. The change to the second person plural forms in vv. 29-34 might suggest a reading in the cult which served to interpret the ritual for the people. Thus, the description of the performance of the ritual is placed in the context of the cultic community, suggesting that the directions are now not only directed to the priests, but also to the community.[1] The final clause, v. 34b, is the typical execution formula, stating that Moses 'did just as Yahweh commanded him'.

The History of the Text

It is generally recognized that Leviticus 16 has a complex history of growth behind its present form.[2] There are literary tensions in the text that suggest multiple hands. It has, in fact, been suggested that there are multiple traditions represented in the text that were originally independent.[3] The question of the literary development of the chapter is compounded when the various levels of Leviticus 16 are placed within a larger scheme concerned with the growth of the Priestly strata.

While it is important to recognize the complexity of the chapter's growth, it is also important to examine the current

---

1   The phrase עולם לחקת לכם והיתה occurs in Lev. 16.29, 34, while the simple חקת עולם is found in Lev. 16.31. Elsewhere in P these phrases have primary reference to cultic matters: the priesthood and certain of its rights and duties (Exod. 27.21; 28.43; 29.9; Lev. 7.36; 10.9; 24.3; Num. 18.23); the observance of festivals (Exod. 12.14, 17; Lev. 23.14, 21, 31, 41); the uncleanness communicated to those coming into contact with the ashes of the red heifer or the waters of purification (Num. 19.10, 21); the prohibition of eating blood (Lev. 3.17); the command to bring sacrifices to the door of the tent (Lev. 17.7 [H]); and various other sacred matters; the use of the trumpets (Num. 10.8); the inheritance of land (Num. 27.11); laws concerning the murderer (Num. 35.29); the insistence on one law of offering for all (Num. 15.15). In all of these uses, it is clear that these are prescriptions that are concerned with sacred issues and are directed to the whole of the nation, and not simply to the priests. See R. Hentschke, *Satzung und Setzender* (BWANT 83; Stuttgart: Kohlhammer, 1963), pp. 42-45, 64-65.

2   For a review, see R. Rendtorff, *Die Gesetze in der Priesterschrift* (FRLANT [n.s.] 48; Göttingen: Vandenhoeck und Ruprecht, 1954), pp. 59-62 and Elliger, *Leviticus*, pp. 200-10.

3   See, for example, Noth, *Leviticus*, pp. 122-26; E. Otto and T. Schramm, *Festival and Joy* (BES; Nashville: Abingdon Press, 1980), pp. 85-92.

dynamics of the text as a self-contained unit of meaning. The
current shape of Leviticus 16 represents an important level of
development in any proper understanding of the history of
Israelite traditions. Any traditio-historical analysis of the text
that would try to arrange the different elements of this text
into a historical, chronological order is well-nigh impossible
because of the nature of the material. Even if one does
separate, from a traditio-historical perspective, for example,
the elements of the ritual concerned with the cleansing of the
sanctuary and those elements concerned with the two goats, it
is still important to understand the resulting structure of
meaning when the two are brought together. Is there a
conceptual framework behind the ritual and operative in the
ritual that is capable of holding together in a meaningful way
disparate traditions? Thus, the present analysis is concerned
with the ritual structure that is now prescribed in the text,
although it is recognized that the present structure has
evolved over a period of time.

The Elements of Ritual 1

Materials and Objects
There are four categories of materials and objects used in the
ritual described in Lev. 16.1-28. First, there is the ritual
clothing prescribed for the priest who performs the ritual.
These are generally described in v. 4 as 'the holy garments'
(בגדי־קדש). There are four distinct elements (v. 4): the holy linen
coat (כתנת־בד קדש); the linen breeches (מכנסי־בד) to be worn on
his flesh;2 the linen sash (אבנט בד); and the linen turban
(מצנפת בד).3 These are distinct from the glorious apparel of the
priest as described in Exodus 28, although in Exod. 28.42 the

---

1 T.P. van Baaren ('Theoretical Speculations on Sacrifice', *Numen* 11 [1964],
   pp. 3-12) gives a very helpful analysis of some of the formal elements
   involved in sacrifice which has influenced the discussion of ritual elements. He discusses six elements in sacrifice: the place and time of sacrifice; the manner or method of sacrifice; the recipient of the effects of the
   sacrifice; and the motivation or intention for offering sacrifice.
2 This phrase is concerned with the covering of the priest's sexual organs
   (cf. Exod. 28.4; Lev. 15.2-3, 7; Ezek. 16.26; 23.20).
3 For a full discussion of the clothing of the priests, see Haran, *Temples*,
   pp. 65-74.

linen breeches are also prescribed for Aaron's sons. An
important element in a correct understanding of this ritual is
the reason for this simple dress. Why is it prescribed for this
occasion?

There are two classes of ritual objects that need to be
distinguished. First, there are objects which are used to prepare for or to lead into a separate and distinct ritual action in
the larger ritual process.[1] In this category may be placed the
lots (גורלוֹח) cast over the two goats and the censer (מחתה) used to
burn the incense. The lots are used to determine the use of the
two goats in the ritual process, while the censer is used to burn
the incense which provides for the priest's safe entry into the
holy place. In both cases, it may be said that the objects
function primarily to prepare for another ritual act and are,
thus, not final ritual acts but instrumental ritual acts that
presuppose further ritual activity.

A second class of ritual objects consists of objects that are
used in the execution of a segment of a ritual and serve to
bring that segment of ritual to a state of completion. Such
objects serve as the focal points of ritual actions. The first of
such objects is the הכפרת which is located on the ark (v. 2: אשר
על־הארן)[2] in the inner sanctum. The blood sprinkling rite associated with it in Leviticus 16 is a central element of the ritual

---

1 For convenience, a ritual process, indicating the whole ritual, may be
   understood to be made up of several distinct ritual segments. A ritual
   segment refers to a self-contained series which brings to completion one
   step of the ritual process. Thus, in Lev. 16, the sections involved in the
   purgation of the sacred structure, or the actions involved with sending the
   one goat into the wilderness, may be referred to as ritual segments.
2 Verse 13 says הכפרת אשר על־העדות. This phrase is related to its use as a
   container for the tablets of the law (Exod. 25.16; 40.20). It is not necessary
   to review all the suggestions that have been made for understanding the
   כפרת (see Haran, *Temples*, pp. 246-59 and T.N.D. Mettinger, *The Dethronement of Sabaoth: Studies in the Shem and Kabod Theologies* [CB, OT series
   18; Lund: CWK Gleerup, 1982], pp. 87-88. Regardless of the original
   function of the כפרת, the latter has two primary notions associated with it
   in P. The first sees it as the point of meeting between Yahweh and Moses
   and the place where Yahweh will issue the commandments for Israel
   (Exod. 25.22). The second, emphasized in Lev. 16, sees it as a focal point of
   the *kipper*-act (obviously cognates) and may be simply understood as 'the
   place where the *kipper*-act is performed'.

and this is the only ritual in which the כפרת is involved.¹ A
second object that receives action in this ritual is the tent of
meeting (v. 16: אהל מועד).² It is also to receive the *kipper*-act as
did the כפרת in the holy place. Finally, the altar before Yahweh
(vv. 18-19) is to be the object of the *kipper*-act. This refers to
the altar of the burnt offerings that stands outside the tent.
These three objects play a role in one of the major segments of
the ritual (described in vv. 11-19) and it is only after the priest
has finished performing the *kipper*-act on these objects that
the ritual phase concerned with the live goat may begin (v. 20).

The final category of ritual elements consists of materials
used in the performance of the ritual. There are three classes
of materials that may be distinguished. First, there is water
which is used for bathing by the priest both before the ritual of
the *kipper*-acts and after (vv. 4, 24). Verse 24 specifies that the
final washing is to take place in a holy place.³ The one who lets
the goat go to Azazel is also to wash his clothes (יכבס בגדיו) and
bathe his body (רחץ את־בשרו) in water, before returning to the

1 This raises a question with regard to the relationship of the two roles
associated with the כפרת—the place of divine communication with Moses
and the place of the *kipper*-act. There is a tension between the statement
that the high priest alone is to enter the most holy place and then only once
a year and the idea that Moses regularly appears before the כפרת to receive
divine communication. Two points should be made with reference to this.
It is not impossible that the high priest's entry be limited as it is, while
Moses is allowed easier access. The reasons for their entry are distinct,
and the function of an object, and the beliefs associated with it, may vary
according to situations. Second, it may be that Moses is allowed entry into
the most holy place because of his role as mediator of the commandments
of Yahweh, necessary in order to receive the instructions for the operation
of the cult. Moses as the voice of Yahweh in establishing the cult stands
above the priests who are part of the cultic institution as prescribed by
Yahweh. Thus, there need not be a tension between Aaron's entry into the
most holy place *once* a year for the purpose of performing the *kipper*-act
and Moses' regular entry to receive the divine instructions.
2 For a review of scholarship on the traditions of the tent of meeting, see M.
Görg, *Das Zelt der Begegnung. Untersuchung zur Gestalt der sakralen
Zelttraditionen Altisraels* (BBB 27; Bonn: Hanstein, 1967), pp. 1-7; and for
the tent in P, see V. Fritz, *Tempel und Zelt: Studien zum Tempelbau in
Israel und zu dem Zeltheiligtum der Priesterschrift* (WMANT 47;
Neukirchen-Vluyn: Neukirchener Verlag, 1977), pp. 112-66.
3 It is probable that the bronze laver described in Exod. 30.17-21 is associated
with the washing of the priest described in Lev. 16.

camp (v. 26). The same procedure is prescribed for the one who burns, outside the camp, the skin, the flesh, and the dung of the bull and goat of the חטאת (v. 27).

A second type of material is the incense and its associated materials: the coals on which it is burnt (v. 12) and the cloud that issues from the burning incense (v. 13). The incense is specified as קטרת סמים דקה, sweet-smelling and finely ground incense. Lev. 16.12 is the only place the incense is described with the word דקה. Elsewhere, incense is specifically associated with the golden altar beside the veil marking off the most holy place, the incense altar (Exod. 30.6-9; 40.26-27). Haran argues that incense was used in the Israelite cult in three distinct ways.[1] First, it was used to supplement the grain offering. The normal spice for this was 'frankincense' (לבנה; Lev. 2.1, 15; 6.8; and elsewhere). The second use is the burning of incense in a censer (Lev. 10.1; Num. 16.6; and elsewhere). Haran argues that such usage was limited to the priests and was confined to the sacred area, although he does note the exception in Aaron's use of a censer in the camp in Num. 17.11-12.[2] The final use of incense was its burning on the altar of gold near the veil before the most holy area (Exod. 30.1-10). The incense burned on this altar was a distinct incense, described in Exod. 30.34-38, and is *most holy*. Hence, its domain is in the inner recesses of the sacred area. [3] This is the incense that Aaron would use in entering the most holy area in the ritual of Leviticus 16.

In Leviticus 16 the incense is to be burned on the coals drawn from the altar (v. 12), thus combining two elements set apart to the sacred area before Yahweh. The purpose was to create a cloud of smoke. This cloud was to act as a veil of protection for the priest upon entering the most holy area, *lest he die* (Lev. 16.13). It should be noted, however, that such 'veiling' at the same time is a 'revealing'. In the ritual act, the need for the incense and its presence in the inner sanctum

---

1 *Temples*, pp. 230-45.
2 *Ibid.*, pp. 238-41.
3 *Ibid.*, pp. 241-45.

communicate the reality of the divine presence in the inner sanctum.[1]

A final class of materials consists of the animals used for sacrifices and offerings in the ritual. A young bull (פר בן־בקר) is to be used for a חטאת and a ram (איל) for an עלה. Two goats (שעירי עזים) are also to be taken for a חטאת and a ram (איל) for an עלה. The bull is the חטאת for Aaron and his house, while one of the goats will serve as a חטאת for the people. The rams are to be burnt offerings for Aaron and his house and for the people. The blood of the bull and the goat is used in the central *kipper*-act by the priest. It is also prescribed that the fat of the חטאת be burned on the altar (v. 25) and the skin, flesh, and dung of the bull and goat offered as a חטאת, be taken outside the camp and burned.

Ritual Roles

There are three specific roles identified in the ritual of Leviticus 16. First, there is the role of the high priest, Aaron, who leads in the enactment of the ritual. As described in Leviticus 16, the ritual is presented as newly commanded by Yahweh and, hence, is enacted here for the first time. It is thus appropriate to understand Leviticus 16 as a paradigmatic account of the ritual of יום הכפרים and, thereby, supplies the script for all future enactments of the ritual. Aaron's role will subsequently be filled by the high priest. This is made clear in the summary statement of vv. 29-34. The priest who is anointed and dedicated to be priest in his father's place (הכהן אשר־ימשח אתו ואשר ימלא את־ידו לכהן תחת אביו) shall perform the ritual while wearing the linen garments (v. 32). A second role consists of the one who is to lead the goat into the wilderness. A third role is found in the one who takes the refuse of the bull and goat outside the camp for incineration. Little is said about these last two roles except that those who fill them must bathe before returning to the camp.

The summary statement of vv. 29-34 makes it clear that this ritual is a communal affair. While there are no specific

1 See T.W. Mann, *Divine Presence and Guidance in Israelite Tradition: The Typology of Exaltation* (JHNES; Baltimore: Johns Hopkins University, 1977), p. 257 and his 'The Pillar of Cloud in the Reed Sea Narrative', *JBL* 90 (1971), pp. 15-30; Cohn, *The Shape of Sacred Space*, pp. 50-51.

prescriptions for the people in vv. 1-28, their participation is enjoined by the prescriptions calling for a cessation of labor (v. 29), for self-affliction and humility (vv. 29, 31), and for a Sabbath of solemn rest (v. 31). In this way, the ritual takes on the character of a national day of purgation. The community becomes the participant on whose behalf the ritual is enacted, and evidence for this is found in the prescriptions for their participation through humility, affliction, and rest, and, at the same time, the one before whom the ritual is enacted. The ritual thus serves as an example of communal self-reflection which operates within the dynamics of defilement, purgation, and elimination.

Spatial Categories
There are three specific spatial categories involved in this ritual that call for interpretation.[1] These are categories that play a meaningful role in the enactment of the ritual and are crucial to its effectiveness. The first of these categories is the holy of holies. The holy of holies is crucial in this ritual precisely because this is the one ritual moment in the year when the high priest enters this area with the blood of sacrifices. The importance of this entry is underscored by the focus of the opening verses on Aaron's safe passage into this categorically distinct area. As will be argued, it is precisely a concern for the integrity of this most holy place that is at the heart of this ritual.

A second spatial category operative in the ritual is *the camp boundary*. This is seen in two ways. First, the instructions specify that the refuse of the burned חטאת is to be taken outside the camp (vv. 27-28). This suggests a concern for the integrity of the camp boundaries. In addition, this concern for the integrity of the camp boundaries is reflected in the prescription that the goat chosen for Azazel, bearing the sin of the people, be taken outside of the camp and released. Second, a concern for the integrity of the camp may be seen in the very

---

1 See D.P. Wright, 'The Disposal of Impurity in the Priestly Writings of the Bible with Reference to Similar Phenomena in Hittite and Mesopotamian Cultures' (PhD. Dissertation; University of California, Berkeley, CA, 1984), pp. 212-29, for an important discussion of spatial categories and the disposal of impurity in P.

fact that the ritual is a communal ritual designed to purge the holy area of the defilement of the people's sin *and* a ritual designed to effect the elimination of the sins of the people. This concern for the sin and defilement of the community clearly reflects a concern for the integrity of society and, hence, of the camp boundaries.

Finally, *the wilderness* functions as a meaningful spatial category in Leviticus 16. As will be demonstrated, it is an 'interpreted' space, the place of chaos, and serves as a means for ordering the categories of order and chaos. The sin of the people, the major cause of cosmic, social, and cultic chaos is sent to the wilderness, the place of chaos. The ritual is not designed to remove chaos from actual existence, but to 'order' it and put it in its 'proper' place. The spatial category of the wilderness functions as a means for ordering chaos.

Temporal Categories
The primary temporal category associated with the ritual of Leviticus 16 is the prescription that it take place once a year (v. 34). The opening statement in v. 2, that Aaron is not to enter בכל־עת, suggests a translation, 'at just any time'.[1] There is only one appropriate time for entry into the inner sanctum, behind the veil, and that time is ritually prescribed and constructed. Verse 29 specifies that this one day is the tenth day of the seventh month.

Time is also treated here in a qualitative sense. It is a Sabbath of solemn rest (שבת שבתון) and a day in which the people are to humble themselves (v. 31: ועניתם את־נפשׁתיכם). Thus, not only is the time of the ritual prescribed in terms of when it is to take place, but also the quality of the time as a time of rest and humiliation is prescribed. The reason for the day is further stated in v. 34: 'because of your sins'. Thus, the mood or tone of the ritual is established by the reason for the ritual.

---

1 For problems associated with this phrase, see N. Kiuchi, *The Purification Offering in the Priestly Literature: Its Meaning and Function* (JSOTS 56; Sheffield: JSOT, 1987), pp. 78-81.

The Structure and Actions of the Ritual

I. Introduction (vv. 1-3a): These verses place the ritual in the context of the issue of Aaron's entry (יבא) into the holy place behind the veil.

II. Ritual preparations (vv. 3b-5): Verse 4 concentrates on the preparations of Aaron: He will bathe (רחץ) his body in water and put on the holy garments.

III. Presentation of the two live goats and the casting of lots for them (vv. 7-10): Two goats will be taken (לקח) and stood (העמיד) before Yahweh at the door of the tent of meeting (v. 7). Aaron will cast lots (נתן גרלוח) for the two goats: one lot for Yahweh (ליהוה) and one lot for Azazel (לעזאזל) (v. 8). Aaron will present (הקריב) the goat for Yahweh and offer it (עשהו) as a חמאת (v. 9). Aaron will stand (העמיד) the live goat for Azazel before Yahweh in order to *kipper* upon it (לכפר עליו) (v. 10).

IV. The חמאת sacrifices, the *kipper*-act, and the entry into the holy place (vv. 6, 11-19):

A. The חמאת bull for Aaron and his house (vv. 6, 11-14): Aaron will present (הקריב) the bull of the חמאת which is for himself and *kipper* for himself and his house (v. 11a). He will kill (שחמ) the bull (v. 11b).

1. The incense and the initial entry into the holy place (vv. 12-13): Aaron shall take (לקח) a censer full of coals of fire from the altar before Yahweh and two handfuls of incense and bring (הביא) it behind the veil (v. 12). He will put (נתן) the incense on the coals before Yahweh that the cloud of incense might cover (כסה) the כפרח (v. 13).

2. The manipulation of the blood of the bull of the חמאת (v. 14): Aaron will take (לקח) some of the blood of the bull and sprinkle (הזה) it with his finger on the front of the כפרח, that is eastward. Before the כפרח he will sprinkle (יזה) some of the blood seven times with his finger (v. 14).

B. The חמאת goat which is for the people (vv. 15-16a): Aaron shall kill (ושחמ) the goat of the חמאת for the people. He will bring (הביא) its blood behind the veil and he will do (ועשה) with its blood just as he did with the blood of the bull. He will sprinkle it (והזה) on the כפרח and before the כפרח (v. 15). Thus shall he *kipper* for the holy place (v. 16a).

V. The *kipper*-act for the tent and outer altar (vv. 16b-19): So also will he do for the tent of meeting (v. 16b). Then he shall go out (ויצא) to the altar which is before Yahweh and *kipper* on it (וכפר עליו). He shall take (ולקח) some of the blood of the bull and goat and put it (ונתן) on the horns of the altar round about (v. 18). He shall sprinkle (והזה) some of the blood upon it seven times with his finger and cleanse it and consecrate it (וטהרו וקדשו) from the sins of the children of Israel (v. 19).

VI. The goat for Azazel (vv. 20-22): When Aaron finishes performing the *kipper*-act for the holy place, the tent of meeting, and the altar, he shall present (הקריב) the live goat (v. 20). He shall lay (וסמך) both of his hands on its head and confess (והתודה) over it all the iniquities of the children of Israel, all their transgressions, and all their sins. He will put (ונתן) them on the head of the goat and send it (ושלח) to the wilderness (v. 21).

VII. The burnt-offerings (vv. 23-24): Aaron shall come into (ובא) the tent of meeting, take off his holy garments, and leave them in the tent (v. 23). He shall then bathe (ורחץ) his body in water in a holy place, put on clothes, and come out (ויצא) and perform (ועשה) the burnt-offerings. Thus, will he *kipper* for himself and for the people (v. 24).

VIII. Concluding actions (vv. 25-28): Aaron shall burn (יקטיר) the fat of the חטאת on the altar (v. 25). The one who released the goat for Azazel shall wash (יכבס) his clothes and bathe (ורחץ) his body in water and then come (יבוא) into the camp (v. 26). The skin, flesh, and dung of the bull and goat which were offered as a חטאת shall be brought out (יוציא) of the camp and burned (ושרפו) with fire (v. 27). The one who burns them shall wash (יכבס) his clothes and bathe (ורחץ) his body in water and then come (יבא) into the camp (v. 28).

There are three central elemments in the enactment of this ritual: the *kipper*-act, the actions associated with the goat for Azazel, and the offering of the burnt offerings. All the other actions are either preparation for these acts or results of these acts.

The Meaning of the Ritual and its Enactment

The ritual of Leviticus 16 draws together two issues and shows how they interact in ritual. The first of these is the question of

how the high priest, who, it will be argued, acts as the
representative of the people in this ritual, can gain access to
the holy place, the place from which Yahweh has said that he
will meet and speak with Moses. The second issue is associated
with the question of how the Israelites, through their representative the high priest, can effect an annual 'cleansing' of
cult and camp. The juxtaposition of these two issues in the
ritual of Leviticus 16 demonstrates the integral relationship
between them, and the ritual is, at one level, an attempt to
address both of these issues. At its heart, this ritual is a
cleansing or purgation ritual. This ritual purgation, however,
can only be accomplished by the yearly entrance of the high
priest into the holy place. In this way the ritual suggests that
the question of the annual cleansing of the sanctuary can only
be answered in relation to the yearly entry into the holy place.
The nature of the ritual cleansing or purgation, then, is an
important element for a proper understanding of this ritual.

The ritual of Leviticus 16 has often been referred to as 'the
day of atonement', since the central act was understood to be
an act of atonement for the people. In such an interpretation,
the chief end of the *kipper*-act was to effect a change in the
status of the people. It is better, however, in light of the work of
Milgrom and Levine, to speak of the ritual as a ritual of
'cleansing' or 'purgation', and to speak of the 'day of purgation'.[1]

Milgrom notes four distinct uses or possible uses of the verb
כפר.[2] The first is found in the context of the חטאת sacrifice. Here
כפר has the meaning of 'purge' and refers either to the object
which is purged by the blood of the חטאת (כפר followed either by
a non-human direct object or the prepositions על or ב with a
non-human object) or the person or persons on whose behalf

---

1 Milgrom, 'Sacrifices and Offerings', pp. 764-70; 'Atonement in the OT',
   pp. 8-82; 'Israel's Sanctuary', pp. 390-99; 'Two Kinds of Hatta't', *VT* 26
   (1976), pp. 333-37; Levine, *In the Presence*, pp. 123-27. A more complete
   discussion of the root כפר and its use throughout the Old Testament may
   be found in F. Maass, כפר *kpr* pi. sühnen', *THAT* 1 (1971), pp. 842-57. An
   important recent treatment may be found in B. Janowski, *Sühne als Heilsgeschehen. Studien zur Sühntheologie der Priesterschrift und zur Wurzel
   KPR im Alten Orient und im Alten Testament* (WMANT 55; Neukirchen-
   Vluyn: Neukirchener Verlag, 1982), pp. 183-265.
2 'Atonement in the OT', *IDBSup* (1976), pp. 78-80.

the purgation is made (כפר followed by אל or בעד with a human object).[1] A second use understands כפר as a denominative verbal form derived from *kopher* which means 'ransom, substitute'.[2] A third possible meaning sees in כפר the idea of 'cover' and understands the act of *kipper* primarily as a covering of sin.[3] While possible, Milgrom generally argues against such a view. A final meaning of כפר noted by Milgrom is the abstract and figurative notion of 'expiation'. This is a late development which comes to refer to 'the process of expiation in general' and is the meaning of *kipper* in conjunction with sacrifices other than the חטאת.[4]

The major contribution of Milgrom in his discussion of the use of כפר is its meaning as 'purgation' in the context of the חטאת. This will serve as a starting point for the present analysis. Two issues, however, need further development and analysis. The first is concerned with the meaning of 'purgation'. It will be argued that the meaning of 'purgation' must be broadened in the context of the חטאת. A second issue is whether the meaning of כפר can always be limited to a single idea. If the world view of the Priestly writers is understood as a complex structure with significant relations among its parts, then Priestly ritual will produce effects throughout the larger structure. In terms of the three elements of cosmos, society, and cult, this means that a change of status in the cultic element, for example, can be expected to have some corresponding effect in the other elements. If the *kipper*-act is understood to be *the* ritual act that holds the Priestly ritual

---

1 This use of כפר is derived from the Akkadian cognate *kaparu*, which in the D-stem means 'to rub, wipe', and comes to mean 'to wipe clean'. See Levine, *In the Presence*, pp. 56-59; G. Gerleman, 'Die Wurzel *kpr* im Hebräischen', *Studien zur alttestamentlichen Theologie* (Heidelberg: Lambert Schneider, 1980), pp. 11-23.
2 See also Levine, *In the Presence*, p. 61.
3 For this view, see P. D. Schötz, *Schuld- und Sündopfer im alten Testament* (BSHT 18; Breslau: Müller & Seiffert, 1930), pp. 102-44; J. Stamm, *Erlösen und Vergeben im alten Testament: Eine begriffsgeschichtliche Untersuchung* (Bern: Franke, 1940), pp. 59-66.
4 'Atonement in the OT', p. 80.

system together,[1] then the meaning of כפר may be more complex in a given ritual than any single meaning would allow. Thus, while it may reflect a fairly consistent function in Priestly ritual, it may well be differently nuanced according to its role in specific ritual contexts.

It is obvious that a shift in meaning for כפר from 'atone' to 'purgation' necessitates a shift in the understanding of the effects of sin. Impurity is produced by sin and is understood by Milgrom as 'an aerial miasma which possessed magnetic attraction for the realm of the sacred'.[2] Levine's view is similar. He writes, '... expiation addressed itself to the presence of impurity, the actualized form of evil forces operative in the human environment'.[3] Expiatory rites, distinct from the sacrificial gift, in Levine's view, were necessary 'because Yahweh demanded that the forces of impurity, unleashed by the offenses committed, be kept away from his immediate environment'.[4] It may be said, then, that the primary concern of the חטאת is with the purgation of the sacred precincts of the impurities that have arisen through the offenses of the people and which were attracted to the sacred area. The chief threat thereby posed is that the

1 On single, unifying ideas in cultic systems, see van Baaren, 'Theoretical Speculations on Sacrifice', p. 12; E.E. Evans-Pritchard, 'The Meaning of Sacrifice Among the Nuer', *JRAI* 84 (1954), p. 29.
2 'Israel's Sanctuary', pp. 392-95. For similar discussions of defilement, see P. Ricoeur, *The Symbolism of Evil* (Boston: Beacon, 1967), pp. 33-40; J. Middleton, *Lugbara Religion: Ritual and Authority among an East African Tribe* (London: Oxford University Press, 1960), pp. 100-16; F.A. Arinze, *Sacrifice in Ibo Religion* (Ibadan, Nigeria: Ibadan University, 1970), pp. 34-36.
3 *In the Presence*, pp. 77-78.
4 *Ibid*. It is difficult, however, to agree with Levine when he says that the forces released by offenses are not only 'dynamic' but also 'demonic', so that the blood of the חטאת is not only purgative, but also protective. Such blood, he argues, protects Yahweh from the attack of demonic forces (pp. 77-90). Such an interpretation is problematic, as Milgrom points out ('Israel's Sanctuary', pp. 394-95), because the ritual shows no particular concern for the entry ways. The issue is not the conflict between Yahweh, representing the forces of good, and the demonic forces, representing the forces of evil. The issue is the impurity of the people which attaches itself to the sanctuary and thereby threatens the presence of Yahweh within the community. At a still deeper level, the concern is with the 'conflict' between order and chaos.

impurity arising from the sins of the people might force
Yahweh, the holy one, to withdraw his presence from the holy
area and hence from the midst of the nation.[1] This would
bring about a collapse of the sacred order, a breakdown in the
structuring lines of demarcation, and bring about the eruption
of chaos.[2]

The view that sin produces dynamic effects is well attested
in the biblical material. In Lev. 20.3 the offering of children to
Molech in fire is forbidden, because it might defile (טמא) the
sanctuary (מקדש) and profane (לחלל) the holy name. Lev. 15.31
exhorts those with some form of a bodily discharge to purify
themselves 'lest they die in their uncleanness (בטמאתם) by their
defiling my tabernacle which is in their midst (בטמאם את־משכני
אשר בתוכם)'. This passage shows the close connection of sinful
impurity and ritual impurity that is at work in the Priestly
writings. Num. 19.20 cites the person who is not cleansed from
corpse-contamination as an offender of purity and defiler of
the sanctuary ('that one shall be cut off from the midst of the
assembly because he has defiled the sanctuary of Yahweh',
כי את־מקדש יהוה טמא; cf. Num. 20.13). It is clear that a central
concern of defilement in Israel was the threat that such
defilement posed to the sacred precincts.

In this regard, Milgrom has argued that various grades of
sin are capable of penetrating the sacred structure in various
degrees.[3] There are four categories of offenses that may be
noted in this regard: (1) inadvertent, individual; (2) inadvertent, high priest or communal; (3) wanton or unrepented,
individual; (4) wanton or unrepented, communal. For the first

---

1 See Milgrom, 'Israel's Sanctuary', pp. 396-99.
2 On the question of the confusion of categories, see Douglas (*Purity and
Danger*, pp. 94-113), who states: 'These are pollution powers which inhere
in the structure of ideas itself and which punish a symbolic breaking of
that which should be joined or joining that which should be separate. It
follows from this that pollution is a type of danger which is not likely to
occur except where the lines of structure, cosmic or social, are clearly
defined' (p. 113). Such structural categories, cosmic, social, and cultic, are
operative in the Priestly ritual materials. See also Zuesse, 'Taboo and the
Divine Order', pp. 490-504.
3 'Israel's Sanctuary', pp. 392-94. See also his 'The Cultic שגגה and its
Influence in Psalms and Job', *JQR* 58 (1967), pp. 115-25; *Studies in
Levitical Terminology*, pp. 38-43; 'Sacrifices and Offerings, OT', pp. 766-68.

category, the blood of the חטאה is applied to the outer altar
(Lev. 4.25, 30). The second category requires the blood of the
חטאה to be applied to the inner altar of incense and before the
פרכת before Yahweh (Lev. 4.5-7, 16-18). The last two
categories require that the blood of the חטאה be applied to the
כפרת, tent, and altar. The last two categories are the most
dangerous and are only dealt with on the great day of
purification as described in Leviticus 16.

This clearly suggests that order is achieved through
separations and distinctions. The tabernacle is by definition a
holy and clean place. This is made clear in the ritual of
Leviticus 8 in which the tabernacle cult is established. The
tabernacle as set apart cultic site is a bounded area and its
boundaries, the conceptual lines that mark it off from all other
sites, must be protected against the intrusion of impurity and
defilement. If these boundaries are not protected and impurity
and defilement are allowed to enter into and remain in the
sacred area, then the order that was attained through the
separation of the holy and the profane, the clean and the
unclean, will be lost and disorder and chaos will arise. With
Douglas, this may be said to be a confusion of categories. Since
the cultic order is established through separations and distinctions, that order may be said to be lost when the separations
and distinctions are not maintained. Order is lost and is
replaced by confusion, disorder, and chaos.

Sin and its resulting impurity, then, may be said to cause the
breakdown of the divinely created order. When one crosses
over or ruptures one of the prescribed boundaries of that
order, one does not just damage oneself, but the whole of the
divinely prescribed social order. When the boundaries of the
divine order, or part of that order, are thus ruptured or
broken, then society is faced with the breakdown of that order,
and hence of the wellbeing of society, and is faced with the
possibility of societal chaos. The divinely created societal order
is thereby threatened by the non-order, or chaos, present
before Yahweh brought society into being. If the created order
of society, created by Yahweh through the divine prescriptions, is at the same time integrally related to the order of
the cosmos, also created by Yahweh, then societal disorder
may be reflected in cosmic disorder as well. Leviticus 16

describes the yearly ritual in which the center of the divinely created order, Yahweh's presence in the midst of the nation, was guarded. This ritual was performed to help maintain and sustain the divinely created order and was, as such, a means by which humans participated in the maintenance of the divinely created order.

How is the ritual of Leviticus 16 effective in accomplishing this? The first step is the offering of the sacrifices so that their blood may be used in the cleansing of the sanctuary. Three elements of this phase of the ritual are of particular importance in understanding the effects of this ritual: the use of the blood of the sacrifices, the function of the incense, and the role of the high priest.

The חטאת Sacrifice

In Leviticus 16, the חטאת sacrifices have as their primary purpose the purgation of the כפרת, the tent of meeting, and the outer altar of burnt offerings. These need to be cleansed because they have become defiled through the sins of the nation. The blood of the sacrifices serves to absorb the impurities that have been attracted to the sanctuary and thereby purge the objects on which the blood is placed.[1] It is for this reason that the flesh of these sacrifices must be burned outside the camp. Because the blood of these animals has absorbed the impurity of the gravest sins, those that can defile the inner sanctum, the flesh of these animals must be burned outside the camp. The flesh itself has become dangerously polluted.[2] Thus, the prescriptions regarding the remains of the חטאת sacrifice in Lev 6.23 state: 'None of the חטאת whose blood is brought into the tent of meeting in order to כפר in the holy place shall be eaten. It will be burned with fire'.

In Lev. 16.16, the reason for the חטאת sacrifice of the people is specifically noted: 'And he will כפר the holy place because of the defilements (מטמאת) of the sons of Israel, and because of their transgressions (ומפשעיהם), for all of their sin (לכל־חטאתם)'. This makes clear that the חטאת for the people is necessary because

1 Milgrom, 'Sacrifices and Offerings', p. 767.
2 *Ibid.* It can be seen here, that the principle of *pars pro toto* is operative. The whole animal partakes of the impurity absorbed by the blood. The same idea is indicated in Lev. 4.11-12, 21.

of the defilement of the holy place brought about by their transgressions and sins. The root פשׁע has been understood to mean primarily 'rebellion' and has been interpreted, in the context of sin, to refer to the presumptuous sins of Israel.[1] Hutton, however, notes that this is simply one sub-category of meaning for the word, but is hardly *the* basic meaning of the term.[2] He cites its use with related terms (מרד, עלילה, טמא, and שׁקר) and suggests, with Knierim, that its basic meaning 'has to do with 'breaking with' a person (neighbor or God), withdrawing from him, taking from him property, robbing him'.[3] The פשׁעים of Lev. 16.16, then, refer to the most flagrant acts against Yahweh and against the societal order created by Yahweh. These acts are the high-handed breaking of the divine prescriptions, breaking away from Yahweh, and such acts threaten to break the harmonious relations of Yahweh and the people.

The range of meaning associated with the root חטא is broader and refers to any act which 'breaks a partnership'.[4] In P these types of acts come to have primary reference to situations in which Yahweh is one of the partners. Thus, this type of offense is concerned with any act which is directed against the holy things of Yahweh[5] and is associated with acts that are particularly defiling. Indeed, in Lev. 16.16 it serves as a summation ('for all their sin') and includes as one of its main types of sin the פשׁעים.

The first act of the purgation ritual using the blood of the חטאת sacrifices is the manipulation of the blood in the inner sanctum behind the veil. Aaron first takes the blood of the bull, which is designated for the priesthood, and applies it to the כפרת. It is clear that the defilement of the priesthood must be dealt with at the beginning of the ritual. This insures that the

---

1 See R.P. Carroll, 'Rebellion and Dissent in Ancient Israelite Society', *ZAW* 89 (1977), pp. 176-204; Milgrom, 'Sacrifices and Offerings', p. 767.

2 R.R. Hutton, 'Declaratory Formulae: Forms of Authoritative Pronouncement in Ancient Israel' (PhD. Dissertation; Claremont Graduate School, Claremont, CA, 1983), pp. 102-103. See also R. Knierim, *Die Hauptbegriffe für Sünde im Alten Testament* (Gütersloh: Gerd Mohn, 1965), p. 180.

3 'Declaratory Formulae', pp. 102-103.

4 Knierim, *Hauptbegriffe*, p. 57.

5 Hutton, 'Declaratory Formulae', pp. 99-100.

priest will be effective in performing rituals on behalf of the rest of the community. It serves, in one sense, to insure that the priest stands in his official and sacred status in the sacred area.

The prescriptions for the use of the blood are detailed in Lev. 16.14. 'He will take some of the blood of the bull and sprinkle it with his finger on the face of the כפרת, eastward (קדמה) and he will sprinkle some of the blood seven times before the כפרת with his finger'. The manner in which the prescription is formulated indicates that there are two distinct sprinkling acts. The first one takes place on top of the כפרת and the second one in front of the כפרת, seven times.[1] It is important to clarify the exact nature and purpose of the 'sprinkling-act' in Priestly ritual,[2] and more particularly when a 'seven-fold' sprinkling is specified.

In Lev. 4.6, 17, the sprinkling rite is used in connection with the חטאת ritual for the high priest or community. Initially, the blood is to be sprinkled seven times before Yahweh, before the veil of the holy place. Some of the blood is then to be placed on the horns of the altar of incense which is before Yahweh inside the tent of meeting, while the rest of the blood is to be poured out at the base of the altar of burnt offerings. As will be discussed below, this sprinkling rite is best understood as an act of presentation of the blood to Yahweh.

In Lev. 8.11, the seven-fold sprinkling act is used in the consecration rites of the altar and its various implements. In this instance, it is the anointing oil (שמן המשחה, v. 10) that is sprinkled on the altar seven times. The purpose of this sprinkling is clearly stated in v. 11: לקדשם. It is to 'make holy' or 'to consecrate' the altar and its related instruments. The result is determined, however, by the material that is sprinkled—the anointing oil.

In Leviticus 14, the seven-fold sprinkling act is found in the cleansing rituals for a recovered leper (vv. 7, 16, 27) and a

---

1 Wright ('The Disposal of Impurity', p. 15) suggests that the second act of sprinkling takes place on the floor before the כפרת. Although not so specified in the text, this is a probable suggestion.
2 See T.C. Vriezen, 'The Term *hizza*: Lustration and Consecration', *OTS* 7 (1950), pp. 201-35; Milgrom, 'The Paradox of the Red Cow (Num. xix)', *VT* 31 (1981), p. 66.

house declared free of leprosy (v. 51). Several distinct acts of sprinkling are described in these rituals. In v. 7 the blood of a slaughtered bird is sprinkled on the recovered leper who is then declared clean (טהר). In vv. 16, 27 the priest sprinkles oil, to be used in the cleansing of the leper and to be distinguished from the holy anointing oil of Leviticus 8, toward the front of the tent of meeting (the ceremony takes place 'outside' the camp). This act serves to prepare the oil for use in the cleansing ceremony.[1] Verse 51 concerns the sprinkling of the blood of the slaughtered bird on a house to be cleansed. There are, then, two distinct functions associated with the seven-fold sprinkling rites in Leviticus 14: (1) to prepare the oil for the cleansing ritual and (2) to cleanse by the application of blood.

In Num. 19.4 the sprinkling act is found in the ritual preparation of the waters for cleansing corpse-contamination. In this instance, the blood of the slain cow is taken by the priest (Eleazer) and sprinkled seven times toward the front of the tent of meeting (אל־נכח פני אהל־מועד). Again, the purpose is the preparation of the blood and cow for further ritual use.

In Leviticus 16 the seven-fold sprinkling act occurs twice (vv. 14, 19, and it may be assumed for the act described in v. 15). In v. 14 (and assumed in v. 15), the blood is sprinkled *on* the mercy seat and then seven times *before* it. In v. 19, the blood of the חטאת sacrifice is sprinkled on the altar of burnt offerings seven times. Some of the blood is then placed on the horns of the altar. The result of the blood manipulation is clearly stated: 'and so will he cleanse it (וטהרו) and consecrate it (וקדשו) from the impurities of the sons of Israel'.

Four distinct ritual effects, then, are produced by the rite of sprinkling.

1. When the material that is sprinkled consists of the anointing oil, the purpose is primarily that of consecration, to set something apart and make it holy. This act of sprinkling serves to place an object or person in the realm of the holy (Exod. 29.21; Lev. 8.11, 30).

2. The rite of sprinkling may serve to prepare some material for further use in ritual (Lev. 14.16, 27; Num. 19.4).

---

1 Vriezen, 'The Term *hizza*', p. 208; Milgrom, 'Paradox', p. 66.

3. The sprinkling rite may be used in a purifying ritual to effect the cleansing of an individual who is in an impure state (Lev. 14.7 [blood], 51 [blood on house]; Num. 8.7 [sprinkle the water of the חטאת[1] on the Levites to purify them]; 19.18, 19 [waters of impurity to purify the corpse-contaminated]).

4. The sprinkling of the blood of a חטאת sacrifice is intended to effect purgation of an object (Lev. 4.4, 17; 14.14, 15) or, in two instances, to cleanse and 'consecrate' (Lev. 8.15; 16.19).

The sprinkling of the blood of the חטאת bull *on* and *before* the כפרת functions to purge the כפרת of the defilement caused by the sin of the priesthood. This is in line with Milgrom's argument that the blood of a חטאת sacrifice purges the object on which it is placed. A question remains, however, about the particular form of the rite. Why is the blood sprinkled on the כפרת *and* before it? An answer to this question requires an examination of the form of the rites associated with the חטאת blood found elsewhere in Priestly texts.

In Lev. 4.6-7, the חטאת ritual for the anointed priest, and Lev. 4.17-18, the חטאת ritual for the whole congregation of Israel, the blood of the חטאת is used in three ways. First, it is sprinkled seven times before Yahweh in front of the כפרת. Second, its blood is applied to the horns of the altar of incense. Finally, the rest of its blood is poured out at the base of the altar of burnt offerings. This sequence is operative when the blood is taken *into* the tent for the purging of the sins of the high priest or whole community. A similar sequence is followed for the manipulation of the blood of a חטאת offered on behalf of an individual as described in Lev. 4.25, 30, 34. In this case, however, there is no entry into the tent and thus no sprinkling rite before the כפרת and no application of the blood to the incense altar. Rather, some of the blood is applied to the horns of the altar of burnt offering, outside the tent, and the rest is poured out at the base of the altar.

A slightly different form of this rite is found in connection with the manipulation of the blood of a bird offered as a חטאת as

---

1 This is the only occurrence of this phrase and its precise meaning is uncertain.

described in Lev. 5.9. Some of the blood of the bird is sprinkled
on the *side* of the altar and the rest is poured out at the base of
the altar. These actions are functionally equivalent to the two
actions associated with the blood of the חטאת described in
Lev. 4.6-7, 17-18. The difference is simply that the blood of a
bird is placed on the side of the altar rather than on its horns.
This is supported by Lev. 1.15 which states that the blood of a
bird offered as an עלה is to be placed on the side of the altar. In
the עלה, however, all the blood is poured on the side of the altar
and none is poured at the base of the altar. The manipulation
of the blood of a bird offered as a חטאת reflects the same form as
a חטאת from the herd.

In Lev. 8.14-15, Moses' manipulation of the blood of the חטאת
bull in the ordination ritual for the priesthood follows this
same form.

> Moses took the blood of the bull and with his finger put some
> of it on the horns of the altar round about and purified (חטא)
> the altar. Then he poured out the rest of the blood at the base
> of the altar and consecrated it (קדש). Thus, he *kippered* on it.

It is clear that the rite in this instance conforms to the twofold
structure noted already. These verses, however, clearly indicate the purpose of the two actions associated with חטאת blood.
The blood placed on the horns of the altar is purgative, while
the blood poured out at the base of the altar functions to (re-)
consecrate the altar. It is particularly important to note that
this explanation comes precisely in the first offering of a חטאת
sacrifice. In the founding ritual for the cult, the writers
include an explanation for the two distinct actions associated
with the manipulation of the חטאת blood.

The use of the חטאת blood is explained in the same way in
Lev. 16.19. Aaron is to take some of the blood of the bull and the
goat, both חטאת sacrifices, and sprinkle it seven times with his
finger on the horns of the altar. Thus shall he cleanse it (טהר)
and (re-)consecrate it (קדש) because of the uncleannesses
(טמאה) of the people of Israel. There is a problem, however, in
that in this instance the blood is not poured out at the base of
the altar. Before addressing this question, it will be helpful to
see the specific structure of the rites, based on spatial categories, associated with the חטאת blood.

I. Inner Sanctum (vv. 14-16a)
   A. The blood of the bull: the חטאת for the priest (v. 14)
      1. Sprinkle it on the front of the כפרת
      2. Sprinkle it seven times *before* the כפרת
   B. The blood of the goat: the חטאת for the people (v. 15)
      1. Sprinkle it *on the front of* the כפרת
      2. Sprinkle it seven times before the כפרת
   C. Concluding notice: 'Thus shall he כפר for the holy place' (v. 16a)

II. The Tent (v. 16b)
   Summary notice: 'So shall he do for the tent of meeting, which is established with them in the midst of their uncleanness'.

III. The Outer Altar of Burnt Offerings (vv. 18-19)
   A. Introductory notice: 'Then he shall go out to the altar which is before Yahweh and כפר for/on it' (v. 18a).
   B. Blood of the bull and goat (vv. 18b-19)
      1. Put it on the horns of the altar round about
      2. Sprinkle some of it seven times upon the altar
   C. Concluding notice: 'Thus he shall cleanse it (וטהרו) and (re-)consecrate it (וקדשו) because of the uncleannesses of the people of Israel' (v. 19b).

It is clearly stated in both Lev. 8.14-15 and Lev. 16.19 that the manipulation of the blood functions both as purgative and consecratory rite. Furthermore, Lev. 8.15b clearly associates the pouring of the blood at the base of the altar with the (re-)consecration of the altar. Finally, Lev. 8.15 clearly indicates that both aspects are considered to be part of the *kipper* process. The same is suggested by the concluding notice in Lev. 16.16a. How, then, can the absence of the act of pouring the blood at the base of the altar in Lev. 16.18-19 be explained?

First, it must be recalled, following Milgrom, that the חטאת blood purges by contact with the defiled object, i.e., by absorption of the impurity. Hence, it is necessary that the blood be placed on the object to be cleansed. The same need not necessarily hold true for the ability of the blood to effect (re-)consecration. There are basically three forms of the ritual to be explained:

1. חטאת for anointed priest or whole congregation: the blood is placed on the horns of the altar of incense and the rest

of the blood is poured out at the base of the altar of burnt offerings;

2. חטאת for ruler or common people: the blood is placed on the horns of the altar of burnt offerings and the rest of the blood is poured out at the base of the altar of burnt offerings;

3. חטאת for priest and people on day of purgation: the blood is placed on top of the כפרת and before it, and then the blood is placed on the horns of the altar of burnt offerings.

The (re-)consecration of the holy area is effected either by sprinkling the blood seven times before the כפרת, as in Lev. 16.14, or by pouring out the blood at the base of the altar of burnt offerings, as in Lev. 4.7, 18, 25, 30, 34. This is done at the כפרת on יום הכפורים because the defilement has penetrated the most holy place and the blood is brought into the most holy place. In the normal חטאת, the action takes place at the altar of burnt offerings. These two points, the כפרת and the outer altar of burnt offerings, represent the boundaries of the tabernacle structure. The כפרת in the most holy place and the outer altar mark the extreme bounds of the sacred structure. Thus, the logic of the rite of (re-)consecration relates to spatial categories —the act of reconsecration, of refounding, takes place at the boundaries of the holy complex of the tabernacle. This is in line with the idea that the purpose of reconsecration is precisely to re-establish the boundaries of the holy realm—the bounds of the holy place are re-established at the boundaries.

Such a dual purpose for the חטאת blood appears necessary given the priests' concern for both holiness *and* cleanness, categories that are related but not equivalent. When the defilement caused by the sin of the people penetrates the tabernacle precincts, an area consecrated, set apart, and bounded, the founded and established order of the tabernacle area is disrupted. The conceptual categories that define that area, i.e., holy, clean, have been contaminated by the intrusion of elements which are, by definition, distinct from them. To put this in other terms, the boundaries that separate the tabernacle area from all other areas have been broken or ruptured and distinct conceptual categories have been confused. The structure and order of the sacred area have been disrupted and defiled. It is necessary for ritual not only to purge the sacred area, but also to reconsecrate it and restore the sacred boundaries that mark off and separate the sacred, cultic site.

Thus, in terms of Leviticus 16, the act of sprinkling the חטאת blood *on* the כפרת serves as a purgative rite. The act of sprinkling the blood *before* the כפרת is functionally equivalent to the pouring of the blood at the base of the altar. It serves to re-establish the structure of the sacred area and, thereby, to maintain the integrity of the cultic order. Thus, the top of the כפרת is functionally equivalent to the horns of the altar and the area before the כפרת is functionally equivalent to the base of the altar.

The Role of the Incense
The role of the incense is made clear by the writer of Leviticus 16. Aaron is to burn the incense 'that the smoke of the incense might cover the כפרת which is on the testimony, 'lest he die' (v. 13b). The smoke of the incense is a protective agent for the priest in order that he might secure safe entry into the inner sanctum. The fact that the text specifies that the incense is to be burned 'lest he die', suggests that this is considered a dangerous time for the priest. This is not surprising in that the high priest at this point enters 'the most holy place', a place categorically set apart and distinct from all other space. It is the dwelling-place of Yahweh. As will be demonstrated below, the time between the high priest's bathings is best understood as a liminal time, a time normally fraught with danger.

At the same time, the smoke is a symbol of Yahweh's presence. The smoke of the incense has connections with the smoke in the wilderness and the smoke on Mt Sinai associated with the glory of Yahweh by the priests. In both cases, it may be said that the smoke veils while it reveals. It acts as a material sign of Yahweh's presence in the inner sanctum and in the midst of the nation. The smoke of the incense, as a symbol of Yahweh's presence, indicates that the ritual is effective. Yahweh *is* present in the inner sanctum and the ritual insures that he will remain there.

The Role of the High Priest

The high priest undergoes two bathings and changes of clothing in this ritual. In preparation for the ritual, he is to bathe his body and then put on the holy linen clothes (v. 14). After the ritual of the goat for Azazel, Aaron is to enter the tent of meeting, take off the holy linen clothes, bathe his body with water in a holy place, and put on clothes before offering the burnt offerings (vv. 23-24). These bathings and changes of clothing mark Aaron's entry into and exit out of a prescribed ritual state. In this ritual, the bathings mark off or set boundaries upon a period of marginality or liminality[1] for the high priest and serve to emphasize two things: (1) the centrality of the rites involving the חטאת blood and the goat sent to Azazel and (2) the status of the high priest as the representative of the people.

In discussing the marginal time associated with the high priest, it should be noted that the ritual of Leviticus 16, in its total structure, may be understood as a communal rite of passage. As such, the whole day may be understood as a marginal time for the community as the following diagram indicates:

Normal time-------// Marginal time //-------Normal time

The day exhibits characteristics often associated with marginal time in rites of passage: a cessation of labor, humility, a solemn rest.[2] Embedded within this larger ritual structure, however, is a marginal time specifically associated with the high priest, marked off by his bathings.

In the ritual of Leviticus 16, it is clear that the bathings of Aaron bracket a central segment within the larger ritual. The rites within this period serve to purify the cultic area and to remove the sins of the Israelites from the camp. The bathings serve to mark the beginning and ending of a marginal status of the high priest within the ritual. In this time, Aaron may be said to stand outside the normal ritual structures associated

---

1 See van Gennep, *Rites of Passage*, pp. 1-13; V. Turner, *The Forest of Symbols*, pp. 93-111; *The Ritual Process*, pp 94-130; *From Ritual to Theatre*, pp. 20-60; 'Variations on a Theme of Liminality', in *Secular Ritual*, pp. 36-52; Douglas, *Purity and Danger*, pp. 94-113.
2 van Gennep, *Rites of Passage*, pp. 178-88.

with the high priest. Aaron's ritual status is changed in this time as he becomes the representative of the people.

Two elements of the ritual suggest Aaron's representative role within this ritual. The first concerns the linen clothing Aaron is to wear during his marginal time. As noted earlier, it stands in sharp contrast to the vestments described in Exodus 28. These plain linen clothes mark him off, in that they are distinct from his normal vestments; they make him 'common'. His distinctiveness on this day is his commonality, his indistinctiveness,[1] and this indistinctiveness serves to emphasize his identification with the people.[2] Second, this view receives support from the fact that it is the high priest who confesses over the goat for Azazel all the iniquities of the sons of Israel, all their transgressions, all their sin (v. 21). The act of confession is generally undertaken by the guilty party (e.g., Lev. 5.5; 26.40; Num. 5.7). Thus, the priest performs the act of confession as the representative of the people.

Finally, such a viewpoint is supported by the description of the status of the people during the ritual as found in vv. 29-31. It is a time when they are to humble themselves and do no work; it is a solemn rest. The nation as a whole is to enter into a common experience of humility. The normal workaday life of the people is to be abandoned (the daily structures of society are lost as in a liminal period) in favor of a day of ritual humility. The humility of the people is reflected in the more humble clothes which the high priest wears on this day, which are a reflection of his status as representative of the people.[3] The entry of the people into a marginal status, their obser-

1 Thus, the idea of Turner that the differentiation found in normal structures is broken down in the liminal period is suggested by the priest's identification with the people (*Dramas, Fields, and Metaphors*, pp. 273-74).

2 See D. Davies, 'An Interpretation of Sacrifice in Leviticus', ZAW 91 (1979), p. 394.

3 For a discussion of status reversal in ritual and its relationship to liminal phases and communitas, see V. Turner, *The Ritual Process*, pp. 166-203. He states, 'Rituals of status reversal, either placed at strategic points in the annual circle or generated by disasters conceived of as being the result of grave social sins, are thought of as bringing social structure and communitas into right mutual relation again' (p. 178). Elsewhere he states that such rituals have 'the effect of regenerating the principles of classification and ordering on which social structure rests' (p. 180).

vance of a day separated from other days which reverses the normal forms of life witnessed on other days, is reflected in and paralleled by the priest's entry into the marginal realm during the ritual.

The high priest's entry into this marginal state presents a dangerous situation because, as has often been emphasized, margins always hold danger within them. Margins are dangerous because they are 'betwixt and between' the normal structures of life and, thereby, present ambiguous situations. As Douglas states, 'Danger lies in transitional states, simply because transition is neither one state nor the next, it is undefinable'.[1] Ritual structures, however, not only create these margins, they also present means by which the margins may be safely entered and exited. For Aaron, the greatest point of danger comes when he passes behind the veil into the inner sanctum. This is clear from the opening warning of v. 2, which indicates that passage behind the veil into the inner sanctum holds the possibility of death. This danger is created because the veil marks a qualitative break between the holiness of the inner sanctum and all spaces outside the inner sanctum. To penetrate the 'inner' sanctum with that which is from the 'outer' area would pollute the inner area, for this would be a confusion of categories.[2] Thus, the priest must 'cleanse' himself, through his ritual bathing, of the 'outer' dirt so as not to pollute the 'inner' sanctum. It is clear that in this case spatial categories are intimately related to the categories that construct Aaron's marginal status. Indeed, a major element of the marginal situation consists of Aaron's passage into the most holy *place*.

The marginal status of Aaron, however, extends beyond his time in the inner sanctum and includes the rites associated with the goat for Azazel. Indeed, the fact that the rites associated with the tabernacle are bracketed together with the rites associated with the goat for Azazel by Aaron's bathings, suggests the important structural relationship of these rites and causes problems for any interpretation that would sepa-

---

1 *Purity and Danger*, p. 97. See also Turner, *The Ritual Process*, pp. 94-130; *The Forest of Symbols*, pp. 93-110; *Dramas, Fields, and Metaphors*, pp. 231-71.

2 See Douglas, *Purity and Danger*, p. 113.

rate them. In this way, the danger that exists for Aaron in his entry into the inner sanctum may be said to extend into the rites associated with the goat because the two are linked together in the ritual by the marginal situation associated with the high priest.

The final bathing of Aaron marks his exit from his marginal status. Having entered into a marginal status, in which he passes into the inner sanctum and also confesses the sins of the people over the head of the goat for Azazel, Aaron must bathe before exiting this status. Before reentering what may be called his 'normal' ritual status, Aaron must take ritual precautions. These precautions guard against the confusion of categories that would result if Aaron reentered his normal ritual status without ritual safeguards.

There are two elements, in particular, associated with Aaron's marginal status that demand the ritual precaution of an exit bathing. The first is concerned with the boundary between the most-holy area, the inner sanctum, and all other areas. Having entered this qualitatively distinct area, Aaron cannot safely enter into any other area without risking the danger of category confusion, taking the 'most holy' out of its prescribed boundaries. Just as he cannot safely enter this area without bathing, he cannot safely exit it without bathing. Indeed, he does come outside to perform the rites of confession associated with the goat for Azazel, but he may 'safely' do this because he is still in his marginal state. Having completed the rites associated with his marginal status, however, he bathes, in part, to wash away qualities attracted to him during his time within the marginal state.

This suggests that 'holiness' is itself understood as a dynamic quality, in the same way discussed above with reference to defilement caused by sin, which attaches itself to persons or objects penetrating its boundaries. There is danger in crossing over the line that marks the boundary of the most holy. To bring the 'profane' into the sacred breaks the structures which determine and set apart the 'holy' and thus 'releases' the holy without bounds. At the same time, to being the 'holy' into other categories of existence 'releases' the power of the holy from its controlled bounds and endangers those exposed.

A second element of Aaron's ritual status that suggests the need for his exit bathing is his contact with 'sin' through his role as confessor. While this could be construed as 'merely' a matter of words, the language used to describe the action suggests a more direct contact with the nation's sin by Aaron. 'And Aaron shall lay (סמך) both his hands upon the head of the live goat and confess over it all the iniquities of the people of Israel, and all their transgressions, all their sins. And he will place (ונתן) them upon the head of the goat' (v. 21). This can be understood to mean that through Aaron's contact with the goat, he actually 'places' the sins of the nation on the goat. If so, Aaron's contact with the sin may be understood in, what may be termed, a physical sense. By the act of confession, an act of speech, Aaron 'creates' the sins of the nation for ritual manipulation. Having thus brought the sins into being, he is able to place them on the head of the goat on the basis of his marginal status and role as primary executor of the ritual. In doing this, however, Aaron comes into direct contact with the sins of the nation and becomes 'polluted'. Such a viewpoint adds support to the contention that Aaron's marginal status is a dangerous time. Through such 'contact' with sin, Aaron bears the danger associated with its polluting power.

The dynamics of Aaron's marginal status in the ritual of Leviticus 16 are quite complex. The rites involving Aaron's entrance into the inner sanctum and his placing of the sins of the nation on the goat for Azazel subject him to two elements that present danger. By entering into the most holy area he contracts the qualities associated with that set apart and qualitatively distinct area. By coming into direct contact with the sins of the nation he contracts the defilement associated with those sins. Both of these elements present a danger to Aaron and the community if left unattended. Of key importance, however, is the way in which the high priest, in his marginal status, is able to hold together qualities that are diametrically opposed—holiness and defilement. Aaron embodies the breakdown of the normal boundaries of order and structure in his marginal status in order that through the ritual he enacts he may reconstruct the world of order and meaning and well-being.

Both of the qualities with which Aaron comes into contact are 'polluting' powers when seen from the context of normal societal structures. Both acts—Aaron's entry into the inner sanctum (holiness) and his placing the sins on the goat (defiling sin)—are necessary for the effective accomplishment of the ritual. Without these actions, the national existence would be threatened because the defilement of the tabernacle complex and the sins of the people are capable of bringing about a breakdown in societal order. Aaron, as representative of the people, purifies the sanctuary and banishes the sins of the people.

The final bathing of Aaron, then, may be understood as an exit bathing from his marginal status. Because of the dangers of the qualities contracted in that time, the bathing must be understood as a cleansing rite, a depolluting rite. It allows for Aaron's safe passage from his marginal status to a more normative ritual status. This bathing marks Aaron's passage from the dangerous time associated with the marginal status to the safe time of his normal ritual status and can, thus, be understood to establish a boundary between these two states. As such, it serves as a means of maintaining order over against the threat of chaos that is contained in the marginal state.

The Goat for Azazel

The rites associated with the goat led into the wilderness for Azazel (vv. 20-22) are, as already indicated, of central importance in the ritual of Leviticus 16. Two goats are brought to the door of the tent and lots are cast over them. One lot is for Yahweh and one lot for Azazel (vv. 7-8). The wording of this action is important: גורל אחד ליהוה וגורל אחד לעזאזל. It can be seen that there is a parallel structure between these two clauses. The goat designated 'for Yahweh' is to be offered as a חטאת on behalf of the people. The goat designated 'for Azazel' is to be presented before Yahweh to *kipper* on it (לכפר עליו) to send it to Azazel, to the wilderness (v. 10). Thus, the writers considered the sending of the goat into the wilderness as part of the *kipper*-process.

Aaron is instructed to lay both of his hands (יסמך אהרן את־שתי ידו) on the head of the goat and confess over it the sins of the

people. 'Thus shall he put them on the head of the goat'
(v. 21b). There are three distinct uses of the act of laying hands
on a person or object: in the offering of various sacrifices (Exod.
29.10; Lev. 1.4; 4.4, 24, 29, 33; 8.14; Num. 8.10, 12); in the
imparting of blessing (Gen. 48.14); and in ordination ceremonies (Num. 27.18, 23; Deut. 34.9).[1] Four basic inter-
pretations of the act have been suggested for its use in rituals
of sacrifice and offering: transference, identification, consecration or dedication, and ownership.[2]

The hand-laying rite in Lev. 16.21 is best understood as an
act of 'transference', by which the sins of the Israelites are
placed on the head of the goat. This rite has been understood as
the interpretive key to the hand-laying rite in the Hebrew
Scriptures so that all hand-laying rites are understood as acts
of transference. Milgrom, however, has suggested that there
are actually two distinct rites found in Israel's rituals.[3] One
rite, which uses two hands, is primarily a transference rite,
capable of transferring either impurity (Lev. 16.21; Num.
24.14) or authority (Num. 27.18). The second rite, which uses
only one hand, is found exclusively with sacrifices (Lev. 1.4;
3.2, 8, 13; 4.4, 24, 29, 33) and is an identification rite which
identifies both the owner of the sacrifice and the type of
sacrifice.

An important issue for understanding this specific ritual
segment is the meaning of לעזאזל. A number of different
suggestions have been made with regard to the meaning of the

---

1 See J.T. Maertens, 'Un Rite de pouvoir: L'imposition des mains, I', *SR* 6
   (1976-77), pp. 637-49; R. Péter, L'imposition des mains dans l'Ancien
   Testament', *VT* 27 (1977), pp. 48-55.
2 For an interpretation of the rite as transference, particularly with reference to Lev. 16, see Wenham, *Leviticus*, p. 233; for identification in the
   sense of substitution, see E.R. Leach, *Culture and Communication* (1976;
   rpt. Cambridge: Cambridge University Press, 1982), p. 89; for union
   between offerer and animal, see C. Stuhlmueller, 'Leviticus: The Teeth of
   divine will into the Smallest expectations of human courtesy', *BibT* 88
   (1977), p. 1084; for identification in the sense of the type of sacrifice, see
   Milgrom, 'Sacrifices and Offerings', p. 765 and Péter, 'L'imposition des
   mains', p. 54; for dedication or consecration, see Evans-Pritchard, 'The
   Meaning of Sacrifice', p. 28; for ownership, see R. de Vaux, *Studies in Old
   Testament Sacrifice* (Cardiff: University of Wales, 1964), pp. 28-29.
3 'Sacrifices and Offerings', p. 765. See also Péter, 'L'imposition des mains',
   pp. 54-55.

word: 'to Azazel' a supernatural being;[1] 'to a rocky precipice';[2] 'to a place of destruction';[3] and 'to the goat that has gone away'.[4] The first view, which appears most probable in light of the parallel syntax 'for Yahweh'/'for Azazel', has often been opposed on the ground that it seems to run contrary to biblical faith. Israel, it is argued, would not recognize such a figure. Further, Israel would not offer a 'gift' or 'sacrifice' to such a figure if it did exist.

It is clear, however, that Israel did recognize the existence of wild demonic figures in light of the statement in Lev. 17.7: 'And they shall no longer sacrifice their sacrifices to the goat demons (שעיר) with which they play the harlot'. True, this is a prohibition, but it is a prohibition against the offering of sacrifices to such beings. Is the goat sent to Azazel considered a sacrifice? In v. 5, it is stated that Aaron will take two goats as a חטאת. This could be read to mean that both goats are a חטאת, but it may also be read to mean that from the two goats brought, one only will be offered as a חטאת. Indeed, if the חטאת is a sacrifice which is killed to obtain blood for purgation, it is difficult to see how the *live* goat can fulfill such a role. It is improbable that it should be termed a 'sacrifice' at all, since sacrifice normally includes the act of slaughter when concerned with animals.[5] The purpose of the live goat is specified in v. 10: to *kipper* on it. Thus, the live goat for Azazel need not be interpreted as a חטאת or sacrifice; rather, it must be understood as part of the larger *kipper*-process.

---

1 Levine, *In the Presence*, pp. 77, 91; Milgrom, 'Day of Atonement as Annual Day of Purgation in Biblical Times', *EncJud* 5 (1971), pp. 1385-86; S. Talmon, 'The "Desert Motif" ', in *Biblical Motifs: Origins and Transformations* (ed. A. Altmann; Cambridge: Harvard University, 1966), p. 44; H. Tawil, ''Azazel the Prince of the Steepe: A Comparative Study', *ZAW* 92 (1980), pp. 43-59.

2 G.R. Driver, 'Three Technical Terms in the Pentateuch', *JSS* 1 (1956), 97-98; *Mishna*, 'Yoma' 6.6.

3 D. Hoffmann, *Das Buch Leviticus* I (Berlin: Poppelauer, 1905-1906), p. 444; Wenham, *Leviticus*, p. 235.

4 N.H. Snaith, *Leviticus and Numbers* (rpt Greenwood, S.C.: Attic, 1977), p. 79.

5 See Firth, 'Offering and Sacrifice', *JRAI* 93 (1963), p. 13; J. van Baal, 'Offering, Sacrifice and Gift', *Numen* 23 (1976), p. 161; van Baaren, 'Theoretical Speculations on Sacrifice', p. 9; V. Turner, 'Sacrifice as Quintessential Process: Prophylaxis or Abandonment?' *HR* 16 (1977), p. 190.

The function of the goat led to Azazel is best understood in terms of banishment.[1] In confessing the offenses of Israel over the goat and sending the goat out into the wilderness, Aaron banishes the offenses of the people to a place outside the camp where they cannot again affect the sanctuary. Thus, the *kipper*-act must be understood in this context to include the act of banishment, and reflects a concern with the effects that sin has *on the people*, and not only its effects on the sacred precincts. It is clear, however, that in this ritual, these two aspects are inseparable.

This suggests, then, that the phrase 'to Azazel' refers to an actual being. This viewpoint, however, must be examined in conjunction with the meaning and significance of the spatial category 'the wilderness'. The wilderness holds an important place in the biblical traditions as the region in which the nation wandered for forty years in its flight from Egypt to the promised land. Cohn has examined this segment of the biblical narrative (Exod. 12.37–Num. 25.18 plus Deuteronomy) in terms of Turner's discussion of liminality.[2] One of Cohn's conclusions is that from the traditionists' viewpoint within the 'structure' of society, the wilderness was a time of disorder (non-structure).[3] As such, it was a dangerous time in which there was a breakthrough of chaos into cosmos, of disorder into order.[4]

Thus, the wilderness came to represent the wild, the untamed, and the dangerously chaotic.[5] In Num. 20.5, the wilderness (see v. 4) is described by the people as 'this evil place. It is no place for seed, or fig, or vine, or pomegranates; and there is no water to drink'. In Isa. 34.9-16, land turned into wilderness is described as a land of thorns and thistles; the home of the hawk, the hedgehog, raven, owl, jackal, ostrich,

---

1 Milgrom, 'Day of Atonement as Annual Day of Purgation', pp. 1385-86; Wright, 'The Disposal of Impurity', p. 29.
2 *The Shape of Sacred Space*, pp. 7-23.
3 *Ibid.*, p. 20. See also L.T. Thompson, 'The Jordan Crossing: *Sidqot* Yahweh and World Building', *JBL* 100 (1981), pp. 355-58.
4 Turner, *From Ritual to Theatre*, p. 46.
5 See J. Pedersen, *Israel: Its Life and Culture* (1926; rpt. London/ Copenhagen: Oxford University Press/Banner Og Korch, 1946), 2, pp. 454-57; Talmon, 'Wilderness', *IDBSup* (1976), pp. 946-48.

and hyenas; the place where the שעיר cry to one another and
where Lilith finds a resting place. Jer. 4.23-26 describes the
fruitful land turned wilderness as תהו ובהו; a return to the non-
order present before creation (cf. Gen. 1.2). It is to this land
that the goat for Azazel is to be sent bearing the sins of the
nation.

With reference to the word עזאזל, Tawil has argued that it is
a compound form of *'zz* and *'l*, or 'a fierce god'.[1] This is a
prominent epithet for the god Mot in several Semitic myths.
Mot

> was depicted as a demonic creature, who characteristically
> ...personifies all evil, destruction and desolation, wars and
> bloodshed, wounds and plagues, diseases and sicknesses. He
> is the foremost and ultimate ruler of the netherworld, and...
> was conceived to be *šar ṣēri*, 'the king of the steepe' [*ṣēri* =
> Heb. *mīdhbār*].[2]

Thus, by sending the goat to Azazel, Israel was sending its sin,
the cause of cosmic, social, and cultic disorder, into the realm
of chaos. In this way, the nation once again saw the triumph of
order over chaos, and, thereby, the reestablishment of order in
the world via the cult.[3]

The wilderness, then, is a distinct spatial category in this
ritual and acts as a symbol for non-order and chaos. The sins
of the nation, understood as the chief cause of chaos, are sent
on the head of the goat to the realm of chaos and non-order. By
sending the chief cause of chaos to the realm of chaos in a rite
of banishment, the ritual is able to establish societal order and
announce to the community that this has taken place. The
wilderness is contrasted in this ritual with the holy place, a
symbol for order and well-being in society.[4] These two spatial

1 Tawil, ''Azazel', pp. 58-59.
2 *Ibid.*, p. 59.
3 Davies ('An Interpretation of Sacrifice', p. 394) states with regard to the
 goat that 'it passed from the realm of ordered society, from the holiness of
 the tabernacle into the chaos, into the symbolic nothingness which
 obtained outside the community of God's people'. It should be specified
 that the wilderness is a symbol for the realm of chaos over aginst the order
 of the social realm.
4 It should be noted that these two spatial categories correspond to the two
 qualities contracted by Aaron in his marginal status. Both the spatial
 categories and Aaron's ritual actions serve to emphasize that this ritual is

categories represent two possibilities for national existence. Thus, in Leviticus 16, the ritual to effect *kipper* is concerned with purgation within the community, restoration of the realm of the holy, and banishment from the camp of sin and defilement.

The Burnt Offerings

After the חטאת ritual and the banishment of the goat, Aaron concludes the larger ritual process by the offering of burnt offerings. This is also said to be part of the *kipper* process (v. 24). A full discussion of the meaning of the burnt offerings will be presented in Chapter 4, where the discussion of Leviticus 8 provides more details for interpreting the burnt offerings. There it will be argued that the burnt offerings are a means of averting the wrath of Yahweh.[1]

Concluding Instructions

There are final instructions given in Lev. 16.26-28 which are concerned with the two other active participants in the ritual other than the high priest—the one who leads forth the goat and the one who burns the refuse of the חטאת sacrifice. In both instances, the instructions directed at these roles emphasize the need to protect the boundaries of the camp, that is, the boundaries of society.

The one who bears the sin-laden goat into the wilderness must bathe his body and launder his clothes before reentering the camp (v. 26). This suggests that the goat was thought to bear the sins placed on its head and could, thereby, transfer the impurity of these sins to anyone who came into contact with it. Here again, the contagious nature of sin can be seen. This is a dangerous process, but it is made possible, made safe, by the ritual structures. It shows how ritual structures events to make what is normally dangerous into a safe process. The real danger is, of course, to the camp because the one who leads the goat into the wilderness could contaminate the camp upon his

concerned with the establishment of a proper state of affairs between the holy and the non-holy, between order and chaos.

1 See below, pp. 124-28.

return. Thus, the washing of body and clothes serves to cleanse the possible dangers from the individual.

The situation is the same with regard to the other 'dirt-bearer' who takes the refuse of the חטאת sacrifices out of the camp (v. 27). Here again the contagious nature of impurity forms the background for the instructions. The question must be raised as to why parts of the animals not actually used in the ceremony would be polluted. There are two ideas being evidenced at this point. The first is that the whole animal is understood to be represented by the part used in the ritual (*pars pro toto*). Thus, if the blood of the animal is used, the whole animal is affected. Secondly, this suggests that the blood applied to the sacred precincts absorbed the impurities in accomplishing its purgative purpose. This explains the paradoxical nature of this blood. The blood purifies the contaminated, but after its application to the sacred objects, it contaminates those who come into contact with it. Thus, when the blood has absorbed the impurities of the shrine, the animal remains must be removed from the camp to guard against further contamination within the camp boundaries. The one who undertakes this removal must be ritually cleansed before reentering the camp since the pollution absorbed by the blood and thus passed on to the rest of the animal's parts is itself now capable of polluting and the remover of the refuse materials exposed to that pollution.

Conclusion

Leviticus 16 details an annual ritual in which the divinely created order is restructured and, as such, is the ritual enactment of world order. Reflecting the marginal period of a rite of passage, the ritual provides the occasion for the recognition and enactment of the breakdown of world order so that it might be restructured and restored. As such, this day is a day fraught with danger as the high priest enacts the ritual while standing outside the normal structures of life.

The breakdown and reestablishment of order is seen particularly in the high priest, who, on this day, acts as the representative of the people. In a marginal status, marked out by his two bathings, the high priest embodies the breakdown of order by holding together in his person categorically distinct states: order/chaos, holy/profane, clean/unclean. The high priest, through this embodiment of the breakdown of order, ritually manipulates these states and through the ritual re-establishes the separations called for between these states in the divinely created order.

Thus, the ritual serves to reestablish the divinely created order by enacting the re-ordering of cosmos, society, and cult. 'Chaos', which threatens the well-being of Israel's existence, is placed in the wilderness, the place of chaos. The holiness of the tabernacle is reestablished, thereby insuring Yahweh's continued presence in the midst of Israel. The defilement of the tabernacle, caused by the sin of the people, is purged and the realm of the holy is cleansed. The holiness of the tabernacle is restored, the community is cleansed and sin eliminated, and chaos is removed to its proper place. Leviticus 16, thus, restructures and reestablishes the three orders of creation. On this day, the divinely created order is 'newly created' in the context of ritual enactment.

Chapter 4

LEVITICUS 8

Introduction

Leviticus 8 describes the ritual of the ordination of Aaron and
his sons into the priesthood. It depicts for the Priestly writers
the moment when the priesthood was instituted in Israel. As
such, it marks the passage of Aaron and his sons from a non-
institutional status into the ritually and institutionally defined
status of priests. It can thus be viewed as an institutional rite of
passage.

The ritual serves, however, not only to pass Aaron and his
sons into their status as priests, it also serves to establish the
institution of the priesthood. The ritual functions not only as a
rite of passage of persons, but as a ritual of the founding of a
social institution. There are two reasons that suggest that
Leviticus 8 is best understood as a rite of founding and not only
as rite of passage. First, the ritual conjoins the consecration of
sacred space, the tabernacle, its furnishings, and the altar, and
the consecration of persons, Aaron and his sons. Spatial
categories are ritually integrated with status. Thus, the ritual
not only serves to pass Aaron and his sons into the priesthood
but to consecrate and, in one sense, establish by consecration
the holy place.

A second reason is based on the redactional activity of the
Priestly traditionists. As Moses enacts the ritual of ordination,
the text emphasizes that he did it 'just as Yahweh commanded
him'. This refrain occurs seven times in the chapter and

serves as a concluding marker of the various phases of the ritual (vv. 4, 9, 13, 17, 21, 29, 36). The use of this execution formula may be explained, in part, by the relationship of this chapter to Exodus 29. Levine argues that Leviticus 8 represents a tradition that is distinct from Exodus 29. Leviticus 8 stands as an original narrative descriptive ritual, while Exodus 29 is a later addition.[1]

While recognizing such differences, it is still difficult to deny that the final redactor intended an 'instruction–execution' relationship between these chapters.[2] The institution of the priesthood functions as part of the divine process of the creation of order. The actively functioning tabernacle cult, requiring an ordained and set-apart priesthood, is a central element of the meaning of the created order for the Priestly traditionists. The founding of the priesthood is related by the speech of Yahweh to the founding of cosmos. Creation serves as context for cult; cult serves as one means of actualizing creation. Thus, the ordination of the priests in Leviticus 8 is related to the construction and enactment of world order.

Thus, the ritual of Leviticus 8 must be seen not only as an institutional rite of passage, but also as a ritual of founding which serves to bring into existence and operation one of the elements essential to an operational cultic space. This raises the following interpretive question: How does the ritual of Leviticus 8 function to accomplish this founding of cult and institutionalization of the priesthood? This chapter will seek to demonstrate the way in which this ritual functions to accomplish these things by presenting arguments for the following theses:

1. Leviticus 8 is a ritual of founding in which there is a convergence of the consecration of sacred space and the institutionalization of the status of the priesthood in such a way that the meaning of sacred space and the meaning of priesthood are interrelated.
2. In Leviticus 8, Moses, depicted as the inaugurator of the tabernacle cult, offers the Ur-sacrifices of the cult and

---

1 'Descriptive Tabernacle Texts', pp. 311-12.
2 On the importance of the 'instruction-execution' formulae in P, see above, pp. 39-52.

in this ritual the basic movement *and* meaning of the sacrifices and offerings of the tabernacle are presented.

3. The key ritual action that effects the passage of Aaron and his sons into the status of the priesthood is the placing of the blood of the ram of ordination on their right ear, thumb, and big toe and this ritual act symbolizes the role of the priests as those who mediate between death and life.

Type of Material

Leviticus 8 narrates the execution of instructions given by Yahweh to Moses concerning the ordination of Aaron and his sons. The precise relationship of this chapter to Exodus 29 remains uncertain.[1] As noted earlier, Levine sees two distinct traditions in these texts, Leviticus 8 being the earlier of the two and having a special interest in Aaron. He argues that Leviticus 8 is best understood as a 'descriptive narrative' text.[2]

In that the chapter is descriptive narrative, it might well be understood to provide the structure for a regularly occurring ordination ritual which would be enacted, for example, at the ordination of the high priest. It is difficult to envision Leviticus 8 as a model for such a ritual for two reasons. First, it is difficult to find a person in Israel who could have filled the role of Moses as depicted in Leviticus 8. Second, it is difficult to envision a ritual being enacted regularly in which the priests were ordained en masse. In addition, the ritual of Leviticus 8 also establishes the consecrated status of the holy place. Thus, Leviticus 8 is best understood as a founding ritual, the enactment of which was placed by the Priestly writers in the period of Israel's liminal sojourn in the wilderness,[3] which served to give institutional status to the Aaronides from the initial

---

1 For discussions, see K. Koch, *Die Priesterschrift von Exodus 25 bis Leviticus 16* (FRLANT (n.s.) 53; Göttingen: Vandenhoeck & Ruprecht, 1959), pp. 67-68; R. Rendtorff, *Studien zur Geschichte des Opfers im Alten Testament* (WMANT 24; Neukirchen-Vluyn: Neukirchener Verlag, 1967), pp. 12-13; Noth, *Leviticus*, pp. 68-69.

2 'Descriptive Tabernacle Texts', pp. 311-12.

3 R.L. Cohn (*The Shape of Sacred Space*, pp. 7-23) discusses the wilderness as a liminal state drawing on the work of Turner.

institution of the wilderness cult. It functions, however, not only as description of a past event, but also as a paradigm for what is to be.[1] The ritual serves as a statement about the cultic order and its proper structure and status. What is effected in this ritual is a permanent and ongoing element of the Israelite cult and ultimately the divinely created order.

History of the Text

Leviticus 8 is generally recognized to have had a complex literary growth.[2] As with Leviticus 16, the matter is further complicated by the necessity of relating its parts to a larger literary scheme concerning the growth of P. As noted above, it does have a redactional relation to Exodus 29, although it may have been an independent tradition at one time.

Levine suggests that two distinct rites have been combined in Leviticus 8.[3] One is an anointing and consecration rite concerned with Aaron and the tabernacle. The other is concerned with the ordination of the priesthood. The former, for Levine, stands as an independent tradition in Leviticus. Noth understands Leviticus 8 to be a secondary addition to Pg along with Exodus 35–39.[4] Elliger, however, argues that parts of Leviticus 8 were found in his Pg, and sees the heart of that material in the legitimation of Aaron and his sons as priests.[5] Their legitimacy is confirmed by the appearance of Yahweh at the tabernacle in response to their ordination.

The text now plays an important role in the larger structure of the Priestly narrative regardless of its pre-history. It narrates the establishment of the priesthood and, as such, functions as part of the Priestly construction of world. The ritual presented, however, serves not only to give legitimacy to the

1 N. Lohfink ('Die Priesterschrift und die Geschichte', *VTSup* 29 [1978], pp. 203-25) suggests that P has turned 'history' back into myths or paradigms which serve to present the ideal form of the world. See also T.E. Fretheim, 'The Theology of the Major Traditions in Genesis-Numbers', *RevExp* 74 (1977), pp. 305-11.

2 Koch, *Priesterschrift*, pp. 67-69; Rendtorff, *Geschichte des Opfers*, pp. 12-13; Noth, *Leviticus*, pp. 67-68; Elliger, *Leviticus*, pp. 104-20.

3 'Descriptive Tabernacle Texts', p. 311.

4 *Leviticus*, p. 68.

5 *Leviticus*, pp. 113-14.

Aaronide priesthood, but also to give legitimacy to the cult. Without this narrative, the tabernacle cult stands only as an unrealized possibility.

The Elements of the Ritual

Materials and Objects

Leviticus 8 exhibits a wide range of materials and objects in its execution. Both Aaron and his sons receive special 'priestly' clothing in this ritual. As will be argued, the clothing performs an important role in the total purpose of this ritual by marking the passage of the individuals into their status as priests. In v.2 the garments (הבגדים) are part of the materials to be gathered in preparation for the ritual. The garments for Aaron, the high priest, are detailed in vv.7-9. The instructions for the making of these garments are found in Exod. 28.5-39 and the actual making of them is described in Exod. 39.1-31. The following items are listed for Aaron in vv.7-9: הכתנת, the coat; האבנט, the sash; המעיל, the robe; האפד, the ephod; חשב האפד, the band of the ephod; החשן, the breastplate; in the breastplate was placed the האורים והתמים, the Urim and Thummin; המצנפת, the turban; and on the front of the turban was the golden plate, the holy crown, ציץ הזהב נזר הקדש.

Haran has argued with reference to Exod. 28.5-39 and Exod. 39.1-31 that there are basically eight articles of clothing, four especially designed for the high priest and four shared by all the priests.[1] The four articles that belong exclusively to the clothing of the high priest are the ephod, the breastplate, the robe of the ephod, and the golden head-dress. They correspond in sanctity to the inner part of the tent and are worn when the high priest functions *inside* the tent.[2] Haran notes three specific ritual acts performed regularly by the high priest inside the tabernacle: the daily offering of the incense of *sammim* on the golden altar of incense (Exod. 30.7-8), the regular tending of the lamps (Exod. 27.20; Lev. 24.2), and the

---

1 *Temples*, pp. 165-74, 208-15.
2 *Ibid.*, pp. 166-69. He develops this thesis by comparing the types of materials used in constructing the tent and garments and the type of workmanship found in each.

arrangement of the loaves of bread on the table of gold
(Lev. 24.5-9).[1] There are also four garments common to all the
priests: the tunic (that of the high priest is somewhat
ornamented, see Exod. 28.4), the sash, the turban (that of the
high priest is distinct, see Exod. 28.39-40), and the linen
breeches (Exod. 28.42; 39.28). These garments are not suitable,
by themselves, for ministering inside the tabernacle, but are
the clothes worn for ritual *outside* the tent.[2] Thus, Haran sees
two primary areas of Priestly ritual acts which are correlated
with two types of priestly attire.

Such a distinction is consistent with the ritual of Leviticus 8.
In conjunction with the anointing of Aaron with the special
anointing oil, his special clothes serve as a symbol of his
passage into the status of high priest, while, at the same time,
serving to locate him in his special 'place' of institutional work.
The same will be true with reference to the clothing of Aaron's
sons (Lev. 8.13).[3] Thus, the primary issue is the role that the
clothes play in the specific ritual described in Leviticus 8 and
not in the general significance of the various parts of the
priestly attire.

There are several objects in Leviticus 8 that receive ritual
activity. Specific objects are to be anointed with the special
anointing oil: the tabernacle (המשכן, v. 10); the altar and its
utensils (המזבח ואת־כל־כליו, v. 11); the laver and its base (הכיר
ואת־כנו, v. 11). Verse 30 speaks of the use of a mixture of the
anointing oil and blood, used for the anointing of Aaron and his
garments and his sons and their garments.

The horns of the altar and the altar itself are the objects of
blood application and the burning of offerings. The blood of the
bull of the חמאת is applied to the horns of the altar and poured
at its base in v. 15. In v. 19 the blood of the ram of the עלה is
thrown round about the altar. The blood of the ram of
'ordination' is thrown round about the altar in v. 24. The
following rites of burning are performed on the altar: the fat of
the entrails, the appendage of the liver, the kidneys and their

1 *Ibid.*, pp. 208-10.
2 *Ibid.*, pp. 169-71.
3 Only three items are specifically mentioned: כתנות, the coats; אבנט, the sash;
   and מגבעות, the caps. It may be assumed, both here and with reference to
   Aaron's clothing, that the breeches are already being worn.

fat from the bull of the חמאת (v. 16); the pieces of the ram of the עלה, its head, the washed entrails and legs of this ram (vv. 20-21); the fat, the fat tail, the fat of the entrails, the appendage of the liver, the two kidneys with their fat, and the right thigh of the ram of ordination with one unleavened cake, one cake of bread with oil, and one wafer (vv. 25-26, 28).

There are four types of materials used in this ritual: water, the anointing oil, the basket of unleavened bread, and the animals and their parts. Water is used in the washing of Aaron and his sons at the beginning of the ritual (v. 6). This is followed by the clothing of Aaron in his special high priestly garments (vv. 7-9). The conjunction of ritual bathing and dressing was also found in Leviticus 16. It is also noted that the entrails (הקרב) and hind legs (הכרעים) of the ram of the עלה are washed with water before the ram is offered on the altar (v. 21). This washing is undertaken to remove the waste of the animal, and thereby purify it, before it is offered to Yahweh.[1]

The anointing oil plays a central role in the ritual. It is used to anoint the tabernacle and its contents, the altar and its utensils, the laver and its base, and it is used to anoint Aaron (vv. 10-12). In each instance the purpose of the anointing is made clear—'to make holy' (לקדש; vv. 10, 11, 12). The making of this oil is described in Exod. 30. 23-33 where it is termed a holy anointing oil (שמן משחת־קדש, v. 25). In Exod. 30.26-28 a more extended list of items to be anointed is found: the tent of meeting, the ark of the testimony, the table and all its utensils, the lampstand and its utensils, the altar of incense, the altar of burnt offerings and its utensils, and the laver and its base. Again, the purpose of this anointing is to consecrate (קדש) the items (v. 29). It is further added, however, that this is done to make them most holy (קדש קדשים). It is also noted that anyone who touches these objects shall be holy (כל־הנגע בהם יקדש v. 29). Further, it instructs that Aaron *and* his sons are to be anointed with this oil to make them holy that they may serve Yahweh as priests (v. 30). The sole purpose of this holy anointing oil, then, is to 'make holy' objects and persons which are anointed with it.

---

1 Snaith, *Leviticus*, p. 31; Wenham, *Leviticus*, p. 54; Noth, *Leviticus*, p. 23.

The mention of a basket of unleavened bread for use in ritual is found only in Lev. 8.2, 26, 31; the instructions for the ritual ordination of priests in Exod. 29. 2-3, 23, 32; and in the ritual for a Nazirite in Num. 6.15, 17, 19. In the ritual for the priests, the use of the bread from the basket is found in conjunction with the offering of the ram of ordination, while its use in the Nazirite ritual is associated with the offering of the ram of the שלמים. There are definite similarities between the ram of ordination and the שלמים offerings as will be discussed below.[1]

There are three animals prescribed for this ritual which are used for three types of sacrifices. First, there is a bull for a חטאת (פר החטאת , vv. 2, 14-17). The blood of the bull is used to *kipper*, which is further defined as purification (חטא) and 'consecration' (קדש) (v. 15). The fat of the entrails, the appendage of the liver, and the kidneys and their fat are burned on the altar. The bull, its skin, flesh, and dung are burned outside the camp. Second, there is a ram for a whole burnt offering (עיל העלה, vv. 18-21). The blood is thrown round about the altar (v. 19) and then it is cut into pieces. Moses then burns the head, the pieces, and the fat on the altar, along with the washed entrails and hind legs (vv. 20-21). Finally, there is the ram of ordination (איל המלאים, vv. 22-26). Part of the blood of this animal is applied to the right ear, thumb, and big toe of Aaron and his sons, while the rest is thrown round about the altar (vv. 23-24). Moses then takes the fat, the fat tail, the fat of the entrails, the appendage of the liver, the two kidneys and their fat, and the right thigh, combines them with an unleavened cake, a cake with oil, and a wafer and places all of this in the hands of Aaron and his sons for a תנופה (vv. 25-27). These are all then burned on the altar as an 'ordination offering' (מלאים, vv. 25-28). The breast is given to Moses as his portion (v. 29).

Ritual Roles

There are two primary roles in this ritual. First, there is Moses who, in this instance, undertakes and guides the enactment of the ritual. While Moses in this ritual functions as a priest, it is difficult to say that he is here depicted as priest

1 See Excursus I, pp. 141-49.

in light of the fact that the ritual is concerned with the ordination and establishment of the priesthood. Moses, as is often the case, is here depicted as one standing outside of the normal institutional structures and role. As will be argued below, Moses' role in Leviticus 8 is best understood as inaugurator of the tabernacle cult.

The second role is filled by Aaron and his sons. They are the ones on whose behalf the ritual is enacted. They are the participants who receive the effects of the ritual. The congregation is mentioned in v. 3 as observer of the ritual, but is not given any specific role to play in the enactment of the ritual. It is clear, however, that the congregation, understood as the larger Israelite society, may also be said to receive effects from the ritual in that it is a ritual concerned with the establishment of an institutional, and therefore societal, status.

Spatial Categories
The number of spatial categories operative in this ritual is not as great as in Leviticus 16, but they are no less important. A minor spatial note concerns the precautionary instruction to burn the remains of the חטאת outside the camp (v. 17). The reason for this is clearly to guard the camp from further contamination from this defiled material.

More important is the prescription that the ritual be enacted at the door of the tent of meeting (vv. 3, 4, 31, 33, 35). This is where the ritual begins (vv. 3, 4) and where the ritual ends (vv. 31, 33, 35). As suggested above, this ritual is a rite of passage that serves to move Aaron and his sons, the priesthood, into their institutional status. The fact that the performance of the ritual is focused at the door of the tent of meeting suggests a convergence of status and space. The priesthood is instituted in its ritual space, its sphere of influence.[1] The

---

1 A distinction must be made between the prescriptions for the priests to be brought to the door of the tent of meeting and the prescription that the congregation be assembled at the door of the tent of meeting. Aaron and his sons are brought near, or 'presented' (קרב; vv. 6, 13, 24), and are the recipients of ritual activity. The congregation is assembled as observer. The presence of the congregation is important to contextualize the larger ritual process within the larger social body—one of society's institutions is being brought into existence. The ritual acts, however, are focused on Aaron

injunction for the priests to remain at the door of the tent for seven days, a typical number of days for rituals of major purification,[1] suggests that the institution of the priesthood is significantly related to the spatial category of the tent of meeting. This conjunction of status and space is further supported by the dual anointing of Aaron and the sacred precincts with the holy anointing oil. They are, thereby, brought into a common ritual status.

Temporal Categories

The only explicit temporal notice in the chapter is the prescription that Aaron and his sons remain at the door of the tent of meeting for seven days, 'until the days of your ordination are completed, for it will take seven days to ordain you' (v. 33). Expression is given here to the idea that the period of seven days, the week, is necessary for the full completion of the ordination process. Exod. 29.35-37 adds that during these seven days a bull is to be offered as a חטאת every day to *kipper* for the priests and for the altar. Also, the altar is to be anointed everyday to make it holy. Thus shall the altar be most holy (קדש קדשים).

A second temporal element may be implicit in this ritual. Exod. 40.2 instructs Moses to erect the tabernacle on the first day of the first month. If Leviticus 8 is read as a continuation of the account of the setting up and establishment of the wilderness cult, then the priesthood would begin its process of ordination on that day. Blenkinsopp has suggested that this date corresponds to the day on which the world emerged from the flood (see Gen. 8.13), and would also correspond to the first week of creation in Gen. 1.1–2.4a as the first week of the liturgical year.[2] Thus, a larger temporal framework may be operative in this ritual which serves to connect the establishment of the wilderness cult with the creation of the world and

and his sons and are concerned with a change of status for Aaron and his sons.

1 Cf. Lev. 12.2 for a woman after giving birth to a son; Lev. 14.8 for a leper; Lev. 15.13 for a man or woman with a bodily discharge; Lev. 15.19 for a menstruant; Lev. 15.24 for a man who has (sexual) contact with a menstruant; Num. 19.11, 14, 16 for one who comes into contact with a corpse.

2 'The Structure of P', pp. 283-84.

thereby present the ordination of the priesthood in that same context. This lends further support to the argument that the creation of the cult, and hence of Israelite society, is related to the creation of the world.

The Actions of the Ritual

For the present purposes this ritual may be divided into ten phases or segments.

I.   *Preparations* (vv. 2-4): Moses is instructed by Yahweh to take (קח) Aaron and his sons, the various materials to be used in the ritual, and the congregation, and assemble (הקהל) them at the door of the tent of meeting.

II. *Washing of Aaron and his sons* (vv. 5-6): Moses presented (ויקרב) Aaron and his sons and washed (וירחץ) them in water.

III. *The clothing of Aaron* (vv. 7-9): And Moses put (ויתן) on him the coat, and he girded (ויחגר) him with the sash, and clothed (וילבש) him with the robe. Then he put (ויתן) on him the ephod, and he girded (ויחגר) him with the band of the ephod; and bound (ויאפד) it on him. Then he put (וישם) the breastplate upon him, and he placed (ויתן) in the breastplate the Urim and Thummin. Then he put (וישם) the turban on his head and he put (וישם) the golden plate on the front of the turban.

IV. *The anointing with the anointing oil* (vv. 10-12): And Moses took (ויקח) the anointing oil and he anointed (וימשח) the tabernacle and all its materials, and he made them holy (ויקדש). And he sprinkled (ויז) some of the oil on the altar seven times and anointed (וימשח) the altar and all of its utensils as well as the laver and its base, to make them holy (לקדשם). Then he poured (ויצק) some of the anointing oil on Aaron's head and anointed (וימשח) him, to make him holy (לקדשו).

V.   *The clothing of Aaron's sons* (v. 13): And Moses presented (ויקרב) the sons of Aaron, and he clothed them (וילבשם) with coats, and girded (ויחגר) them with sashes, and bound (ויחבש) caps on them.

VI. *The bull of the* חטאת (vv. 14-17): Then Moses brought near (ויגש) the bull of the חטאת and Aaron and his sons laid (ויסמך) their hands on its head. And Moses slaughtered (וישחט) it and took (ויקח) some of its blood and placed (ויתן) it on the horns of the altar round about with his finger. Thus he purified (ויחטא) the altar. He poured (יצק) the rest of the blood at the base of the altar. And he made it holy (ויקדשהו), to *kipper* (לכפר) on it. Then he took (ויקח) all the fat of the entrails and the appendage of the liver, and the two kidneys and their fat, and he burned (ויקטר) it on the altar. The bull, its skin, its flesh, and its dung he burned (שרף) with fire outside the camp.

VII.   *The ram of the* עלה (vv. 18-21): And Moses presented (ויקרב) the ram of the עלה. And Aaron and his sons laid (ויסמכו) their hands on its head. And Moses slaughtered (וישחם) it and tossed (ויזרק) the blood on the altar round about it. Then he cut (נתח) the ram into pieces and he burned (ויקטר) the head and the pieces and the fat. And he washed (רחץ) the entrails and the hind legs in water and burned (ויקטר) all of the ram on the altar.

VIII. *The ram of ordination* (vv. 22-29): And Moses presented (ויקרב) the second ram the ram of ordination. And Aaron and his sons laid (ויסמכו) their hands on its head. And Moses slaughtered (וישחם) it and took some of its blood and put (ויתן) it on the tip of Aaron's right ear, on the thumb of his right hand, and on the big toe of his right foot. And he presented (ויקרב) the sons of Aaron. And Moses put (ויתן) some of the blood on the tips of their right ears, on the thumb of their right hand, and on the big toe of their right foot. Then Moses tossed (ויזרק) the blood on the altar round about. And he took (ויקח) the fat, the fat tail, all the fat on the entrails, the appendage of the liver, the two kidneys and their fat, and the right thigh. And from the basket of unleavened bread which was before Yahweh he took (לקח) one unleavened cake, one cake of bread with oil, and one wafer, and he placed (וישם) them on the fat and on the right thigh. Then he put (ויתן) all of this into the hands of Aaron and his sons and elevated (וינף) them as an elevation offering (תנופה) before Yahweh.[1] Moses then took (ויקח) them from their hands and burned (ויקטר) them on the altar of burnt offerings. And Moses took (ויקח) the breast and lifted it (ויניפהו) as an elevation offering before Yahweh. It was Moses' portion from the ram of ordination.

---

1 For this meaning of תנופה, see Milgrom, *Studies in Cultic and Levitical Terminology*, pp. 133-58.

IX. *The anointing with blood and oil* (v. 30): And Moses took
(ויקח) some of the anointing oil and some of the blood which
was on the altar and sprinkled (ויז) it on Aaron and his
clothes and on his sons and their clothes. And he made
holy (ויקדש) Aaron and his clothes along with his sons and
their clothes.

X. *Final instructions for Aaron and his sons* (vv. 31-36): And
Moses said to Aaron and his sons, 'Boil (בשלו) the flesh at
the door of the tent of meeting and eat (תאכלו) it there along
with the bread that is in the basket of ordination. And what
is left over of the flesh and the bread, you shall burn (ושרפו)
with fire. And you shall not go out (לא תצאו) from the door of
the tent of meeting for seven days, until the days of your
ordination are full, because you will become ordained
(ימלא את-ידכם) in seven days. You shall remain (תשבו) at the
door of the tent of meeting seven days and nights and you
shall perform (ושמרתם) the services of Yahweh lest you die'.

The Meaning of the Ritual and its Enactment

The Introduction (Lev. 8.1-4)
Moses is instructed in verses 1-2 to gather the necessary
materials for the enactment of the ritual. More importantly,
the opening verses state that the ritual is to take place in the
context of the whole congregation at the door of the tent of
meeting. This indicates that the ritual has communal significance and lends support to the view that this ritual is a
founding ritual. The ordination of the priesthood and the
establishment of sacred space are social concerns which must
be ritually enacted in the context of the whole community. The
cult is founded in the context of the community and the
community is defined, in large part, by its orientation with
reference to the cult. The door of the tent of meeting functions
as a symbol for this convergence of cult and community. It is
at this place where Israel will bring its sacrifices and offerings
to Yahweh and where the priesthood will serve in its role as
mediators between the people and Yahweh.

The Washing of Aaron and His Sons (v. 6)

After the materials are gathered, the first act of the ritual is the washing of Aaron and his sons by Moses (v. 6). In Leviticus 16, the ritual bathing of Aaron serves to mark off Aaron's marginal status.[1] In the present ritual, the washing of Aaron and his sons marks their entry into the state in which the ritual to be performed will have its intended effect on them. It is clear that in both rituals the washing is designed to put the persons washed into an appropriate ritual state for the enactment of the ritual.

A distinction must be made between 'bathing' and 'washing' on the basis of context. Both acts are expressed in Hebrew by the Qal form of רחץ.[2] Three distinct, although related, types of רחץ-rites may be distinguished. The most common type is the washing found in rites of purification. This 'bathing' is normally found with the added prescriptions that the clothes be laundered (כבס) and that the unclean person remain unclean until evening (see Lev. 14.8, 9; 15.5, 6, 7, 8, 10, 11, 13, 16, 18, 21, 22, 27; 16.26, 28; 17.15, 16; 22.6; Num. 19.7, 8, 19). In these examples, the bathing forms the heart of the purification act. It also serves, however, to mark off the one for whom the effects of the rite are intended.

A second type of רחץ-rite is evidenced in Exod. 30.18-21 and Exod. 40.30-32. In these passages the priests are instructed to wash their hands and feet in the water of the bronze laver before entering the tent of meeting or approaching the altar to burn an offering by fire to Yahweh. The purpose of these washings is to purify those parts of the body that will come into contact with 'the holy things' involved in the ritual. There is no indication that this rite is concerned with marking off the priests as the ones who will receive the effects of the rite.

The final type of רחץ-rite is evidenced in Lev. 16.4, 24 and 8.6. This rite is distinct because it is joined with a prescribed change of clothing. The change of clothes is symbolic of a

---

1 See above, pp. 90-95.
2 A distinction is made in *BDB* (p. 934) between a transitive and intransitive use of the word.

ritually constituted change of status.[1] In Lev. 16.4, 24 Aaron's bathings mark off his marginal status, symbolized by his change of clothes, within the larger ritual process. In Leviticus 8, Moses washes Aaron and his sons and they subsequently are clothed in their priestly garments. It is clear that this washing is part of the ritual being undertaken on behalf of Aaron and his sons. Moses enacts the ritual and as part of that process he washes those who are to become priests through the ritual.[2] At one level, it is clear that this may be understood as a purification rite for Aaron and his sons which begins the larger ritual process that will effect their status as priests. At the same time, the washing serves to mark out Aaron and his sons as the ones upon whom the effects of the ritual will fall. Finally, it should be emphasized that there is no second washing in this ritual. In Leviticus 16, Aaron bathed at the time of his entry into a new status and then bathed when he exited from that status. The fact that there is no complementary exit washing in the ritual of Leviticus 8 is an indication of the permanency of the status attained through this ritual. This is a 'perpetual' status for Aaron and his sons.

The Ritual Focused on Aaron (vv. 5-12)
The Ritual Act of Clothing. After Aaron and his sons have undergone their רחץ-rite, the ritual shifts its focus to Aaron. First, Aaron is clothed in the special attire of the high priest. The concern here is not to find any particular symbolic

---

1 In this case it is not only a change of status from defiled to clean, a state that may be changed through further defilement, but a change of one's standing and status within the structure of society.

2 It should be noted that Moses does not undergo a רחץ-rite of any type before enacting the ritual of Lev. 8. This would be expected if the רחץ-rite were considered essential for those performing rituals. It is probable, however, that Moses needs no ritual bathing because, as inaugurator of the cult, he stands outside of the normal ritual structures. Indeed, as the mediator of the instructions of Yahweh for the establishment of the wilderness cult, he transcends the normal structures of the cult which will only become operative *after* the cult has been fully established. See Excursus I.

meaning for each item of clothing;[1] rather, the concern is to
see the ritual importance of *the act of clothing*. As already
suggested, the clothing rite serves as a marker of Aaron's
passage into his new status. It does not in and of itself effect
that passage, but is one part of the larger ritual process of
passage. The clothes are a symbolic statement about his
status.[2] They give tangible evidence of his changed position in
society and serve as a symbol of his unique status.[3]

The Anointing Ceremony. The rite of clothing is followed by
the anointing ceremony involving the sacred precinct and
Aaron. This anointing with the special anointing oil serves to
pass objects and persons into a similar ritual state. The
description of the composition of the oil and the way it is to be
used found in Exod. 30.22-33 makes this clear. It is Yahweh's
holy anointing oil (v. 31). It is placed on Aaron and his sons in
order to 'consecrate' them to be priests to Yahweh (וקדשת אתם
לכהן לי; v. 30). It is not to be placed on the flesh of any other man
(v. 31). Finally, it is specifically stated that the purpose for
anointing the cultic objects is to 'consecrate' them that they
may be most holy (קדש קדשים), an act of 'consecration' that
parallels the anointing of Aaron and his sons. This parallel
purpose for the anointing is also evident in Lev. 8.11-12.

The anointing rite functions primarily to place Aaron and
the anointed objects in a common ritual state.[4] The common

1 For an attempt to explain the symbolic significance of Aaron's clothes, see
   C.F. Keil, *Manual of Biblical Archaeology*, 1 (trans. P. Christie;
   Edinburgh: Clark, 1887-1888), pp. 230-37.
2 See Leach, *Culture and Communication*, pp. 55-56; Grimes, *Beginnings*,
   pp. 28-30.
3 These clothes are referred to as 'holy garments' (בגדי-קדש) in Exod. 28.2 and
   further stated to be for glory and beauty (לכבוד ולתפארת) in the same verse.
   Verse 4 states that the clothes of Aaron and his sons are holy garments so
   that they might serve Yahweh as priests. Thus, it is recognized that the
   garments are distinct and, thereby, serve as markers of the priestly
   status.
4 It is common to distinguish between an early anointing rite in which the
   people anointed a leader and a later anointing rite in which a prophet
   anointed a leader for Yahweh (E. Kutsch, *Salbung als Rechtsakt im Alten
   Testament und im Alten Orient* [BZAW 87; Berlin: Töpelmann, 1963],
   pp. 55-58; R. Knierim, 'The Messianic Concept in the First Book of
   Samuel', in *Jesus and the Historian* [ed. F.T. Trotter; Philadelphia:

anointing also serves to emphasize that these are the primary 'spaces' of Aaron's cultic officiating as high priest. This is not to say that all of the anointed objects are the private domain of the high priest; rather, it is to indicate the *primary* places of his service and to mark the outer bounds of his service. Thereby, the ritual emphasizes that his sphere of cultic influence will not extend beyond these bounds. As such, the altar marks the outer boundary of the high priest's activity. At the same time, the rite gives expression to the common ritual state of Aaron and these objects. They are 'made holy' or 'set apart' to a common state of being. In this way, the area and its functionary share common boundaries and status; cultic space and correct cultic activity are coordinated through this dual anointing with the holy anointing oil.

A wide range of expressions are used in this anointing rite.

> v. 10: And Moses took (ויקח) the anointing oil and he anointed (וימשח) the tabernacle and all which was within it; thus he consecrated (ויקדש) them.

> v. 11: And he sprinkled (ויז) some of it on the altar seven times; thus he anointed (וימשח) the altar and all its utensils, the laver and its stand, in order to consecrate them (לקדשם).

> v. 12: And he poured (ויצק) some of the anointing oil on Aaron's head; thus he anointed (וימשח) him in order to consecrate him (לקדשו).[1]

The syntax of these verses suggests that 'sprinkling' and 'pouring' are parallel means for accomplishing the ritual act

---

Westminster, 1968], pp. 26-28). The latter rite forms the basis for the theology of the anointed Davidic king. In the post-exilic period, this rite was transferred to the high priest who took over many of the rights and duties of the king, according to Noth (*The Laws in the Pentateuch and Other Essays* [trans. D.R. Ap-Thomas; Philadelphia: Fortress, 1966], pp. 235-38). The general tendency is to emphasize that the anointing of the high priest serves to sanctify him and make him cultically clean (Kutsch, *Salbung als Rechtsakt*, pp. 22-27). It is necessary, however, to place the anointing of the high priest in the context of the anointing of the tabernacle precincts and the founding of the wilderness cult. The anointing of the high priest is not only an act of purification, but also an act of (institutional) location.

1 The *waw* on וימשח in vv. 11, 12 is understood as an explicative *waw* (see *GKC*, par. 154).

of 'anointing'. The mode of the anointing is, thereby, decided by
the object which is anointed. The use of קדשׁ with the ל of purpose in vv. 11 and 12 clearly indicates the purpose of the
anointing—'in order to קדשׁ' the person or object on which the
anointing oil is placed. Thus, the common anointing of the
tabernacle, altar, and Aaron serves to place them in a common
state of קדשׁ.

It is clear that the idea of 'setting apart' is central to this rite.
The anointing oil has as its purpose the 'setting apart' of the
objects on which it is placed. To put this in other terms, it
serves to place people and objects in the realm of the holy and
thereby sets bounds around them that distinguish them from
the ordinary categories of existence. In this case the category
is conceptual—the realm of the holy—but it is, in part, made
objective by its connection with the holy *place*.[1]

Ritual Focus on Aaron's Sons

After Aaron, and the cult site, and cultic objects are anointed,
the sons of Aaron are once again introduced into the ritual.
They are clothed in their special priestly clothes (v. 13). The
separation of the clothing rite of Aaron and the clothing rite of
his sons serves to emphasize that the anointing of Aaron and
the sanctuary was a special anointing of the high priest and
his office. It is the special anointing ritual that separates the
high priest from the other priests, and this is communicated
by their different clothes. The clothing of the sons serves to

---

1 Lev. 21.10-12 (H) should be noted in this context. It defines the high priest
   as the one on whose head the anointing oil has been poured and who is
   ordained (ומלא את־יד) to wear the garments (v. 11). Verse 12 further states
   that he shall not go out of the sanctuary (המקדשׁ) nor profane the sanctuary
   of his God. The reason is given: 'Because (כי) the consecration (נזר) of the
   anointing of his God is upon him'. This passage supports the view that the
   anointing of Aaron along with the cult site and objects serves to place
   them in a similar state. Lev. 10.7 indicates that the period in which the
   anointing oil was upon the priests involved a *time* in which they were
   separated to the *space* of the tabernacle. This suggests that for priests in
   general, the anointing was for a limited time. Thus, the ritual of Lev. 8 is
   an institutional rite of passage which establishes the Aaronide priesthood
   as a permanent institution. Individuals could assume the role of priest for
   a limited time, but the institution itself was permanent.

mark their entry into the ritual and, as with Aaron, marks, in
part, their passage into the priesthood.

The Sacrifices and Offerings
The ritual now turns to a series of sacrifices or offerings: פר
חטאת (vv. 14-17) איל העלה (vv. 18-21), and איל המלאים (vv. 22-29).

פר חטאת
The bull of the חטאת is the first of a series of sacrifices to be
presented. Aaron and his sons begin the sacrificial process by
laying their hands upon the head of the bull (v. 14). Various
explanations of this rite were noted above in the discussion of
Leviticus 16.[1] In Lev. 16.21 the rite is best understood as an act
of transference in which the sins of the people were placed on
the head of the goat for Azazel. It is doubtful if 'transference' is
the purpose of the act in the ritual of Leviticus 8.

This act should be related to its place in the larger ritual
process of the sacrifice. It begins the sacrificial ritual proper. It
has been understood as an act of identification in the sense of
substitution,[2] although such an interpretation lacks textual
support. It could be an act in which the type of sacrifice is
identified[3] or in which the one offering the sacrifice is identified.[4] The latter suggestion operates within the larger framework of sacrifice interpreted as gift. There is no indication,
however, that there was any need to identify the type of sacrifice being offered. Indeed, it appears that the 'type' of sacrifice
was already determined in large part by the animal being
sacrificed and the occasion for the sacrifice. The idea that the
rite intends to identify the offerer and the sacrifice as the
offerer's property makes better sense of the rite in its larger
ritual context.

Such an interpretation emphasizes that the sacrifice is
'given' by the offerer. Seen in this way, the rite operates as an
act of dedication.[5] It marks the passage of the animal from the

1 See pp. 95-96.
2 Leach, *Culture and Communication*, p. 89.
3 Milgrom, 'Sacrifices and Offerings', p. 765.
4 De Vaux, *Old Testament Sacrifice*, pp. 28-29.
5 Evans-Pritchard, 'The Meaning of Sacrifice', p. 28.

grasp of the *sacrifiant* to the hands of the *sacrificateur* . The act transfers the victim from the use of the *sacrifiant* (profane) to the use of the *sacrificateur* (sacred).[1] It is an act of giving in which the offerer hands over to the realm of the sacred an animal to be used in sacred ritual. As such, this hand-laying rite is an act of dedication in which the animal is officially presented and given over to the priest for its use in sacred matters.[2]

Verse 15 describes the use of the blood by Moses. The manipulation of the blood does not follow the prescriptions for an unintentional sin of the anointed priest (Lev. 4.2-7) nor for an unintentional sin of the community (Lev. 4.16-18). Rather, it follows the prescriptions for an unintentional sin of a leader or common person (Lev. 4.22-26, 27-31, 33-34). Moses takes some of the blood with his finger and puts it on the horns of the altar, clearly the outer altar of the burnt offerings, and then he pours out the rest of the blood at the base of the altar. Thus, the blood is not taken into the tent. That this sacrifice follows the pattern for the common people is consistent with the view that Aaron and his sons are *not yet* priests. They are *in the process* of passage into the priesthood. This is made clear by the statement of v. 33 which states that the full period of their ordination is seven days.

Lev. 8.15 adds several explanations for these acts.

> And Moses placed some of the blood on the horns of the altar round about with his finger; thus he purified the altar (ויחטא את־המזבח). Then he poured the blood at the base of the altar; thus he consecrated it (ויקדשהו), in order to *kipper* on it.

---

1 This distinction was made by H. Hubert and M. Mauss (*Sacrifice: Its Nature and Function* [trans. W.D. Halls; Chicago: University of Chicago, 1964], pp. 9-10, 22-25). The *sacrifiant* is 'the subject to whom the benefits of sacrifice thus accrue, or who undergoes its effects' (p. 10). The *sacrificateur* is the intermediary, the priest, who performs the sacrifice.

2 It is tempting to see in this interpretation the meaning of 'filling the hand' (= ordination) with reference to the priests. The offerer empties his/her hand of the animal in transferring it to the realm of the sacred and in so doing fills the hand of the priests who represent the realm of the sacred. Indeed, the priests receive the material benefits, when possible, of such offerings.

As argued above with reference to the anointing procedure, the *waw* on וידא and the *waw* on ויקדשהו are best understood as explanatory; they further define the ritual actions of putting blood on the altar and pouring the blood at the base of the altar. There is confirmation, then, of the argument that the two acts involving the blood of the חטאת represent two distinct functions.[1] The blood placed on the horns serves as a purgative or purificatory rite, while the blood poured at the base of the altar serves to reconsecrate the altar and, thus, to reestablish the sacred boundaries. Again, לכפר serves to give the purpose (ל of purpose) for the blood acts: 'in order to *kipper* on it'. Thus, in this instance, the *kipper*-act serves (1) to purify the altar *and* (2) to reestablish the structure of the holy.[2]

If this reasoning is correct, it means that the act of *kipper* is a complex act that cannot be reduced to a single idea. *Kipper* involves not only purification or cleansing, but also a restructuring of the realm of holiness. It involves a restoration of the boundaries that surround and protect the holy things. Thus, it involves maintenance of the holy. *Kipper* entails not only elimination of defilement, but also realignment and maintenance of the created cultic order. Sin and defilement bring about a disruption of the holiness of the cultic site, a state of holiness demanded by Yahweh and understood as part of Yahweh's created order. The boundaries created in the setting apart of this area, thus, have been broken and must be repaired. Ritual, thereby, becomes a means for human participation in the maintaining and sustaining of the divinely created order.

Moses then takes the fat of the entrails, the appendage of the liver, and the kidneys with their fat and burns them on the altar. The blood is used for the ritual acts of purification and

1 See above, pp. 81-89.
2 It may be that this verse is the foundational explanation of the purpose of the חטאת. The explanation is not included in Lev. 1-7 because it is given here in the Ur-חטאת. Indeed, this is the description of the cult inaugurator making the ur-offerings in order to establish and make operative the cult. While Lev. 9 will narrate the inauguration of the sacrificial cult by the priests, Lev. 8 describes the sacrifices and offerings necessary for the passage of Aaron and his sons from the status of common people to the status of priests. Such passage, as all ritual passages in the Priestly cult, must be accompanied by sacrifices and offerings.

consecration, but the fat belongs to Yahweh (Lev. 3.16-17;
7.22-27). The blood and the fat are not for human consumption. They have been removed from human intake by their
role in ritual. Verse 17 states that the refuse of the bull is to be
taken outside the camp and burned. When the blood of the
חמאת was taken inside the tent, the remains were to be burned
outside the camp.[1] The priests, however, cannot eat the
remains in this instance because theoretically the priesthood is
not yet established. Beyond this, however, is the probability
that they could not eat sacrifices which they offered for themselves.[2] It may be asked why Moses does not eat the normal
priestly portion in this instance? Moses does receive the breast
of the ram of ordination (Lev. 8.29), although he does not
receive the thigh as is customary for the priest in sacrifices (cf.
Lev. 7.28-36). This might be seen as evidence that Moses is not
perceived as priest in this ritual. While the evidence is incon-
clusive, the reason would seem to be that the bull of the חמאת is
placed in the context of the establishment of the priesthood and
is, for that reason alone, removed from human consumption
and must, therefore, be burned.

איל העלה

The next phase of the ordination ritual (vv. 18-21) consists of
the offering of a ram as an עלה. The precise nature of the עלה is
unclear. The problem is compounded by the uncertainty of the
historical development of this type of offering. It is generally
agreed that this was the earliest of the offerings and as such
had a broad range of effects. It is specifically said to *kipper* in
Lev. 1.4 and 16.24. In Lev. 9.7 and 14.20 it is said to *kipper* in
conjunction with the offering of a חמאת in a larger ritual
process.

In Lev. 8.18-21 there are several distinct elements prescribed for the ritual.

---

1 Following Milgrom, 'Two Kinds of *hatta't*', pp. 333-37.
2 Cf. Lev. 6.16. So Milgrom, *ibid.*, p. 337.

v. 18:   Presentation of the ram: Aaron and his
sons lay their hands on the head of the ram[1]

v. 19:   Moses kills the ram: Moses throws (זרק) the blood on the
altar round about

v. 20:   The ram is cut into pieces: Moses burns the head, the
pieces, and the fat

v. 21:   The entrails and hind legs are washed with water: the
whole animal is burned on the altar[2]

v. 21:   'It is an עלה, a pleasing fragrance; it is an offering of
fire to Yahweh'.

As can be seen, there are three major elements in this ritual:
presentation, the blood manipulation, and the burning. An
important indication of the purpose of the עלה is found in the
final phrase: 'it is an עלה to Yahweh, a pleasing fragrance'.
This suggests that the sacrifice must be understood primarily
by its effect upon Yahweh,[3] and this as part of the *kipper*
process. The presentation and the laying on of the hands are

---

1 Lev. 1.4 adds תרצה לו לכפר עליו. Similarly, in Lev. 1.3 the offerer presents the
animal at the door of the tent of meeting לרצנו לפני יהוה. The verb רצה is used
in P in Lev. 1.4; 7.18; 19.7; 22.23, 25, 27. The related form רצון is found in P
in Exod. 28.38; Lev. 1.3; 19.5; 22.19, 20, 21, 29; 23.11. In several cases it is
clear that the verbal form refers to the acceptability of the animal for sacrificial purposes (Lev. 1.4; 19.7; 22.23, 25, 27). The related form is clearly
used this way in Lev. 22.20, 21. In Exod. 23.38, it refers to the gold plate to
be placed in the high priest's turban 'to be acceptable for them (on their
behalf [referring to the Israelites]) before Yahweh'. In Lev. 17.18 the form
ירצה (N stem) is used in conjunction with a prohibition against eating the
flesh of the זבח שלמים on the third day: 'the one who presents it will not be
accepted'. This form elsewhere refers to the sacrifice and not the offerer.
Milgrom (review of G.J. Wenham, *The Book of Leviticus, JBL* 100 [1981],
p. 628) argues that in 1.3 the meaning is 'for acceptance on his behalf'
rather than 'may accept him'. He bases this on the obvious meaning in the
expanded phrase in Lev. 22.20: כי לא לרצון יהוה לכם. The dominant idea
associated with the term in P is the acceptance of the animal and not the
offerer. Thus, the idea in relation to the עלה is clearly that the animal is
accepted on behalf of the offerer. This also suggests that the act of the
offerer in laying his hands on the head of the animal is primarily an act of
giving over the animal so that it might be accepted by the priest for use in
the ritual.

2 See Rendtorff (*Studien*, pp. 114-15) and Ringgren (*Sacrifice*, pp. 14-15) for a
reconstruction of the original form of the עלה sacrifice.

3 Wenham, *Leviticus*, p. 56.

the normal acts associated with the dedicatory giving of the animal for use in ritual matters. The act associated with the blood is necessary because of the *kipper* function of the sacrifice. Finally, the burning of the animal gives the whole animal to the deity in the form of a pleasing fragrance.

Before analyzing these actions, the discussion of the effects of sin as understood by the priests must be expanded. Sin produces effects in four areas. Human sin has an effect on the deity and on the human agent of sin. Sin offends Yahweh with the result that Yahweh's wrath may become aroused.[1] At the same time, sin defiles the human agent of sin.[2] It is also true, however, that such defilement can pollute the sanctuary and threaten Yahweh's continued presence there. Finally, as already noted, sin can threaten the created order by disrupting the structures of the created order.[3] Thus, sin has negative effects on Yahweh, the human agent of sin, the sanctuary, and the created order. The חטאת serves to purge the sanctuary and to reestablish the boundaries of the sacred and created order. The עלה is concerned with the offense to Yahweh caused by sin, and serves to avert the wrath of Yahweh which results from sin.

1 There are several examples in the Priestly traditions (e.g., the Priestly flood story in Gen. 8.11-13). See N. Lohfink, 'Die Ursünden in der priesterlichen Geschichtserzählung', in *Die Zeit Jesu* (ed. G. Bornkamm and K. Rahner; Freiburg: Herder, 1970), pp. 38-57; Westermann, *Genesis*, pp. 416-18. Elsewhere in P this idea is often associated with the wrath (קצף) of God breaking out against sancta offenders (e.g., Lev. 10.6; Num. 1.53; 16.22; 17.11; 18.5). On this use, see Milgrom, *Levitical Terminology*, p. 109, and 'Atonement in the OT', p. 80.

2 While the main concern of defilement was its effect on the tabernacle and holy things, sin was also seen to 'defile' the larger camp area, and the agent of sin as well (see Lev. 11.44; Num. 5.3b). On this, see Milgrom, 'Atonement, Day of', p. 83; Hutton, 'Declaratory Formulae', pp. 172-73.

3 It should be noted that the Priestly account of the flood is a paradigm for this. The disruption of the created order by human violence and corruption brings about the breakdown of the created order and a return to chaos. See E. Würthwein, 'Chaos und Schöpfung im mythischen Denken und in der biblischen Urgeschichte', in *Zeit und Geschichte* (ed. E. Dinkler; Tübingen: Mohr [Paul Siebeck], 1964), pp. 317-27; T. Frymer-Kensky, 'Pollution, Purification, and Purgation in Biblical Israel', in *The Word of the Lord Shall Go Forth* (ed. C.L. Meyers and M. O'Connor; Winona Lake, ID: Eisenbrauns, 1983), pp. 399-414.

The gift aspect of the עלה has often been emphasized.[1] Levine has argued that its primary purpose was to evoke 'an initial response from the deity prior to bringing the primary concerns of his worshippers to his attention'.[2] It is difficult to see such a meaning in the Priestly ritual, however, because of the almost complete lack of 'concerns' brought by the worshipper. The Priestly concern is with the ritual attempt to maintain right order. Thus, the עלה becomes a permanent part of the regulated sacrifices of the sacred calendar.[3]

The first part of the ritual presents the animal to the sacred area to secure its effective use in the ritual. The splashing of the blood on the altar is the primary act of *kipper*, here related to *kôphar*, which serves to avert the wrath of Yahweh and to keep it from breaking out against the human agent of sin *and* the community.[4] The burning of the animal acts as a gift to Yahweh and serves to secure right relations with Yahweh established when the divine wrath is averted.

The ritual process presented thus far with regard to Leviticus 8 shows the following development. The חטאת is offered to purge the sanctuary and reestablish the sacred boundaries. The defilement of the sanctuary represents the gravest threat to the community in that a breakdown in the cultic order would entail a breakdown in the created order. Thus, the structures that serve to order life are first established. The עלה is then undertaken to insure that the wrath of Yahweh is averted and that the threat of a destructive reaction by Yahweh is negated. A gift is offered to Yahweh to insure that right relations are established.

איל המלאים

The Meaning of מלאים

In analyzing this part of the ritual, three issues in particular need attention. First, the meaning of מלאים needs to be examined. Second, the relation of the איל המלאים to the זבח שלמים

1 H.H. Rowley, *Worship in Ancient Israel: Its Forms and Meanings* (1967; rpt. London: SPCK, 1976), pp. 120-21.
2 *In the Presence*, p. 22.
3 Num. 28-29; Exod. 29.38-42. See Chapter 7.
4 See Milgrom, 'Atonement in the OT', p. 80.

must be addressed. Third, the significance of the placing of the
blood on the right ear, thumb, and big toe of Aaron and his sons
needs explanation.

Lev. 8.22-29 is concerned with the second ram, the איל
המלאים. Various suggestions have been offered to explain the
meaning of מלאים, derived from the verb meaning 'to be full, to
fill'. 'To fill the hand' is used to refer to one who is established
as priest (Exod. 28.41; 29.29; Lev. 8.33; 16.32; 21.10; Num. 3.3).
Snaith relates the idea of 'filling the hand' to that of 'make the
first sacrifice'.[1] Cody relates the phrase to the story of the
Levites in Exod. 32.25-29.[2] Acting in response to Moses' call for
fidelity, the Levites take up swords to kill those who had acted
against Yahweh. He translates the call of Moses in v. 29 as
follows: 'Fill your hands today for Yahweh, each man at the
expense of his son and his brother, so that he (Yahweh) may
give you his blessing today'. Thus, Cody continues, 'the Levites,
as a result of their "filling their hands" in the slaying of their
kinsmen, have "filled their hands" in the sense of becoming
priests'.[3] It is probable, however, that this passage is late and
reflects the later attempts of Levites to lay claim to the priesthood.[4] It is difficult to see how a phrase originally applied to the
Levites would be adopted to refer to the whole priesthood. It is
more probable that a pro-Levite traditionist would make use
of a phrase already in use for the priests in order to support the
claim of the Levites. It is preferable to relate the phrase to the
cultic activities of the priests in performing the sacrifices and
offerings. It is possible, although not certain, that the phrase
may be derived from the presentation of the sacrificial animal
or offering to the priest at the sanctuary. The priest receives
the animal, takes it in his hand, thereby showing that the
animal has been accepted and deemed appropriate for its
intended ritual use. The ram of ordination, then, is a sacrifice
that serves to place the priests in their institutional role as
those who offer the sacrifices and offerings.

1 *Leviticus*, p. 57.
2 *Priesthood*, p. 154.
3 *Ibid.*
4 Noth, *Exodus* (trans. J.S. Bowden; OTL; Philadelphia: Westminster, 1962),
   pp. 250-51; B.S. Childs, *The Book of Exodus* (OTL; Philadelphia:
   Westminster, 1974), pp. 570-71.

The Relation of the איל המלאים *to the* זבח שלמים

This sacrifice occurs in the ritual at the place where the זבח
שלמים normally comes.[1] Indeed, Exod. 29.28 coordinates this
sacrifice with the זבח שלמים in order to indicate the portion of
such sacrifices that belong to the priests. Thus, it is appropriate
to interpret this sacrifice, in part, as a זבח שלמים. At the same
time, however, there are important differences. In particular,
the placing of the blood of this animal on the right ear lobe, the
right thumb, and the right big toe of the priests must be
explained. Indeed, this would seem to be *the* distinctive act that
brings about the name of this sacrifice as the 'ordination
sacrifice'.

The rite consists of the following elements.

1. Presentation of the ram and the laying on of the hands (v. 22)
2. Slaughter of the ram (v.23aα)
3. Manipulation of the blood (v. 23aβ-24)
   a. Placed on Aaron's extremities (v. 23aβ-b)
   b. Placed on the extremities of Aaron's sons (v. 24a)
   c. Placed on the altar (v. 24b)
4. The elevation offering (vv. 25-28)
   a. The elevation of the various materials (vv. 25-27)
   b. The burning of the materials (v. 28)
5. Moses' elevation offering of the breast (v. 29)

If this sacrifice is an adaptation of the זבח שלמים, then some
understanding of such sacrifices will be necessary in order to
interpret the rite in Leviticus 8. There has been no consensus
reached on the significance and purpose of the זבח שלמים. In
part, the problem has been complicated by the attempt to find
a single basic meaning for these sacrifices. It is probable that a
single type of sacrifice would have a broad range of meanings
and functions depending on the ritual process of which it was
a part.[2]

---

1 See Levine, 'Descriptive Tabernacle Texts', pp. 307-18; A.F. Rainey, 'The
  Order of Sacrifices in Old Testament Ritual Texts', *Bibl* 51 (1970), pp. 485-
  98.
2 This would seem to be implied in the instructions of Lev. 7.12-17; 22.21-23,
  29-30 which state that the sacrifice was appropriate in connection with a
  sacrifice of praise (תודה), a free-will offering (נדבה), and as a votive offering
  (נדר).

The LXX offers three translations of the word that already reflect the interpretive process:[1] τὸ σωτήριον and related forms which suggest a rendering related to 'that which saves' or 'preserves'; τελείωσις and related forms which suggest a rendering related to 'wholeness, completeness, perfect'; εἰρηνικός and related forms which suggest a rendering related to 'peace'. These ideas have been developed further in modern scholarship. One view sees the שלמים זבח as a communion sacrifice and emphasizes the meal associated with the sacrifice.[2] Related to this idea is the view that it represents a 'peace offering'.[3] Others see in this type of sacrifice a covenant sacrifice and meal concerned primarily with the establishment and maintenance of the covenant.[4] Rendtorff argues that it means simply 'concluding offering'.[5] Levine has suggested that the שלמים should be related to the idea of gift on the basis of Ugaritic *slmm*, and argues that in early Israel this type of sacrifice functioned primarily as part of royal and/or national celebrations which were particularly concerned with acts of dedication and beginnings. Its incorporation into the regular cult was a later development.[6]

As already indicated, it is doubtful if any *one* meaning does justice to all the biblical material. Indeed, as Israelite religion developed, it is probable that standard ritual acts would be adapted to cover new situations as they arose. Levine's suggestion certainly does more justice to the המלאים איל sacrifice, interpreted in part as a שלמים זבח, in Leviticus 8. The ram of ordination is associated with the idea of dedication to a new situation, the institutionalization of the priesthood. It serves to mark the beginning of the priesthood and announce the establishment of their cultic status.

---

1 See S. Daniel, *Recherches sur le Vocabulaire du Culte dans la Septante* (EC 61; Paris: Librairie C. Klincksieck, 1966), pp. 273-97.

2 See, for example, de Vaux, *Studies*, pp. 27-51.

3 Wenham, *Leviticus*, pp. 76-81.

4 R. Dussaud, *Les origines Cananéennes du sacrifice Israélite* (Paris: Leroux, 1921), pp. 96-115; R. Schmid, *Das Bundesopfer in Israel* (Munich: Kösel-Verlag, 1964); W. Eisenbeis, *Die Wurzel š-l-m im Alten Testament* (BZAW 113; Berlin: Töpelmann, 1969), pp. 285-96.

5 *Studien*, pp. 119-62.

6 *In the Presence*, pp. 8-52.

The ritual process of the ordination of the priesthood, then, presents the following development and structure.

A. Anointing of the holy place and Aaron to establish the sacred area and to mark the one whose primary institutional *setting* is the holy place.

B. The bull of the חטאת to purge the sacred objects and insure the integrity of the sacred boundaries.

C. The ram of the עלה to avert the possible outbreak of the wrath of Yahweh and to secure the bond, the 'safe' relation, between the offerer and Yahweh.

D. The ram of the מלאים to dedicate the priests to public, institutional status.

The Daubing Rite

This leaves the placing of the blood on the lobe of the right ear, the right thumb, and the right big toe to be explained. This procedure is only found in one other ritual—the re-entry of the recovered leper into the camp in Leviticus 14.[1] In Leviticus 8, the blood of the ram of ordination is placed on the extremities of Aaron and his sons. In Leviticus 14 it is the blood of the lamb offered as an אשם that is placed on the extremities of the recovered leper. This takes place on the eighth day of the cleansing process after the individual has returned to the camp (vv. 8-14). It is followed by the placing of oil on the same extremities (vv. 15-18).

The issue that must be addressed in order to understand the ritual of Leviticus 8 is what the priestly ordination accomplishes that is also accomplished in the ritual of the recovered leper. One common feature is that both rituals effect a passage. As already suggested, the priestly ordination is a ritual intended to give passage to Aaron and his sons across the boundary separating non-institutional status to institutional status. This is primarily a socio-conceptual boundary, but one that is given objective focus by its relation to the sacred precincts. The recovered leper is passing over spatial boundaries—from outside the camp (see Lev. 13.46) to inside the camp. The thesis here is that in both cases the passage is

---

1 See below, Chapter 5, for a detailed analysis of this ritual.

understood as passage across the conceptual boundary between 'death' and 'life' and, as such, is a dangerous passage.

Feldman has shown that the leper was understood in terms of one who had suffered a kind of death.[1] Leprosy placed the victim in a situation like death, like a corpse. This is suggested by Num. 12.10-12 where Miriam becomes leprous (מצרעת, v. 10). In Aaron's plea for Moses' help, he says, 'Let her not be as one dead (כמח), who, when he comes out of his mother's womb, has his flesh half eaten' (v. 12). Further, Lev. 13.45 describes the appropriate actions for the leper to be those associated with mourning rites for the dead (cf. Lev. 10.6; 21.10-11).[2]

There are similarities between the rituals of cleansing for the recovered leper and the corpse-contaminated person. Both rituals make use of the three elements of cedar wood, scarlet string, and hyssop. These are the only rituals where these three elements appear together. This, at least, suggests that the defilement of leprosy and the defilement of corpse-contamination were understood to be similar in effect.

It may be said, then, that the recovered leper is understood as one who has come into contact with 'death' and has recovered and returned to 'life'. The boundary between life and death is a dangerous boundary because it always holds the potential for the end of life. The key to the leper's safe passage across this boundary is the placing of the blood on the lobe of the right ear, the right thumb, and the right big toe. This is paralleled in the ritual of the ordination of the priests. At the same time, the ritual for the recovered leper parallels the ritual for purification from corpse-contamination. It may be said that the common element that runs through all three of these rituals is the desire to effect safe passage across the boundary between life and death.[3] The ordination of the priests

---

1 E. Feldman, *Biblical and Post-Biblical Defilement and Mourning: Law as Theology* (LJLE; New York: Yeshiva University/KTAV, 1977), pp. 37-41. See also Frymer-Kensky, 'Pollution', p. 400.

2 Feldman, *Defilement*, pp. 38-39.

3 See G. von Rad, *Old Testament Theology* (New York: Harper & Row, 1962), I, pp. 272-79 for a discussion of clean/unclean and death. He states, 'Thus the life of Israel . . . was bounded by a great tension between clean and unclean and between life and death, for every uncleanness was to some

and the purification of the recovered leper are distinct from
the ritual to purify the corpse-contaminated because they
each have an observable change to mark the passage—the
recovered leper has a change in skin condition while the
priests have a change of clothing which serves to mark their
new status as priests. The one purified from corpse-
contamination shows no outer change in appearance. The
recovered leper and corpse-contaminated are similar in that
both are considered to have come physically into contact with
death, while the priests, on the other hand, do not have such
direct physical contact.

It must now be asked if it is possible to understand the
passage of Aaron and his sons into the priesthood as a passage
between the boundary separating death and life. The stories in
Numbers 16–18 justify such an interpretation. A major
theme of the Priestly traditions in these chapters is the
selection of Aaron to be priest. The rebellion of Korah is
generally understood as Priestly material and will form the
focus of the discussion. The central issue in Korah's rebellion
concerns the issue of who may have commerce with the
sacred area, focused in this story on the issue of the burning of
incense.[1] As v. 5 makes clear, the issue concerns who may
הקריב.[2] The rebels are destroyed by an act of Yahweh and the
'moral' of the story is found in Num. 17.5. The censers of the
rebels, now made holy, are hammered on to the altar so as 'to
be a reminder to the sons of Israel, in order that no unauthor-
ized person who is not a priest, a descendant of Aaron, shall
encroach (upon the priestly duty) to offer incense before
Yahweh, lest he become as Korah and his company'. Thus,
those who perform the cultic act of burning incense before
Yahweh will die unless given safe passage.

In Num. 17.6-15 a plague from Yahweh breaks out against
the people because of further complaint against Moses and

extent already a precursor of the thing that was uncleanness out and out,
death' (p. 277). This idea is developed by W. Paschen, *Rein und Unrein*
(StANT 25; Munich: Kösel-Verlag, 1970), pp. 63-65.

1 Milgrom, *Levitical Terminology*, pp. 18-20.
2 Milgrom (*ibid.*, pp. 16-22) argues that the meaning is not simply 'draw
   near', but 'encroachment upon the priestly function of offering incense'
   (p. 19).

Aaron. It afflicts the innocent as well as the guilty. Moses instructs Aaron to take his censer, put fire from the altar in it, put incense on it, and bring it to the congregation to *kipper*[1] for them, because wrath has gone forth from Yahweh (v. 11). Aaron obeys Moses and stands 'between the dead and the living (ויעמד בין־המתים ובין החיים) and the plague was stopped' (v. 13). Again, Aaron stands in the boundary between life and death in performing his ritual duties.

Finally, Num. 17.16-28 tells how Aaron's house was chosen to be the one which would have access to the tent of meeting and would perform the rituals associated with it. Rods from each of the families were placed in the tent before the testimony over night. The following morning Aaron's rod had sprouted and blossomed. The response of the people is recorded in 17.27-28: 'Behold, we die (גוענו), we are perishing (אבדנו), all of us are perishing (אבדנו כלנו)! Anyone who dares to encroach (הקרב הקרב) upon the tabernacle of Yahweh will die (ימות). Are we all then to die (לגוע)?' The answer to the question is found in the Yahweh speech of Numbers 18. Aaron's household will bear the liability of the sacred area and the priesthood.[2] They are given the responsibility of guarding the sacred boundaries against encroachment (v. 7). The punishment for encroachment is death.

There is a consistent theme in these chapters that those who encroach upon the realm of the holy are liable to death. This is the response of Yahweh to encroachers who cross the boundaries of the sacred improperly. Aaron and his sons have been given safe passage, not only to cross these boundaries, but to stay within them. The crossing of the sacred boundaries is dangerous, but ritual structures make it possible. The priests have stood in the breach between life and death and now live to act as mediators between the sacred and the non-sacred, and between life and death.[3] Israel's existence depends upon the continued integrity of the sacred order, but to enter it without

---

1 This use of *kipper* is related to the noun *kôpher* and suggests a ransom paid for the people. See Milgrom, 'Atonement in the OT', p. 80.

2 See Milgrom, *Levitical Terminology*, pp. 18-20.

3 Rites of initiation or institutionalization reflect the passage from death to life. See van Gennep, *Rites of Passage*, pp. 65-115; Eliade, *Sacred and Profane*, pp. 162-92; Zuesse, 'Taboo and the Divine Order', pp. 500-501.

proper ritual safeguards is certain death. The priests are
ritually instituted to be the ones who stand within the sacred
structures to insure the proper maintenance of these sacred
structures.

The ritual placing of the blood on the extremities of the
priests is the ritual act that provides the priests safe passage
across the dangerous boundaries. It has often been noted that
these bodily extremities represent the whole person. They
form the outer bounds of the person. The whole person must
receive passage because of the severity of the danger in
crossing these bounds. It is quite probable that the blood in this
instance represents 'life'. If so, it may be said to communicate
life to those on whom it is placed. It is an appropriate ritual
symbol for this type of passage.[1] It is even more appropriate
when understood to be derived from the ordination sacrifice.

The Final Anointing
The final act of the ritual is recorded in v. 30. Moses takes
some of the anointing oil and blood from the altar and
sprinkles (נזה) it on Aaron and his garments and on Aaron's
sons and their garments. Thus he made them holy (ויקדש).
Again, the *waw* on the verb functions to define the meaning of
the sprinkling act. A similar rite takes place in Lev. 14.14-18.
The leper has blood placed on his extremities and then oil is
placed on the blood. The major difference is that the blood and
oil in Lev. 8.30 form one mixture and the oil is the holy
anointing oil designed to consecrate the realm of the holy. Also,
the mixture in Lev. 8.30 is sprinkled on the priests and their
clothes as opposed to being placed on the extremities.

The anointing rite in Lev. 8.30 must be understood, in part,
as a parallel to the first act of anointing with the anointing oil
as described in Lev. 8.10-12. Both have as their purpose the act
of making holy (cf. vv. 12b, 30b). The purpose is to effect a
common state for the priests and the altar. The altar is here
seen as the common ritual object of the high priest and the

---

1 See Wolff, *Anthropology of the Old Testament* (trans. M. Kohl; Philadelphia: Fortress, 1974), pp. 60-62; D.J. McCarthy, 'The Symbolism of Blood
and Sacrifice', *JBL* 88 (1969), pp. 166-76; *idem*, 'Further Notes on the
Symbolism of Blood and Sacrifice', *JBL* 92 (1973), pp. 205-10.

other priests. Just as the anointing of vv. 10-12 serves to mark off the area of Aaron's ritual activity, so the altar marks off the area of the priests' ritual activity. This act depicts the construction of the holy and its contents and it serves to place priests, clothes, and altar in the same category.

The fact that the blood from the altar is also used in this sprinkling rite may be a demonstration of the priests' concern with blood manipulation on the altar. That is, the ceremony serves not only to construct the sacred area, but also serves to demonstrate the major concern of the priests in that area. They are the ones who will perform ritual acts involving blood manipulation and the altar. In this way the ritual serves to indicate their sacrificial function in the sacred area. Once again, the conceptual category of the holy is correlated with a specific space. Category construction is here linked to spatial construction and institutional function.

Final Instructions

The remainder of the chapter (vv. 31-36) consists of Moses' instructions to the priests for the completion of their ordination process. There are three basic requirements: the proper eating of the offerings (vv. 31-32), the seven-day stay at the door of the tent (vv. 34-35), and the performance of Yahweh's charge (v. 35).

The priests are instructed to boil the flesh of the ram of ordination at the door of the tent of meeting and to eat it there along with the bread in the basket of ordination offerings. This is in line with the instructions for the זבח שלמים found in Lev. 7.11-18. The fact that the priests are instructed to eat their portion at the door of the tent emphasizes again their institutional location at the area before the tent of meeting.[1] This serves to support the argument that the ordination ritual as a rite of passage is primarily a rite of institutional location.

The priests are further instructed to remain at the door of the tent of meeting for seven days. The reason for this is stated in v. 33: 'You shall not depart from the door of the tent of meeting for seven days, until the days of your ordination are completed, because (כי) it will take seven days to complete your

---

1 Wenham, *Leviticus*, p. 144.

ordination'. Seven days is the necessary time period involved
for purification from major defilement (Lev. 12.2; 14.8; 15.13,
19, 24, 28; Num. 19.11). This does not mean that the ordination ritual is primarily an act of purification. Rather, seven
days is the necessary time period to effect passage from one
status to another when the passage involves a major change in
status.[1] Just as seven days of purification are necessary for
passage from major defilement to purity, so seven days are
necessary for passage from the state of the common to the
state of the holy.

Verse 34 is of interest because of the way in which it explains
and interprets the ritual acts performed by Moses. 'Yahweh
commanded the things that have been done today in order to
kipper on your behalf'. This verse sums up the whole of these
ritual proceedings and speaks against any single interpretation of the *kipper*-act. It suggests that in P the word already
carried a broad meaning which covered several distinct acts:
purgation, purification, averting the wrath of Yahweh,
institutionalization, passage, maintenance of the sacred, and
the solidification of the divine-human relations. Such was
already seen to be the case in Leviticus 16. The effecting of
kipper, by various means and for various purposes, must be
seen as a unifying symbol of the Priestly ritual system.

Finally, Aaron and his sons are instructed to perform what
was charged by Yahweh. The precise meaning of the phrase is
uncertain. It could refer to the instructions in Exod. 29.38-42
for the offering of daily sacrifices.[2] Milgrom argues, however,
that the phrase את־משמרת יהוה refers to the duties of the priests
in watching over the sacred taboos.[3] He notes that the only
'charge' found here is the charge to remain at the door of the

1 It should be noted that the seven-day requirement is found in conjunction
with the recovered leper and the corpse-contaminated, showing once
again a similarity between these three rituals. The other cases demanding
a seven-day purification period are concerned with a bodily discharge, a
menstruating woman, or childbirth. These cases show a common concern
with the loss of life by discharge or, in the case of childbirth, the giving of
life. These may be explained on the basis of their concern with the boundaries between life and death and the crossing of these boundaries. See
Frymer-Kensky, 'Pollution', pp. 400-406.
2 Wenham, *Leviticus*, p. 144.
3 *Levitical Terminology*, pp. 10-11. See Noth, *Leviticus*, p. 73.

tent of meeting. Thus, he understands the phrase as a charge
to begin the priestly duties. This makes sense in that the ritual
of Leviticus 8 not only consecrates the priesthood, but also constructs the sacred area. Once constructed, it must be protected.
This protection is defined by Yahweh's instructions regarding
the taboo and is watched over by the priesthood.[1]

Conclusion

Leviticus 8 is a founding ritual. It depicts when the priesthood
was instituted and 'set apart' in conjunction with the 'setting
apart' of sacred space. This ritual provides the basic categories
of 'set apart' status and 'set apart' space in the way that Gen.
1.1–2.4a provides the basic category of 'set apart' time. As
such, this ritual reflects a moment of origins in the Priestly
traditionists' larger process of establishing the order of creation. The order consists of the three elements of cosmos,
society, and cult, but within that order there are established
the basic categories of set apart space, time, and status.

The ritual functions, through the use of the holy anointing
oil, to establish a mutual state of holiness for the priests and the
places of their priestly activity. More specifically, the ritual
functions to establish the institution of priesthood and to pass
Aaron and his sons into the status of priests. Central to this
passage is the use of the blood of the ram of ordination. Its blood
is placed on the extremities of Aaron and his sons and serves as
the central act of the ritual to move them from their non-
institutional status to their institutional status.

At the same time, it was argued that this passage into the
priesthood reflects parallels to the rites of purification for the
recovered leper and the corpse-contaminated. All three of

---

1 The connection of these two is made explicit in Lev. 10.10-11: 'You [the
   priests] are to distinguish between the holy and the common, and between
   the unclean and the clean, and to teach the children of Israel all the
   statutes which Yahweh has commanded them through Moses'. It should
   be noted that the priestly duties are related to the creative act of Yahweh in
   Gen. 1.1-2:4a. They are to 'separate' (להבדיל) on the basis of Yahweh's
   spoken commandments just as Yahweh 'separated' categories and elements in creation (v. 4: the light from the dark; vv. 6-7: the waters under
   the firmament from the waters above the firmament; vv. 14, 18: the lights
   in the firmament to separate the day from the night).

these passages function within the context of the tension between death and life. All three rituals serve to pass individuals from contact with 'the realm of death' to 'the realm of life'. The priests are established as mediators between death and life for the people of Israel.

They perform this function as mediators in the cult. They act as mediators between the holy and the not-holy, the clean and the not-clean. Because they act as mediators between these categorically distinct states, they are in a dangerous position. They effect commerce between the holy (cultic activity at the sanctuary) and the not-holy (the everyday activity in society). They serve not only to effect ritual restoration of the created order when it has been disrupted because of sin and defilement, but they also serve to maintain the order of creation. As such, they stand in a precarious position—they ritually manipulate the ever-changing conditions of holiness, purity, and order.

The priesthood, then, may be said to be in a permanent liminal state in the context of the structures of ordinary existence. The priesthood is established to stand at the intersection of chaos and order, pollution and purity, the holy and the profane. They are set apart to officiate in the holy place, a place set apart; they are set apart to perform the sacrifices and offerings designed to eliminate pollution and restore order.

EXODUS 34.29-35: MOSES THE EXALTED INAUGURATOR OF THE CULT

Moses is depicted in Leviticus 8 as the inaugurator of the wilderness cult.[1] As such he transcends the normal ritual structures and is thereby able to perform this task. Moses' role as mediator of the divine instructions plays an important role in all the traditions. Exod. 34.29-35 calls for particular comment. A consensus has not formed on the stratum to which the tradition is related. Generally it is recognized as Priestly,[2] although many see it as an independent tradition with Priestly additions.[3] In addition to the source critical problem is the traditio problem of the origin of the pericope.[4]

---

1 See above, pp. 110-11.
2 Beyerlin, *Origins and History of the Oldest Sinaitic Traditions* (trans. S. Rudman; Oxford: Basil Blackwell, 1961), p. 30; Plastaras, *The God of Exodus* (Milwaukee: Bruce, 1966), p. 317; Sellin-Fohrer, *Introduction*, p. 180.
3 Noth, *Exodus*, p. 267; F. Dummermuth, 'Moses strahlendes Gesicht', *ThZ* 17 (1961) pp. 241-48; R. de Vaux, *The Early History of Israel* (Philadelphia: Westminster, 1978) p. 394 (see n. 2); R.W.L. Moberly, *At the Mountain of God: Story and Theology in Exodus 32–34* (JSOT Supp 22; Sheffield: JSOT, 1983) pp. 106-09, 177-80. J. Morgenstern ('Moses with the Shining Face', *HUCA* 2 [1925] p. 12) argues that the passage belongs to J2 and is prior to P.
4 See Gressmann, *Moses und seine Zeit* (Göttingen: Vandenhoeck und Ruprecht, 1913) pp. 246-51; A. Jirku, 'Die Gesichtsmaske des Mose', *ZDPV* 67 (1944-1945), pp. 43ff.; Morgenstern, 'Moses with the Shining Face', pp. 1-27; K. Jaroš, 'Des Mose "strahlende Haut". Eine Notiz zu Ex. 34:29, 30, 35', *ZAW* 88 (1976), pp. 275-80; M. Sasson, 'Bovine Symbolism in the Exodus Narrative', *VT* 18 (1968), pp. 384-85; E. Suhr, 'The Horned Moses', *Folklore* 74 (1963), pp. 387-95; H. Horn, 'Traditionsschichten in Ex 23, 10-33 und Ex 34, 10-36', *BZ* (n. 35) 15 (1971), pp. 203-22; Childs, *Exodus* pp. 609-10, 617-19;

Part of the issue revolves around the meaning of קרן in the phrase קרן עור פני בדברו אתו which describes Moses' appearance when he descended from the mountain and the reason that the people were afraid to come near him (vv. 29, 30, 35). The normal meaning of the word is 'to have horns' and this has led some to see here a reference to a horned mask worn by priests when undertaking cultic duties.[1] As has been noted, however, the Exodus passage would seem to turn this around.[2] Moses removes the veil (מסוה, found only in this passage) when speaking to the people or Yahweh, but wears it at all other times (vv. 33-35). The veil was necessary because Aaron and all the people were afraid when they saw his face (v. 30). The fact that the קרן is associated with עור adds further to the difficulty of seeing this as a reference to a mask. Before deciding the significance of the קרן, it will be helpful to examine the other elements of the passage.

There are, as already noted, several distinct elements of P in the passage: 'Aaron', 'all the leaders of the congregation', and 'the tablets of the testimony'. While these may be excised from the passage as simple Priestly additions,[3] they suggest that the passage has been picked up and meaningfully redacted by, if not actually composed by, the Priestly school.[4] Mann notes that this passage brings together and draws important connections between the ideas of divine presence, Moses' exaltation, and talking and seeing.[5] The most important of these ideas is that of 'speaking', found throughout the passage.[6]

Wayne A. Meeks, 'Moses as God and King', in *Religions in Antiquity* (ed. J. Neusner; *Numen Sup* 14; Leiden: Brill, 1968), pp. 361-65.

1   Gressmann, *Mose und seine Zeit* (Göttingen: Vandenhoeck und Ruprecht, 1913), pp. 246-51; J. de Fraine, 'Moses "Cornuta facies" (Ex 34, 29-35)', *BTFT* 20 (1959), pp. 35-36. See the review of the issue of 'horns' and Moses in L.R. Bailey, 'Horns of Moses', *IDBSup*, pp. 419-20.

2   Childs, *Exodus*, pp. 610, 618; Moberly, *The Mountain of God*, pp. 106-109.

3   Noth, *Exodus*, p. 267.

4   Moberly (*The Mountain of God*, pp. 177-78) raises several important possibilities about how the traditio questions concerning the passage might be addressed, and argues that the P terminology cannot be easily excised from the passage without undermining its basic character (p. 178).

5   *Divine Presence and Guidance*, p. 148.

6   Verse 29: Moses descended with his new appearance 'because he had been speaking with him' (בדברו אתו). Note that the Hebrew leaves the pronouns undefined so it could mean because God had been speaking with Moses or because Moses had been speaking with God. Verse 31: And Moses spoke

There is a constant emphasis on the fact that Moses 'spoke' to the people what 'had been spoken' to him by Yahweh.[1]

It must also be noted that two distinct spatial categories are mentioned in the passage that are significantly related to the speaking of Yahweh with Moses. Verses 29-33 emphasize the words spoken by Yahweh to Moses on Mt Sinai. This act of speech is paradigmatic for the relationship of Yahweh and Moses that brings about the change in Moses' appearance. Verses 34-35 emphasize the *continual* speaking of Yahweh to Moses.[2] This speaking takes place when Moses goes in before Yahweh (v. 34a) and Moses relates the information to the people when he comes out (v. 34b). This 'going in' to hear Yahweh and 'coming out' to speak to the people must be related to Moses' entry into and exit from the tent.[3]

(וידבר) with Aaron and the leaders of the assembly. Verse 32: And Moses commanded (ויצום) all the sons of Israel all that Yahweh had spoken to him (כל־אשר דבר יהוה אתו). This passage suggests that the better understanding of v. 29 is because *God* had been speaking with Moses, thereby emphasizing that Moses was relaying what Yahweh had told him. Verse 33: And when Moses had finished speaking with them (ויכל משה מדבר אתם). Verse 34: But whenever Moses went in before Yahweh to speak with him (ובבא משה לפני יהוה לדבר אתו). Verse 34: And he came out and spoke (ודבר) to the people what he was commanded (יצוה). Verse 35: . . . until he went in to speak (לדבר) with him.

1 The redactional placement of this passage immediately following vv. 27-28 (J material emphasizing the making of the covenant, see Noth, *Exodus*, pp. 265-66) is important to note. Yahweh told (ויאמר) Moses to write these words (הדברים האלה) because it is in accordance with these words (הדברים האלה) that the covenant will be made between Yahweh and Israel. The connection between the 'words' spoken by Yahweh to Moses and related by Moses to the people should not be overlooked. In both traditions the idea of Yahweh's speaking as constitutive for the existence of Israel is emphasized.

2 The shift in v. 34 to the use of the imperfect tense suggests that this is a 'recurring situation' (Moberly, *The Mountain of God*, p. 107).

3 There are similarities between this passage and the account of the tent of meeting in Exod. 33.7-11. This has led Noth (*Exodus*, p. 267) to suggest a relation between the passages as witnesses to a special tradition. That a similar tradition stands behind the two texts is a possibility. A better suggestion is that Exod. 34.29-35 has been redacted by the Priestly traditionists for specific reasons. While the Priestly tradition would disagree with Exod. 33.7-11 on the location of the tent/tabernacle, there is agreement on the idea that the tent was the place of Yahweh's speaking with Moses.

The speaking of Yahweh to Moses in the tent is a central concern of P. This is seen in Exod. 25.21-22. Instructions are given to put the כפרת on top of the ark and to put the testimony (העדת) in the ark. 'And I will make myself known to you there, and I will speak with you (ודברתי אתך) from (מעל) the כפרת, between the cherubim which are on the ark of the testimony, all that I will command you with regard to the sons of Israel' (v. 22). The linguistic and conceptual similarities between this passage and Exod. 34.29-35 are clear. Exod. 25.21-22 already recognizes the twofold nature of Yahweh's address to Moses— on the mountain and in the tent—and, indeed, lays the groundwork for the situation which is explicitly detailed in Exod. 34.29-35.

This observation necessitates a more careful analysis of the redactional placement of this passage. Exod. 34.29-35 marks the close of Moses' journeys up the mountain. It gives clear indication in vv. 34-35 that his speaking with Yahweh will from now on take place by his going into the tent. Thus, there is no longer any need for him to climb the mountain to speak with Yahweh. This, however, will require the construction of the tent and this is precisely what takes place in Exodus 35– 40. Moses has received the instructions, or the model (תבנית, see Exod. 25.9, 40), for the structure of the tabernacle and its appurtenances on the mountain, and in Exodus 35–40 he undertakes the erection of the sacred precinct.[1] Once built, the tabernacle, and more specifically its inner sanctum with the ark of the testimony and the כפרת, will provide *the place* where Yahweh will issue his instructions for Israel. Exod. 34.29-35, then, functions to indicate the transfer of the place of Yahweh's speaking from the mountain to the tent in the midst of the people.[2] This transfer of the place of speaking is paralleled in P by the transfer of the glory from the mountain to the tabernacle, emphasizing the issue of presence rather than

---

1 See R.J. Clifford, *The Cosmic Mountain in Canaan and the Old Testament* (Cambridge: Harvard University, 1977), pp. 123-31 for a discussion of the importance of תבנית.

2 See Blenkinsopp, 'The Structure of P', pp. 277-80.

speaking (cf. Exod. 24.15-18; 25.8; 40.34-35).[1] It is clear, however, that for P these two issues are inseparable.

In terms of cultic practice, P believes that Yahweh is permanently housed in the inner sanctum. At the same time, there are moments when there are public manifestations, or emanations,[2] of the glory: when the glory settles on Mt Sinai (Exod. 24.15-18); when the tabernacle is completed (Exod. 40.34-35); when Aaron offers the first sacrifices (Lev. 9.5-6, 23-24); and in certain crisis situations in the wilderness (Exod. 16.7, 10; Num. 14.10; 16.19). The first three are clearly associated with Yahweh's presence in the cult and community, while the crisis passages are concerned with judgment and legitimation.

1 The issue of the כבוד יהוה in P has received a great deal of attention. A review of earlier treatments may be found in Westermann, 'Die Herrlichkeit Gottes in der Priesterschrift', in *Wort-Gebot-Glaube. Beiträge zur Theologie des Alten Testaments* (ed. H.J. Stoebe, J.J. Stamm, Ernst Jenni; Zürich: Zwingli, 1970), pp. 227-45. A review of more recent discussions may be found in Mettinger, *The Dethronement of Sabaoth*, pp. 80-97. A key issue in the discussion has been whether the 'glory' is thought to be an occasional appearance by Yahweh at the place of meeting (*Begegnungsort*) or a permanent indwelling of Yahweh in a holy place (*Wohntempel*). The former is argued by von Rad (*Old Testament Theology* 1, [New York/Evanston: Harper & Row, 1962], pp. 235-41): *idem*, 'δόξα: כבוד in the OT', *TDNT* 2 (1964), pp. 238-42; Noth (*A History of Pentateuchal Traditions* (trans. B.W. Anderson; Englewood Cliffs: Prentice-Hall, 1972), pp. 243-47); Kuschke ('Die Lagervorstellung der priesterschriftlichen Erzählung', pp. 74-105); Cross, who approaches the issue from the study of משכן ('The Priestly Tabernacle', *BAR* [ed. G.E. Wright and D.N. Freedman; Garden City; Doubleday, 1961], I, pp. 201-28, and *Canaanite Myth and Hebrew Epic* [Cambridge/London: Harvard University Press, 1975], pp. 298-300), and Clements (*God and Temple* [Philadelphia: Fortress Press, 1965], pp. 113-22). There have been those who have argued for a more permanent indwelling of the glory in the tabernacle. These include J. Morgenstern ('Biblical Theophanies', *ZAW* 25 [1911], pp. 139-93, and 'The Tent of Meeting', *JAOS* 38 [1918], pp. 125-39). L. Rost (*Die Vorstufen von Kirche und Synagoge im Alten Testament. Eine wortgeschichtliche Untersuchung* [BWANT 76; Stuttgart: Kohlhammer, 1938], pp. 35-38; R. Schmitt (*Zelt und Lade als Thema alttestamentlicher Wissenschaft* [Gütersloh: Gütersloher Verlagshaus, 1972], pp. 219-28), who distinguishes the אהל מעד as cult site from משכן which refers to the architecture of the cult structure; Wienfeld (*Deuteronomy and the Deuteronomic School* [Oxford: Oxford University Press, 1972], p. 197); Childs (*Exodus*, pp. 534-35); Haran (*Temples and Temple Service*, pp. 218-26); and Mettinger (*Dethronement of Sabaoth*, pp. 80-97).

2 Schmitt (*Zelt und Lade*, p. 224) speaks of 'Hervorscheinen'. See also Mettinger, *Dethronement of Sabaoth*, p. 89.

Yahweh's presence in the cult and community, while the crisis passages are concerned with judgment and legitimation.

Thus, Moses' final descent from the mountain with his changed appearance is associated with two ideas: (1) the transfer of the glory of Yahweh from Mt. Sinai to the tabernacle and (2) the shift of the place where Yahweh will meet with Moses. The establishment of the tabernacle cult is the key image that holds these ideas together.[1] Moses' descent, then, is correlated with these movements in the text.

The phrase describing Moses' changed appearance must be understood in this context. The LXX understood the verb קרן to refer to the glory of Yahweh shining on Moses' face (δεδόξασται). Hab. 3.4 is often adduced as an example of קרן used in the sense of 'light'.[2] The text is full of textual difficulties, however, and can be used only cautiously, at best, to find the meaning of 'light' for קרן. Sasson notes three primary uses of the noun קרן: (1) the horn of a beast; (2) the horns of the altar; (3) 'a metaphor suggesting vanity, pride, force, dignity, and power'.[3] The meaning of the word in Exod. 34.29-35 is certainly to be related to the last usage. Moberly develops this idea and relates the passage to the larger context of Exodus 32–34, emphasizing particularly the golden calf incident.[4] The horn was often a cultic symbol for the bull,[5] and, thus, the horn of Moses was a negative judgment on the golden calf as leader and mediator of the divine presence. Moses is exalted as the true leader and mediator of the divine presence.

A second option, not necessarily opposed to this interpretation, may be offered. While the Priestly writers obviously have an exalted view of Moses, one must question if they

1 See Rolf Rendtorff, 'The Concept of Revelation in Ancient Israel', in *Revelation as History* (ed. W. Pannenberg; London: Collier-Macmillan, 1968), pp. 33-37.

2 So George Coats, 'The King's Loyal Opposition: Obedience and Authority in Exodus 32–34', in *Canon and Authority: Essays in Old Testament Religion and Theology* (ed. G.W. Coats and B. Long; Philadelphia: Fortress, 1977), pp. 104-105. See, however, Jaroš, 'Des Mose "strahlende Haut"', p. 277.

3 'Bovine Symbolism', p. 386.

4 *At the Mountain of God*, pp. 108-109.

5 Moberly, here, draws on the work of J.P. Brown, 'The Sacrificial Cult and its Critique in Greek and Hebrew (I)', *JSS* 24 (1979), p. 171.

would want to confuse Moses and Yahweh? If they had depicted Moses with the 'light' of Yahweh's glory shining on his face, there could have been a misunderstanding of the distinctive nature of Yahweh's glory. Moses is exalted, but not deified. He is exalted as the one who establishes on earth the divine תבנית and inaugurates the operative cult. In this sense he stands outside of and transcends the normally operating cultic structures. He does this, however, as a human being representing Yahweh.[1] The *horn* then, serves as a symbol of Moses' power and authority as the representative of Yahweh.

This would help explain the reversal of the expected function of the veil. Moses removes it when speaking to Yahweh or the people, i.e., in the cultic situation, but wears it at all other times. Moses must display the מסוה, his symbol of authority, in those situations which are concerned with his role as the one who communicates with Yahweh and then speaks those words to the people. His role, it must be noted, goes well beyond that of 'mediator', because he is also the one who institutes Yahweh's plans. His role as receiver of the divine speech and his role as founder of the divine plans cannot be separated.

The symbol of Moses' status, be it horns or a shining face, is a cause of fear among the people. This shows the Priestly

---

1 It may well be that there is operative here a parallel idea to the place and role of human beings in creation as depicted by P in Gen 1.1–2.4a. In Genesis human beings are created in the image and likeness of God and are instructed to rule over the created order. O.H. Steck (*World and Environment* [BES; Nashville: Abingdon Press, 1980], pp. 102-106) so interprets the 'image of God' in P. He sees the role of this representative to be 'the continual establishment and enforcement of order', where order 'is the framework in which individual life develops, but is also restricted for its own good and continuance, as well as for the good and continuance of the whole' (p. 104). 'The function of the human being's task as ruler is to guarantee the continuance of the created world as a whole, laid down by God in the event of creation, and to guarantee it for the benefit of all created life' (p. 106). For similar views see the following: H. Wildberger, צלם *saelem* Abbild', *THAT* 2 (1971), pp. 556-63; J.J. Stamm, 'Zur Frage der Imago Dei in Alten Testament [Gen 1:26f.; Ps 8:6-9]', in *Humanität und Glaube. Gedenkschrift K. Guggisbero* (ed. U. Neuenschwander und R. Dellspergen; Bern/Stuttgart: Paul Haupt, 1973), pp. 243-53; O.H. Steck, *Der Schöpfungsbericht der Priesterschrift. Studien zur literarkritischen und überlieferungsgeschichtlichen Problematik von Genesis 1,1–2,4a* (FRLANT 115; Gottingen: Vandenhoeck und Ruprecht, 1975), pp. 129-58.

writers' tendency to stress the danger of 'drawing near' to speak with, or confront, Yahweh. Moses alone can do this. In doing this, however, Moses himself has become fearful and the people are afraid to 'draw near' to him.[1] The people can, however, bear to draw near to Moses, because the fearful quality of his bearing that has come about through his contact ('drawing near') with Yahweh is now mediated through a human representative. Nonetheless, the danger of drawing near to hear Yahweh's instructions is still emphasized by Moses' fearful features. Thus, Moses 'veils' his face when he is not speaking with Yahweh or the people precisely to emphasize, in those times of 'speaking', his power and authority as the one who speaks for and acts for Yahweh in the cultic community.[2]

Moses thus has special status in the Priestly traditions as the one who draws near to speak with Yahweh, the one who received the divine תבנית for the structure of the cult, and the one who established and founded the cult and began its normative operation. As such, Moses embodies the symbol of his power and authority, but is in no way confused with deity. He is Yahweh's representative on earth who is to found Yahweh's cult in Israel. It is because of this role that Moses stands outside the normal cultic structures and is, therefore, able to inaugurate and found the tabernacle cult.

Such an interpretation of Moses as a liminal figure who passes on the divinely given law and founds the cult, emphasizes his unique role in the wilderness and Sinai traditions. As Cohn has convincingly argued,[3] the wilderness texts reflect

---

1 There may be present here a reflex of the idea of contagion so prominent in P's thought. Moses, having drawn near (נגשׁ) to Yahweh and having come into contact with Yahweh's glorious presence, is 'contaminated'. Since he is 'changed' due to this contact, it is necessary to take (cultic) measures to insure that he is safe for the people. The veil thus serves as a means of bounding his cultic activities and serves as a means of insuring the safety of the people against the outbreak of his own changed status.

2 It is cautiously suggested that the 'veil' of Moses may be a reflex of the 'veil' that separates the holy of holies from the rest of the inside of the tent. Just as it serves as a boundary for the most holy place, and the place where Yahweh will speak to Moses, so Moses's veil serves as a boundary marker of his cult-communicative actions. There are certainly functional similarities between the two objects.

3 Cohn, *The Shape of Sacred Space*, pp. 7-23.

the structure and characteristics of liminal states as described by Turner. Israel's liminal passage from slavery in Egypt to life in the promised land is guided by a complex figure of power and authority who teaches them of life in their new status in the land and establishes those institutions that will give structure to this new status. As Turner has demonstrated, such liminal figures often employ masks and are hedged about with fear and power.[1] Just such a figure was needed to found and inaugurate the cult and teach Israel the meaning of its existence as a cultic community in whose midst dwelt the one revealed in glory.

---

1 *The Forest of Symbols*, pp. 93-111.

Chapter 5

LEVITICUS 14.1-20

Introduction

Leviticus 14 details the ritual to be enacted for a recovered leper. Leviticus 13 notes the various situations which require the priest to declare a person 'unclean' because of leprosy. Lev. 13.45-46 details the resulting situation for one declared 'unclean': 'The leper who has the disease shall wear torn clothes and let the hair of his head hang loose, and he shall cover his lip and cry, 'Unclean, unclean'. He shall remain unclean as long as he has the disease; he is unclean; he shall dwell alone in a habitation outside the camp'. Thus, the person declared 'leprous' and, therefore, 'unclean' by a priest is expulsed from the camp. In this instance, to be 'outside the camp' is to be 'outside' the normal structures of society. As has been noted in recent years, such concerns as evidenced in this ritual reflect a concern for the social body as much as for the individual and illness.[1] The physical body is symbolic of the social body, and, it should be added, the 'cosmological' body.[2]

---

[1] See Zuesse, 'Taboo and the Divine Order', pp. 482-504; B.J. Malina, 'The Individual and the Community: Personality in the Social World of Early Christianity', *BTB* 9 (1979), pp. 126-38; E. Moerman, 'Anthropology of Symbolic Healing', *CurAnt* 20 (1979), pp. 59-66; Malina, *The New Testament World* (Atlanta: John Knox Pess, 1981), pp. 122-52; S. Bean, 'Toward a Semiotics of 'Purity' and 'Pollution' in India', *AA* 8 (1981), pp. 575-95.

[2] See S.K. Postal, 'Body-Image and Identity: A Comparison of Kwakiutl and Hopi', *AA* 67 (1965), pp. 455-60; Douglas, *Purity and Danger*, pp. 114-28;

Leviticus 14 describes the ritual means by which the recovered leper may reenter the camp and, thus, normal social structures. It is clear that 'geography' plays a central role in this ritual. It was argued earlier that the ritual for the recovered leper reflects the conceptual passage of a leper from the realm of 'death' to the realm of 'life'.[1] This is the primary passage effected in this ritual. Such passage is reflected in the outward, physical appearance of the recovered leper, and is symbolically reflected in the repeated ritual shavings. It is clear, however, that this conceptual boundary is made concrete in the boundary of the camp and even the structure within the camp, for the recovered leper must remain outside his tent for seven days after returning to the camp.

This ritual is designed for an individual, as opposed to the community or a group, and is clearly stated to be a ritual for cleansing (14.2). Thus, the ritual for the recovered leper is clearly a rite of passage designed to effect passage for the individual from a state of uncleanness, reflected spatially and socially by the leper's expulsion from the camp, to a state of cleanness, reflected by the leper's return to his own tent within the camp boundaries. In discussing the way the ritual functions to effect this passage, the following arguments will be presented.

1. The rite of cleansing in Lev. 14.1-20 effects the recovered leper's return to normal societal standing and thus reflects the Priestly tradionists' concern for rightly structured social order. The ritual is designed to restore proper societal order to its divinely created status.

2. The passage of the recovered leper from an unclean state to a clean state, primarily understood in socio-cultic categories, is reflected in the ritual in spatial categories as the individual moves from 'outside the camp' to 'inside the camp' to 'inside his own tent'. These socio-cultic and spatial categories reflect the deeper theological concern of the priests in that the passage of

---

idem, Natural Symbols, pp. 93-112; J. Pilch, 'Biblical Leprosy and Body Symbolism', *BTB* 11 (1981), pp. 108-13.

1 See above, pp. 131-35.

the leper is ultimately placed in the context of a passage
from 'death' to 'life'.

3. The crucial symbol in the ritual effecting the recovered
   leper's passage from 'death' to 'life', from 'outside' to
   'inside' the camp, from 'expulsion' from society to
   'inclusion' in society is the blood of the slaughtered bird
   which functions as a symbol of both life and death.

Type of Material

The material in Lev. 14.1-20 is best understood, with Levine,
as a *prescriptive account* of the ritual for a recovered leper.[1]
Its concern is to prescribe the basic ritual by which the
recovered leper returns to society. The chapter is written in an
impersonal ritual style,[2] suggesting, therefore, that the prescribed ritual may be used in any situation that qualifies. The
passage stands in the midst of a larger redactional section (chs.
11–15) concerned with various types of impurity and defilement. This passage provides the instructions, prescribed by
Yahweh (v. 1), for cleansing anyone defiled by skin disease. It
is now widely recognized that מצרע covers a much broader
range of skin ailments than the modern 'leprosy'.[3] It is not
necessary at this point to try and identify the actual disease or
diseases; rather, it is enough to note that such skin eruptions
were considered defiling with regard to society and the cult
and were considered polluting to the degree that expulsion
from the camp (= society) was necessary.

---

[1] See Levine, 'Descriptive Tabernacle Texts', pp. 307-18; *idem*, 'The
Descriptive Ritual Texts from Ugarit: Some Formal and Functional
Features of the Genre', in *The Word of the Lord Shall Go Forth*, pp. 467-75.

[2] Noth, *Leviticus*, p. 104; Elliger, *Leviticus*, p. 174.

[3] For recent discussions of the nature of מצרע, see S.G. Browne, *Leprosy in
the Bible* (London: Christian Medical Fellowship, 1970); E.V. Hulse, 'The
Nature of Biblical "Leprosy" and the Use of Alternative Medical Terms in
Modern Translations of the Bible', *PEQ* 107 (1975), pp. 87-105; J. Wilkinson,
'Leprosy and Leviticus: The Problem of Description and Identification',
SJT 30 (1977), pp. 153-69; *idem*, 'Leprosy and Leviticus: A Problem of
Semantics and Translation', *SJT* 31 (1978), pp. 153-66.

History of the Text
There is general agreement that behind Lev. 14.1-20 stands a pre-Priestly ritual.[1] The heart of this early material is found in vv. 2-9. To this was later added the ritual sacrifices and offerings found in vv. 10-20. Verse 13 is generally recognized as secondary material and reflects the sacrificial instructions found in Leviticus 1–7.[2] Again, while recognizing a process of development in the text, the present analysis seeks to understand the present ritual as a meaningful and coherent ritual in terms of the ritual world of the Priestly traditionists.

The Elements of the Ritual

Materials and Objects
There is no specific clothing involved in this ritual, although clothing does play an important role. On the first day of the ritual (v. 8) and on the seventh day of the ritual (v. 9) the recovered leper is instructed to wash his clothes as part of the rites of purification. While this use of clothing must be distinguished from the ritual clothes associated with the priests, it must be emphasized that the washing of the clothes is an important element in the performance of the ritual.

There is only one item to be classified as an instrumental object in the ritual. This is the earthenware vessel mentioned in v. 5. Its primary purpose is to catch the blood of the slaughtered bird. The blood must be used in the ritual and in order for it to be used it must first be collected in the earthen vessel.

Materials
Water is used in two distinct ways in this ritual. First, it is used in a purification act when the recovered leper is instructed to wash his clothes and bathe his body. 'Running water' (המים החיים) is used in the ritual (vv. 5, 6). One of the birds used in the ritual is to be killed in an earthen vessel over running water.

---

1 Noth, *Leviticus*, p. 104; Milgrom, 'The Paradox of the Red Cow (Num. xix)', *VT* 31 (1981), pp. 69-72; Koch, *Die Priesterschrift*, pp. 83-90.
2 Noth, *Leviticus*, p. 104; Elliger, *Leviticus*, p. 175.

There are several other materials prescribed for the execution
of the ritual. Verse 4 calls for cedar wood (עץ ארז), scarlet
thread (שׁני תולעת), and hyssop (אזב). The use of these elements is
described in vv. 6-7. The priest is to take these materials along
with the live bird, dip them in the blood of the slaughtered bird,
sprinkle the leper seven times, and then set the live bird free.
The only complete ritual parallel to these materials is in
Numbers 19 in the ritual to cleanse the corpse-contaminated
person.[1]

Verse 10 prescribes a cereal offering (מנחה) made up of three
tenths of an ephah of fine flour mixed with oil. Instructions for
the cereal offering are found in Lev. 2; 6.7-11. In P this
offering regularly accompanies the burnt offering (e.g., Num.
28–29), and is noted in the historical books (Judg. 13.19, 23; 1
Kgs 8.64; 2 Kgs 16.13, 15). Finally, the recovered leper is
instructed to bring a unit of oil (v. 10). The unit is לג אחד. The
exact meaning of this unit of measure is uncertain and does
not greatly affect the significance of the oil in the ritual. The
actual amount used is small, however, limited to the palm of
the priest (vv. 15-18). It is to be applied to the lobe of the right
ear, the right thumb, and the right big toe of the recovered
leper (v. 17).

Several animals are called for in the ritual. For the ritual
that takes place outside the camp on the first day, two live,
clean birds are necessary (v. 4). One of these is to be
slaughtered and its blood used in the ritual (v. 7), while the
other one is to be turned loose (v. 7). Neither bird is specifically
identified by name as a particular type of sacrifice or offering.

On the eighth day of the ritual, performed inside the camp,
three animals are involved: two male lambs without defect
and one ewe lamb, a year old, without defect (v. 10). One of the
male lambs is to be offered as an אשם and in conjunction with
the oil is termed a תנופה (v. 12). The blood of this lamb is to be
applied to the lobe of the right ear, the right thumb, and the
right big toe of the recovered leper (v. 14). The female lamb is
then offered as a חטאת (v. 19a) While the text does not specify

---

[1] These elements are also found in the purification rituals discussed
further in Lev. 14 (see vv. 49, 51, 52). For the use of hyssop in purification
ritual, see Ps. 51.9.

which animal is used for the חטאת, it is more appropriate for a
female lamb to be offered as a חטאת than as an עלה (cf. Lev. 1.1-
13, the instructions for the עלה, which require a male animal;
4.27-31, where a female animal is required for the חטאת; Num.
6.14, which specifies that the Nazirite is to bring a one year old
male lamb for an עלה and a one year old ewe lamb for a חטאת).
Finally, the other male lamb is offered as an עלה. It has often
been noted that in this ritual the אשם precedes the other
sacrifices, an act unique to this ritual. The only use of the blood
of these animals is described in conjunction with the
slaughtered bird (vv. 6-7) and the אשם sacrifice (v. 14).

Ritual Language

While no specific quotations are described in the text, it is clear
from the text that the pronouncements of the priest are a
central element of the ritual.[1] It is probable that the priest
issues a statement concerning the condition of the leper after
the examination (v. 3b).[2] The text states that the priest will
examine the leper and if the disease is healed, the priest will
command for the appropriate ritual materials to be brought.
This 'command' in itself constitutes ritual language and may
in and of itself have constituted notice that the leper was
recovered.

Verse 7 states that after the priest sprinkles the recovered
leper with the blood of the slaughtered bird that 'he shall
pronounce him clean' (וטהרו).[3] Elsewhere, the text simply
states that following certain actions the recovered leper 'shall
be clean' (וטהר; vv. 8, 9, 20).[4] Hillers has argued convincingly

---

[1] It will be suggested below that the phrase והובא אל־הכהן in v. 1b, normally
translated 'and he shall be brought to the priest', is better translated 'and
it [the matter of the leper] shall be brought to the [attention of] the priest'.
As such, it could be included as ritual language.

[2] This is suggested by Lev. 13 where the priest after examining a person or
object makes the declaration 'he/it is clean' (vv. 6, 13, 17, 23, 28, 34, 59).

[3] Verse 11 defines the priest who is to perform the sacrifices and offerings
as המטהר, 'the one who pronounces cleanness'. This may be understood,
however, as 'the one who effects cleanness'. This makes clear the close
relationship in ritual between effecting purity and pronouncing purity.

[4] For the etymology and basic meaning of טהר, see J.A. Emerton, 'The
Meaning of אבני־קדש in Lamentations 4,1', *ZAW* 79 (1967), 233-36; J.H.
Eaton, 'Some Questions of Philology and Exegesis in the Psalms', *JThSt* 19

that the Pi'el form of the verb refers primarily to pronouncement and terms this use 'delocutive'.[1] Thus, the Pi'el form of
the verb is concerned with the pronouncement and effecting
of the state of cleanness, while the Qal form is concerned with
the state in which the person stands. While the declaration of
the priest is primarily directed at the issue of ritual cleanness-
uncleanness, it is clear in Leviticus 14 that it is also concerned
with the individual's place in society. Ritual and societal
standing intersect at this point.

Ritual Roles
There are two primary roles in this ritual. First, there is the
recovered leper, the one on whose behalf the ritual is performed. The ritual effects are focused on the recovered leper
and have as their purpose the passage of the individual from a
state of uncleanness to a state of cleanness. The second role is
that of the priest, the one who performs the ritual and effects
the cleansing for the recovered leper.

Spatial Categories
Spatial categories play an important symbolic role in this
ritual. The most important spatial categories have to do with
the camp boundaries. The ritual of the first day takes place
outside the camp (v. 3: אל־מחוץ למחנה). The priest must go
outside the camp to examine the leper and perform the ritual
of the first day, because the leper was banished outside the
camp (Lev. 13.46). As has already been noted, the camp
boundaries represent and reflect the social boundaries. Thus,
banishment 'outside the camp' represents not only ritual
banishment, but also banishment from the normal order of
society.

After the rites of the first day are performed, the recovered
leper is allowed to return to the camp (יבוא אל־המחנה), but now is
instructed to remain outside his tent (וישב מחוץ לאהלו) for seven

---

(n.s.) (1968), p. 605; H.-J. Hermisson, *Sprache und Ritus im Altisraeli-*
tischen Kult (WMANT 19; Neukirchen-Vluyn: Neukirchener Verlag,
1965), pp. 84-95.
[1] D.R. Hillers, 'Delocutive Verbs in Biblical Hebrew', *JBL* 86 (1967), pp. 320-
24.

days (v. 8). This suggests that the effecting of the recovered
leper's cleansing is a *process* that takes place over a period of
time. His full recovery and return to the normal structures of
society entail the full period of cleansing. This temporal
process, as already seen, is paralleled by the temporal process
of the ordination of the priests (Lev. 8.33-35).[1] There is an
important difference, however, which is indicated by the
spatial notices associated with each ritual. Lev. 8.33a states
with regard to the priests, 'you shall not go out (לא תצאו) from
the door of the tent of meeting for seven days', while Lev. 14.8
states with regard to the recovered leper, 'he shall dwell outside [i.e., he shall not go into] his tent for seven days'. These
spatial notices serve to underline the purpose of each ritual.
The priests have already performed the necessary sacrifices
and offerings which brought about their passage into their
institutional setting (they are located in their normal structures); whereas, the recovered leper still has to perform the
necessary sacrifices and offerings to effect fully his final passage into society (he will be re-located in his normal structures). The individual's return to his tent, then, signifies his
ultimate return to society.

Two other spatial categories are important in the performance of the ritual. The first is the place to which the live
bird is released: the open field (v. 7b: על-פני השדה). The second
spatial category is 'before Yahweh, at the door of the tent of
meeting' (v. 11b: לפני יהוה פתח אהל מועד). This is the place where
the recovered leper and the sacrificial materials are to be
brought prior to undertaking the sacrifices and offerings. As is
clear, this is the place par excellence of Israelite ritual. It is the
place where the normal sacrifices and offerings prove to be
effective.

Temporal Categories
As already noted, the temporal process of this ritual is
important. The ritual may be structured according to the temporal notices found in the text as follows:

---

[1] See above, p. 112.

Day One: Ritual outside the camp (Concluding acts:
                      wash clothes, shave, bath)
Seven day period: Dwelling inside the camp, but outside tent
Day Seven: Shave hair, wash clothes, bathe body
Day Eight: Sacrifices and offerings presented

The eighth day plays a prominent role in other rituals of
passage and/or purification. Lev. 9.1 places the priests' first
official offerings and sacrifices in the normative cult on the
eighth day of their ordination. A male child is to be circum-
cised on the eighth day (Lev. 12.3). A man being cleansed from
a discharge is to bring birds for his cleansing on the eighth day,
one for a חטאת and one for an עלה (Lev. 15.14). A woman with
an unusual discharge of blood is likewise instructed in
Lev. 15.29. Num. 6.10 prescribes two birds to be offered on the
eighth day, one as a חטאת and one as an עלה, for the Nazirite
who has someone die suddenly near him and thereby produce
a need for purification.[1] Thus, the temporal framework, seven
days followed by sacrifices on the eighth day, is a common
structure in Priestly rituals of purification.

The Actions of the Ritual

Day One

  I. Preparations (vv. 2b-4): The matter is brought (הובא) to the
     priest. And the priest shall go out (ויצא) of the camp and he
     will look (וראה) and if (והנה) the leprous disease is healed
     (נרפא) in the leper, then the priest will give commandment
     (וצוה). And he will take (ולקח) for the one to be purified, two
     live, clean birds and cedar wood, and scarlet string and
     hyssop.
 II. Ritual Proper (vv. 5-8): And the priest will give
     commandment, and he will slaughter (ושחט) the one bird
     in an earthen vessel over running water. Then he will
     take (יקח) the live bird and the cedar wood and the scarlet
     string and the hyssop and he will dip (וטבל) them and the
     live bird in the blood of the slaughtered bird over running
     water. And he will sprinkle (והזה) it on the one to be
     cleansed from leprosy seven times and he shall be clean

---

[1] Elsewhere in P the eighth day plays an important role in certain
community rituals (Lev. 23.36, 39; Num. 29.35) and is prescribed as the
first day that an animal can be offered as a sacrifice (Lev. 22.27).

(ומהרו). Then he will send forth (ושלח) the live bird over the
face of the field. And the one to be cleansed will wash (וכבס)
his clothes and shave off (וגלח) all his hair, and bathe (ורחץ)
in water, and he will be clean (וטהר). Afterwards, he will
come (ובא) into the camp but he will remain (וישב) outside
his tent seven days.

Day Seven

Ritual Proper (v. 9): And on the seventh day he will shave
off (ינלח) all his hair—his head and his beard and his
eyebrows. He will shave off (ינלח) all his hair. Then he will
wash (וכבס) his clothes and bathe (ורחץ) his skin in water,
and he will be clean (וטהר).

Day Eight

   I. Materials (v. 10): And on the eighth day he will take (יקח)
      two male lambs without defect and one ewe lamb, one year
      old, without defect, and a cereal offering of three-tenths of
      fine flour mixed with oil and one log of oil.
  II. Ritual Proper (vv. 11-20)
     A. Preparations (v. 11): And the priest who pronounces
        cleanness shall stand (והעמיד) the man who is to be
        cleansed and the materials before Yahweh at the door
        of the tent of meeting.
     B. The אשם (vv. 12-18)
        1. Presentation (v. 12): And the priest will take (ולקח)
           one male lamb and present (והקריב) it for an אשם,
           along with the log of oil. And he will elevate (והניף)
           them as an elevation offering before Yahweh.
        2. Slaughter (v. 13): And he will slaughter (ושחט) the
           lamb in the place where he slaughters (ישחט) the חטאת
           and the עלה, in the holy place. For the אשם is like the
           חטאת to the priest. It is most holy.
        3. Blood Manipulation (v. 14): And the priest will take
           (ולקח) some of the blood of the אשם and the priest will
           put (ונתן) it on the lobe of the right ear of the one to be
           cleansed, and on his right thumb, and on his right
           big toe.
        4. The Manipulation of the Oil (vv. 15-18a): Then the
           priest will take (ולקח) some of the log of oil and will
           pour (ויצק) it into the left palm of his hand. And the
           priest will dip (וטבל) with his right finger some of the
           oil which is in his left palm. And he will sprinkle
           (והזה) some of the oil with his finger seven times

before Yahweh. And some of the remaining oil
which is in his palm the priest will put (יתן) on the
lobe of the right ear of the one to be cleansed, and on
his right thumb, and on his right big toe on top of
the blood of the אשם. And the rest of the oil that is in
the palm of the priest he will put (יתן) on the head of
the one to be cleansed.

5. Concluding Formula (v. 18b): Thus will the priest
kipper on his behalf (עליו) before Yahweh.

C. The חמאת and עלה (vv. 19-20a): Then the priest will
perform (ועשה) the חמאת and *kipper* on behalf of the one
who is to be cleansed from his uncleanness. After-
ward, he will slaughter (ישחט) the עלה. And the priest
shall offer up (והעלה) the עלה and the cereal offering on
the altar.

D. Concluding Formula (v. 20b): Thus shall the priest
kipper on his behalf, and he will be clean (וטהר).

There are three major phases in the ritual which may be
separated on the basis of the temporal segments of the ritual. It
begins on the first day, the day of the leper's initial cleansing.
After the rituals of this day, the recovered leper is allowed to
return to camp, but is instructed to remain outside his own
tent for seven days. On the seventh day, a transitional day
with a transitional ritual, the leper undergoes a ritual shaving
and washing in preparation for the ritual acts to performed on
the eighth day. Finally, the third segment, which takes place
on the eighth day, concludes the ritual process and allows the
recovered and cleansed leper to return to the normal forms of
life.

The Meaning of the Ritual and its Enactment

Introduction: The Examination by the Priest

The ritual begins when the priest is notified that there is a case
in need of priestly discrimination (see Lev. 10.10) and pronouncement. Lev. 14.2b is often noted as a problem. The leper
is to be brought to the priest *inside the camp* and then in v. 3
the text states that the priest will go *outside* the camp to the
leper. The form of the verb in v. 2b is a third singular *Hop'al*,
however, and if translated with an unspecified subject can
receive an impersonal translation: 'and it [the matter, the

case] shall be brought to the priest'.[1] It is quite clear that the
expelled leper cannot simply walk into the camp, for it is the
camp boundary that is being so carefully guarded in Leviticus
13–14. Hence, Lev. 14.2b is better understood to mean that the
matter is brought to the attention of the priest. After the
report, the priest then goes to the one who had been pronounced 'unclean' (see Lev. 13) and makes an examination. If
the leprous condition has passed, if it is no longer such as to
demand expulsion from the camp, then the priest gives
commandment to undertake the ritual which will restore the
recovered leper to the camp and society.

The priest gives instructions for the appropriate materials to
be gathered. This ritual involves the use of two live, clean birds,
an earthen vessel, running water, cedar wood, scarlet string,
and hyssop. This particular combination of materials, as
already noted, finds its only close parallel in Numbers 19, the
ritual of the red cow for the cleansing of corpse-contamination. In Numbers 19, the cedar wood, hyssop, and scarlet
string are thrown into the midst of the burning cow (v. 6). The
resulting ashes of this burning (called 'the ashes of the burnt
חטאת', v. 17) are mixed with running water (מים חיים) and
placed in a vessel (כלי). A clean person then takes hyssop and
dips it into the mixture and sprinkles it on the corpse-
contaminated person to effect purification.

It was argued above that leprosy was understood as passage
into the realm of death, particularly in light of the similarity of
the instructions regarding a leper as stated in Lev. 13.45 and
the reference to rites of mourning the dead in Lev. 10.6. In the
context of this ritual, and its conception of leprosy in terms of
death, the categories 'inside the camp' and 'outside the camp'
come to play important symbolic roles. The camp represents
life, wholeness, and health, while the region 'outside' the camp
represents death, brokenness, and disease. The camp represents assimilation into the life of the community, while expulsion from the camp means a life alone and separate from the
community. A similar structure was noted in Leviticus 16.
The camp is the realm of life, order, and blessing, while the
wilderness is represented as a place of chaos and dread. The

[1] Noth, *Leviticus*, p. 107; Elliger, *Leviticus*, p. 174.

importance of life within the order of society is emphasized in both of these rituals. Ritual is, in both cases, a means of maintaining the order of society and one's existence within that order.

It is this conceptual relationship of leprosy and death that explains the similarities between the ritual for the cleansing of the recovered leper and the ritual for the cleansing of the corpse-contaminated person. Thus, the leper is in the same category as one who has come into contact with a corpse. Both are ritually 'unclean' and must be purified from the contamination before once again participating in the normal structures of life. Ritual uncleanness is not merely a prohibition against participation in worship, it also means expulsion from the everyday structures of life and society. Thus, the use of hyssop, cedar wood, scarlet string, and running water in both rituals may be explained by the fact that both rituals are concerned with cleansing and passage from contact with 'death'.[1] It must be kept in mind that the ritual for the recovered leper also has parallel elements to the ritual ordination of the priests as well. The conceptual categories linking these two rituals were discussed above in Chapter 4. Here it may be reiterated that a concern for death runs throughout the rituals described in Leviticus 8, 14, and Numbers 19.

The Ritual of the First Day: Lev. 14.1-9
The ritual of the first day takes place outside of the camp. This is the area to which the leper has been expelled. The priest goes out to the subject, examines the individual, and makes a pronouncement concerning the individual's state. If the priest judges that the leprosy is healed, he then orders that the materials for the ritual be gathered. One bird is killed in an earthen vessel over running water. The remaining materials—the live bird, the cedar wood, hyssop, and scarlet string—are then dipped into the blood of the slain bird and the

---

[1] The precise significance of these elements, beyond their use for cleansing, is unknown. It is probable that 'red' string is required because of the color association with blood, although this is uncertain. There is simply not enough data to go beyond this general statement. See Snaith (*Leviticus*, pp. 73-74) for a discussion of these items.

blood is sprinkled on the recovered leper seven times. After the sprinkling rite the priest pronounces him clean and releases the live bird over the open field. The recovered leper washes his clothes, shaves off all of his hair, and bathes himself in water. He is then allowed to enter the camp.

It is clear that the role of the two live, clean birds is central to this ritual and must be understood if the ritual is to be interpreted correctly. It has often been noted that the use of the two birds in Leviticus 14 is parallel to the use of the goats in Leviticus 16.[1] In both cases one of the animals is killed and the other turned loose. There are, however, significant differences. In Leviticus 16, it is emphasized that the goats are being used in a process that is primarily concerned with the problem of sin and its resulting defilement. The goat that is killed is specifically called the goat of the חטאת and its blood is used for purging the sanctuary. The blood of the slain goat is not placed on the goat sent to Azazel, nor is it sprinkled on any person. Thus, while the ritual use of the two goats in Leviticus 16 is primarily concerned with the issue of sin and its resultant defilement, and the use of the blood is concerned with purgation, the use of the birds and the blood of the slain bird in Lev. 14 gives no indication that this ritual is concerned with sin—it is concerned with cleansing an *unclean person*. It should be emphasized that this phase of the ritual is not a healing rite.[2] The ritual only begins when the priest has examined the victim and made the decision that the leprosy is healed. Thus, this is not a ritual to restore physical health.

It is clear that this part of the ritual is primarily a 'cleansing' rite. Thus, the question must be asked: How does the ritual effect the cleansing? The beginning point is to understand how the two birds function in the process. It is of interest to note that the type of birds to be used is left unspecified. The birds need only be alive and clean. This suggests, however, that there is a conceptual correlation between this ritual and the list of clean and unclean animals in Leviticus 11.

---

[1] Wenham, *Leviticus*, p. 208; Milgrom, 'The Paradox of the Red Cow', p. 70; Frymer-Kensky, 'Pollution', p. 400; Wright, 'Disposal of Impurity', pp. 80-81.

[2] Milgrom, 'The Paradox of the Red Cow', p. 69; Noth, *Leviticus*, p. 107; Wenham, *Leviticus*, pp. 207-208.

One bird is taken and slain over running water in an earthen vessel. There is a practical need for a container to hold the blood of the slain bird since the blood will be used further in the ritual. The precise indication of 'an earthen vessel' (כלי־חרש) is found in ritual texts only in Lev. 6.21; 11.33; 14.5, 50; 15.12; and Num. 5.17. Lev. 6.21 states that an earthen vessel in which the חטאת is boiled shall be broken.[1] A bronze vessel need only be scoured and rinsed. It may be that a very practical and economic reason guides these decisions, but it is clear that an earthen vessel was more easily contaminated. This is most likely due to its being more absorbant. Lev. 11.33 again speaks of an earthen vessel becoming unclean with the prescription that it is to be broken. This time the uncleanness is contracted by contact with one of the unclean 'swarming' animals. Lev. 15.12 states that an earthen vessel is to be broken if touched by one who has had a discharge and is thereby unclean. Hence, there is clearly the belief that earthen vessels are particularly susceptible to uncleanness and impossible to cleanse. They must be broken if unclean. The final ritual text speaking of earthen vessels outside of Leviticus 14 is Num. 15.17. In this instance an earthen vessel is used for holding the water that a woman suspected of adultery will drink.

An earthen vessel, then , has two primary concerns in the Priestly material. It shows particular susceptibility to uncleanness and is to be broken when it has become unclean. It also serves as a container for liquids which are to be used in rituals. It is interesting to note that in the two texts where such a vessel is specified for use, neither text describes the final outcome of the vessel. Whether this type of container is used for economic reasons or whether its particular connection with 'the earth' plays a role in the rituals is uncertain. The evidence is not such as to allow a full determination.

The requirement that the bird be slain over 'living water' (על־מים חיים) does have important implications. This specific designation is also used sparsely, but its few uses in Priestly ritual texts give indications of its significance in ritual. In Lev. 15.13, the man with a discharge who has become

---

[1] On the disposal of such vessels, see Wright, 'Disposal of Impurity', pp. 95-112.

unclean, shall count seven days from his discharge and then shall wash his clothes and bathe himself in 'running water'. Then he shall be clean.[1] In Num. 19.17, a ritual already seen to have parallels with Leviticus 14, the ashes of the burned red cow, mixed with hyssop, cedar wood, and scarlet string, are mixed with running water. This mixture is then sprinkled on the corpse-contaminated person or object to cleanse it. Thus, use of running water is found primarily in rituals of cleansing from uncleanness.[2]

Running water stands in contrast to stagnant water. The use of running water in this ritual serves to emphasize the idea of removal.[3] In this way the ritual notion of cleansing comes to be associated with the idea of removal. It must be noted that the recovered leper will undertake a subsequent bathing so that this 'running water' is not the water with which the subject will cleanse himself.[4] The slaughter of the bird over running water must be interpreted primarily in

---

[1] The Hebrew reads: וכבס בגדיו ורחץ בשרו במים חיים וטהר. The clear parallel of these actions and their outcome to the present ritual adds further support to the understanding of this ritual as a cleansing ritual.

[2] Two points should be noted with regard to the rituals of Lev. 15 and 19. In both cases, the uncleanness is contracted through 'unintentional' means. These are not cases of 'moral' uncleanness concerned primarily with sin. Rather, they are viewed as disruptions of right order. Secondly, both cases involve a specified temporal phase in their enactment. In the case of uncleanness through discharge, the bathing comes on the seventh day free from the discharge, with a final series of ritual acts to follow on the eighth day. In Num. 19, the sprinkling of the corpse-contaminated person is to take place on the third and seventh days.

[3] A similar idea is present in Lev. 16 with regard to the goat that is sent to Azazel. On the symbolism of water, see V. Turner, 'The Waters of Life: Some Reflections on Zionist Water Symbolism', in *Religions in Antiquity*, pp. 509-20.

[4] Lev. 14.51 must be noted. This verse is concerned with the ritual that is to be performed for a house that was previously declared 'leprous'. The bird is slain over running water as in Lev. 14.5, but now the remaining materials of the ritual are dipped not only in the blood of the slain bird but also in the running water. Thus, the liquid sprinkled on the house is a mixture of blood *and* water. The reason for this difference is the basic belief that a cleansing ritual must make use of water. A ritual 'bathing' is necessary. While the individual can perform the bathing by himself, a house obviously cannot do so. Hence, the water is mixed with the blood so that the house is sprinkled with the blood and ritually 'bathed' with water in one act.

terms of its symbolic value in the ritual. It symbolizes that the
ritual to be performed with the blood of the slain bird will
perform its intended purpose—the *removal* of uncleanness. It
displays at the beginning of the ritual the effective outcome of
the ritual and thereby provides an effective context for the
ritual use of blood.[1] The symbolic value of the running water
serves to anticipate the ritual and embody the results of the
ritual from the beginning of the ritual.

The obvious reason for the slaying of the one bird is the
necessity of using blood in this cleansing ritual. This is
extremely important to note in that this is the only cleansing
ritual that applies blood directly to a person in order to effect
cleansing. The only close parallel is Numbers 19. In Numbers
19, however, the blood is not used directly, but is simply part of
the ashes that remain after the burning of the cow. In Num.
19.9 the ashes are mixed with water to form the waters of
impurity, and the elements are called a חטאת (למי נדה חטאת הוא).
This is not true of Leviticus 14. It would not be expected, however, in that the blood of a חטאת is never sprinkled on a person,
only on objects. Its purpose, as already seen, is to cleanse or
purge those objects. From this, however, it is clear that a
common belief is present in the use of the blood of the חטאת and
the blood of the bird in Leviticus 14—the blood is understood as
a detergent, an agent of cleansing.

It could be argued that the ritual of Numbers 19 makes use
of the blood of the חטאת in order to effect its cleansing of an
impure individual. If this is so, however, the blood is not applied
directly but comes in a somewhat altered form by the mixing
of the ashes with the water. Also, the ashes themselves are
understood as a חטאת[2]. Leviticus 14 and 19, then, both understand the blood to be a detergent for cleansing individuals. The
reason for this drastic and unusual measure is the concern of
both rituals with a passage from contact with 'the realm of
death' back to 'the realm of life'. This supports, again, the

---

1 Ritual symbols are powerful symbols and serve to communicate and effect
their purpose. By providing the context of the ritual use of the blood with a
symbol that presents the effective outcome of the ritual, the priests have
provided a guarantee of the ritual's work. On this use of symbols and its
relation to magic, see Douglas, *Purity and Danger*, pp. 58-72.
2 See Milgrom, 'The Paradox of the Red Cow', pp. 66-72.

interpretation of the priestly ordination as a similar type of passage in that the blood of the ram of ordination is applied directly to the extremities of the priests.

In using phrases such as 'the realm of death' and 'the realm of life', it should be clear that the ritual is dealing with more than just physical states. These are interpretive, symbolic, and conceptual categories operative in the thinking of the Priestly writers. Death, for the Priestly writers, was more than simply the description of a physical state. Death was viewed as a disruption of the created order. For the Priestly traditionists, human existence meant life lived in the context of blessing, fertility, and the ongoing maintenance of the divinely created order. Death brought such existence, such possibilities, to an end. The boundary between life and death was absolute and crossing the boundary into death brought to an end human participation in the divinely created order. Its danger arises precisely because of its symbolic reflection of a ruptured order. Thus, 'death' is understood as a state of contagion that reflects the disruption of the divinely created order. When one is contaminated by contact with this realm, strict ritual structures are employed to keep the contamination in check.

It is precisely in this ritual passage from 'death' to 'life' that the tensive symbolic nature of blood, as it is used in the ritual, can be seen. The blood of the slaughtered bird functions in the ritual as a symbol of death *and* life. It is thus a symbol that holds together polar extremes of meaning. The blood is the necessary ritual means for cleansing the recovered leper and passing the individual into the realm of life. In order to acquire the blood necessary for the ritual, the bird must be slaughtered. Thus, the blood reflects the death of the animal, but, at the same time, it reflects the life gained by the recovered leper through the sprinkling of the blood on the individual. Thus, the blood functions symbolically to hold in a tensive balance the categories of death and life and serves as an apt ritual symbol for effecting passage from the realm of death to the realm of life.

Thus, in Leviticus 14 blood serves as a cleansing agent for the individual because of the individual's contact with death contagion. At the same time, it functions to pass the individual into the realm of life and communicate life to the individual. It is clear that this blood is not concerned with the purgation of sin, nor is it specifically identified as one of the major types of sacrifice. The blood serves as a cleansing agent in this ritual because it effectively combines in itself the ideas of life and death and is thus an appropriate symbolic agent for cleansing the individual from the uncleanness of contact with death and, at the same time, for effecting the individual's passage from death to life.

Verse 7 specifically states that the priest is to sprinkle the one to be cleansed from leprosy seven times with the blood. It is probable that the hyssop was used as the sprinkling tool (cf. Num. 19.18). As already discussed, the seven-fold sprinkling rite functions here as a cleansing rite.[1] A clear parallel is apparent between this sprinkling of blood in order to cleanse and the sprinkling of the blood of the חטאת in order to cleanse the sanctuary and its ritual objects.

The second, live bird is also dipped in the blood of the slain bird and is then set free after the seven-fold sprinkling of the recovered leper. The sending of the blood-soaked bird into the open field is best understood as an act parallel to the sending of the goat into the wilderness in Leviticus 16. There are two primary differences, however, but differences that are important for understanding the ritual meaning of the live bird in Leviticus 14. First, in Leviticus 16 the sins of the people are placed on the head of the goat, while in Leviticus 14 the bird to be set free is dipped in the blood of the slaughtered bird which has already been sprinkled on the recovered leper. Secondly, in Leviticus 16 the live goat is sent (שלח) into the wilderness, while in Leviticus 14 the live bird is sent (שלח) into the open field. This suggests that the purpose of these two acts is similar, although nuanced somewhat differently because of the different purposes of the rituals and the differences in the acts.

It was argued above[2] that the live goat in Leviticus 16 was understood to carry the sins of the people and of the camp to the wilderness, a spatial category which functioned symbolically as the place of chaos. The 'sin' of the people, the cause for the breakdown of order, was thus eliminated from the camp

---

1 See above, pp. 82-85.
2 See above, pp. 95-100.

and placed in its appropriate place. Thus, the goat took sin out of the camp to its proper place, the place of chaos, precisely because it was the sin of the people and its defilement which threatened the community with a breakdown of order and an outbreak of chaos.

This suggests that the function of the freeing of the blood-soaked bird must be understood in terms of elimination. In this case, the ritual functions to eliminate the impurity of the recovered leper. The blood of the slaughtered bird serves as a cleansing agent, which is then sent to the open field away from society. This supports the idea, found elsewhere in Priestly rituals, that the blood of an animal is absorbant and communicates its essence to all of its blood even when spatially separated.

Why, however, do the priests think that the impurity of the leper needs to be eliminated? The answer to this question would seem to lie in the nature of the leper's status—one who has come into contact with the contagion of death. The leper is being cleansed from death contagion, is being passed from death to life. Such impurity must be eliminated because of its severe nature.

Although the evidence is uncertain, this may be supported by the statement that the bird is to be sent 'into the open field' (על פני־השׂדה). This precise phrase is found elsewhere in P only in Lev. 14.7,53 and Lev. 17.5. It is found, however, five times in Ezekiel (16.5; 29.5; 32.4; 33.27; 39.5). Each of these is found in a judgment speech: against Jerusalem (16.5); against the Pharaoh of Egypt (29.5, 32.4); against the inhabitants of the waste places in Israel (33.27); against Gog (39.5). In Ezek. 16.5 Jerusalem, depicted as a newborn child, is abhorred and cast into the open field weltering in blood. The other four instances all employ 'the open field' as a place where the Lord's judgment of death will fall on the accursed; it is a place where they will die and be devoured by bird and beast. While the evidence is too limited to be conclusive, it suggests that the use of the phrase 'the open field' in Lev. 14.7 may have symbolic significance similar to that of 'wilderness' in Leviticus 16. This is true in two ways. First, 'the open field' is a place associated with death. Since the recovered leper is understood as one making passage from death to life, the bird carrying the impurity is sent to a place associated with death. Secondly, the death associated with 'the open field' is related to the judgment of Yahweh. If, as argued below, the leper is understood as one afflicted because of trespass, then sending such impurity to a place of judgment makes sense of this rite. Thus, 'the open field' may function as a meaningful spatial category in Leviticus 14 in the same way that 'the wilderness' functions in Leviticus 16. It is the place to which the impurity of leprosy, understood in terms of death contagion, is sent in order to eliminate it from the ordered social realm.

It is also important to explore the significance of blood as it is used on the first day of this ritual. The priestly writers do not call the slaughtered bird a sacrifice. This is true because it *cannot* be made at the central altar. In order for this ritual to take place, it is necessary for the blood to be obtained and used *outside* the camp—for that is the place to which the leper has been banished. The blood of the slaughtered bird is necessary in order to pass the recovered leper back to the realm of life. A death is necessary in order to effect life. Thus, the blood in the ritual functions symbolically to hold together several ritual ideas: purity, life and death, social order. First, it serves as a purifying agent when placed on the recovered leper. This is clear in that after sprinkling the individual with the blood the priest pronounces him clean. It is clear, however, that the purification process is not complete at this point in that the total ritual will take eight more days to be completed. Secondly, the blood serves to pass the recovered leper from the realm of death to the realm of life. This passage is reflected in the death of the animal and the return to life by the recovered leper through his return to camp. Third, the blood as agent of both purification and passage, serves as a symbol of social order as it functions to restore the expulsed individual to a standing within the camp and community. This suggests that life is understood to be experienced inside the camp—a right standing within the community.

The recovered leper then washes his clothes, shaves off all his hair, and bathes in water. He may enter the camp at this point, but he must remain outside his tent for another seven days. The first part of the ritual makes it possible for the recovered leper to return to the camp because it has eliminated the dangerous impurity that could be contaminating to the rest of the community. The recovered leper is not yet able to enter into the full structures of community life, however, and must await a further ceremony on the eighth day to be realigned finally and fully into the community.

It is important to note that the ceremonies which take place on the eighth day can only take place *inside* the camp. That is, the offerings and sacrifices that will allow the recovered leper's full participation in the societal structures can only take place at the altar and, therefore, only inside the camp. These sacrifices and offerings are presented on the eighth day because the eighth day is consistently the great day of cleansing from severe impurity, and leprosy is one of the most severe. On the seventh day another shaving, laundering, and bathing are to take place. Thus, once again these ritual acts of washing mark the passage of the individual from ritual state to ritual state.[1]

```
        Unclean                            Clean
        Ritual                             Ritual
        Bathing----------Seven Days----------Bathing
```

The Ritual of the Eighth Day: Lev. 14.10-20

The ritual of the eighth day takes place inside the camp at the doorway of the tent of meeting (v. 11). The materials for the ritual are brought to the doorway of the tent and the priest who pronounces the leper clean is to stand the material and the recovered leper at the door of the tent of meeting. The materials consist of the following: two male lambs without blemish; a year old ewe lamb without blemish; three tenths of an ephah of fine flour mixed with oil; and one log of oil (v. 10). The ritual takes place as follows:

תנופה (v. 12): אשם + the log of oil
אשם (v. 12): one male lamb

---

1   In the context of a rite of passage, these bathings mark off a liminal period. There is no information, however, on what transpires in this phase, and it is of no value to conjecture on this matter. It does appear, however, that the seven days reflect a liminal state, a state when the recovered leper is 'betwixt and between' clearly defined social categories.

Manipulation of the blood and oil (vv. 14-18):
 Blood on extremities of the recovered leper
 Sprinkle oil seven times before Yahweh
 Oil on extremities of recovered leper on top of the blood of the אשם
 Remaining oil on the head of the recovered leper
חטאת (v. 19): one ewe lamb
עלה and מנחה (v. 20): one male lamb

There are major questions that arise with regard to this ritual. First, why is the order of the חטאת and the אשם reversed from normal sequence? Second, what is the significance of the phase of the ritual in which the priest anoints the leper with the blood of the אשם and the oil of the תנופה?

As already noted, the anointing of an individual's extremities with blood has a parallel only in the ordination ritual of the priests (Lev. 8.23, 24). In that ritual the blood was obtained from the ram of ordination. In the present ritual the blood which will be sprinkled on the recovered leper's extremities is obtained from the lamb offered as an אשם. It has already been argued that this rite is concerned with the passage of the individual (or group with reference to Aaron's sons) from the realm of death to the realm of life. This passage can only take place *inside* the camp. This is a key to a correct understanding of the reason for why the אשם comes first in this ritual. This issue will be discussed below after the function of the oil and its use in this ritual have been examined.

There are three distinct acts performed with the oil in Lev. 14.15-18. First, the priest dips his right finger into the oil, which is in his left palm, and sprinkles it seven times before Yahweh. Second, the priest is to take some of the oil and place it on the three extremities of the recovered leper, on top of the blood of the אשם that has already been placed on these extremities. Third, the priest is to take the rest of the oil and put it on the head of the one to be cleansed. At this point, the text reads: 'Thus shall the priest *kipper* on his behalf before Yahweh' (וכפר עליו הכהן לפני יהוה). Once again it is necessary to grant that *kipper* has a broad range of meaning that must be determined in each case by its specific ritual context. It is clear that in this case the seven-fold sprinkling of the oil before

Yahweh serves to prepare it for its further ritual use.[1] It is an act in which the oil is given over and dedicated to its intended ritual purpose.

There is no clear parallel to this rite employing the oil. The closest thing to a parallel comes in the ordination ritual of the priests. In that ritual, Moses takes some of the sacred anointing oil, which is distinct from the oil used in Leviticus 14, and, in conjunction with the anointing of the tabernacle, pours some of it on Aaron's head to consecrate Aaron, to mark him in his special status.[2] Aaron's sons do not receive this anointing. Moses then takes the ram of ordination and places its blood on the extremities of Aaron *and* his sons. Finally, Moses takes some of the anointing oil and some of the blood which was on the altar, and he sprinkles this mixture on Aaron, his sons, and all their garments. Thus, Moses consecrates Aaron, his sons, and their garments (Lev. 8.30).

The difference that makes these two rituals very distinct is the fact that Aaron and his sons are anointed with the special anointing oil. This oil is confined in its use to the sanctuary and its accouterments. It is the means by which the priesthood is joined in spheres of sanctity to the tabernacle and its sacred objects. This oil serves to locate the priests in their special sphere of influence and work. Their passage from life to death is part of their passage from a non-institutional status to an institutional status, and the anointing oil serves to effect this new standing in the institution of the tabernacle cult.

The type of oil used for the anointing of the recovered leper is not specified, but it is clearly distinct from the anointing oil used in Leviticus 8. There is no other place in the Priestly strata where oil is placed on a person.[3] Outside of P, oil is used in the anointing of kings (e.g., 1 Sam. 10.1; 16.13; 1 Kgs 1.39; 2 Kgs 9.3, 6; Ps. 89.21) and with reference to favor, wellbeing, or gladness (e.g., 2 Sam. 14.2; Isa. 61.3; Pss. 23.5; 45.8; 104.15; 133.2; Prov. 27.9; Eccl. 9.8). It is difficult to determine the exact significance of the rite on the basis of these texts. It is possible to

---

[1] See above, pp. 82-85.

[2] On anointing, see above, pp. 118-20.

[3] Elsewhere in P, oil is mentioned in conjunction with lights (e.g., Exod. 25.6; 27.20; 35.14; 39.37) or with reference to the oil added to offerings (e.g., Lev. 2.1, 6, 15; 5.11; 8.26).

interpret this anointing with the oil as a symbol of gladness
and well-being on the 'recovery' of the leper.[1] It is more
probable, however, that the use of the oil is related to some
aspect of the rite as a rite of passage. This would be in line with
the anointing of the kings and would also clarify the relation of
this ritual to the ordination of the priests. In Leviticus 8 and
Leviticus 14, the placing of the blood on the extremities of the
subject of the ritual serves to provide safe passage from death
to life. The anointing oil in Leviticus 8 has as its primary
purpose the consecration of the priests and, therefore, their
location in the institution of the cult. If true, the placing of the
oil on the recovered leper would have as its purpose the
location of the leper back into society. It is part of the ritual
that effects and communicates the individual's passage into a
restored societal standing. Just as the priests move from a
non-institutional status to an institutional status, so the leper
moves from one societal status (exclusion) to another societal
standing (inclusion).

The geography of the ritual supports this type of movement
as the recovered leper gradually moves back inside the camp
boundaries and ultimately back to his own tent. Thus, one's
residence, in this case the tent, is seen to represent one's place
in the community and the society. It is only as one is residing
inside one's own tent that one is understood to be residing
inside the societal order. Thus, it is not only the wholeness of
the individual that is at stake in this ritual, it is the wholeness
of the societal body that is also at stake. The exclusion of the
leper in the first place is an attempt to maintain the wholeness
and well-being of the community, and the ritual readmittance
of the recovered leper reflects the strong feelings of the
Priestly writers toward the need to maintain the integrity of
the community. One cannot simply return to the societal
order when one has been expulsed. One must return carefully
and ritually.

It must now be asked why the normal order of the חטאת and
the אשם is reversed in this ritual. Before addressing this,

---

[1] Wenham (*Leviticus*, p. 211) understands the oil to indicate union with
God. There is no textual evidence, however, in P or elsewhere to suggest
such an interpretation. Noth (*Leviticus*, p. 109) suggests that the purpose
of the oil was to have a life-renewing effect.

however, the purpose of the אשם must be discussed. The basic
situations calling for an אשם are detailed in Lev. 5.14-26 and
the procedures for the offering briefly described in Lev. 7.1-7.
The procedure for offering the אשם is similar to the procedure
for the עלה. The animal is killed and its blood thrown on the
altar round about. Then all of its fat, the fat tail, the fat on the
entrails, the kidneys and their fat, and the appendage of the
liver are to be burned on the altar.[1]

Three major cases are described in Lev. 5.14-26, according
to Milgrom, which require the אשם[2]. The first case deals with
trespass (מעל) upon sanctums that is inadvertent.[3] The second
case (Lev. 5.17-19) is concerned with suspected trespass on
sanctums. The final case (Lev. 5.20-26) is concerned with a
fraudulent act against an individual that is done in conjunction with a false oath to God. Thus, Milgrom understands
the אשם in this context to mean 'reparation offering', made
because of trespass on divine sanctums.[4] For the present study,
it is not necessary to enter into the discussion of the various
uses of the verbal forms of the root אשם.[5]

Such an understanding of the אשם makes sense of the
requirement that the recovered leper must offer it. Leprosy
was understood to be one form of punishment by God for
wrong doing. Indeed, as Milgrom points out, it is specifically
identified as an affliction resulting from מעל in the story of

---

1   It is probable that when an animal was offered as an אשם the offerer laid
    his/her hands on the animal's head as with the עלה. This is not required,
    however, because it was possible under normal circumstances, although
    not so with the leper's אשם, to commute the אשם into money (Milgrom, *Cult
    and Conscience*, p. 15 [n. 48]). The leper cannot commute the אשם because
    of the necessity of the animal's blood in the ritual.

2   *Cult and Conscience*, pp. 13-44, 63-88; 'Sacrifices and Offerings', pp. 768-69
    for a summary. See also his 'The Priestly Doctrine of Repentance', *RB* 82
    (1975), pp. 186-205.

3   See Milgrom, 'The Concept of Ma'al in the Bible and the Ancient Near
    East' *JAOS* 96 (1976), pp. 236-47 and his 'The Cultic שגגה', pp. 115-25.

4   De Vaux (*Studies*, pp. 98-102) understands אשם as reparation offering. See
    also Schötz, *Schuld- und Sündopfer*, pp. 32-35. This idea is also evident in
    the case of the Nazirite who has come into contact with a corpse and
    thereby broken the pure state of the Nazirite vow (Num. 6.9-12). See
    Milgrom, *Cult and Conscience*, pp. 66-70.

5   See Milgrom, *Cult and Conscience*, pp. 3-12; Hutton, 'Declaratory
    Formulae', pp. 107-11.

Uzziah in 2 Chron. 26.16-19.[1] The leprosy that afflicts Uzziah comes as a result of his trespass against Yahweh in entering the temple to offer incense on the the altar of incense. Thus, the contraction of leprosy could suggest that the leper had trespassed on sacred sanctums and needed to offer a reparation offering.

It has already been argued that the blood was a necessary part of this ritual, effecting the individual's passage back into the realm of life. It seems clear that the blood in this ritual indicates the life that the recovered leper has entered into through the ritual process. The blood's symbolic associations with life allow it to be used effectively in passing the person from the realm of death into the realm of life. It may be understood to communicate life to the individual on whom it is placed.

Why is the blood of the אשם used for this procedure? It would not be possible to use the blood of the חטאת for this rite because that blood is reserved for the purgation of the sanctuary. At the same time, the חטאת cannot be effectively offered before the individual has already passed into the realm of life. The same reasoning would hold true for the עלה.[2] The אשם of Leviticus 14, then, serves two functions. First, it provides the blood necessary for the recovered leper's complete passage into life. Second, it makes reparation for a possible trespass upon divine sanctums and, thereby, assures the offerer that he will not be held guilty for a trespass upon Yahweh's divine realm. This אשם is not commutable into currency because of the necessity of acquiring blood for the ritual. It should also be noted that the twofold purpose of the אשם in this instance combines within itself the ideas of sacrifice, blood, and life. Life is the return that the recovered leper gets from payment for reparation.

The אשם is followed by the חטאת and then the עלה. Their function at this point is identical to their function in Leviticus

---

1 *Cult and Conscience*, pp. 80-81.
2 An objection could be raised at this point since the חטאת and עלה both precede the placing of the blood on the extremities of the priests in Lev. 8. In Lev. 8, however, the חטאת and עלה are being offered for the first time, and are part of the procedure for establishing not only the priesthood but also the sanctuary and the sacred boundaries. Thus, the חטאת and עלה are offered first as foundation sacrifices.

8. The חטאת serves to cleanse the altar from possible pollution caused by the 'sin' of the leper, or from the impurity of the leper, and at the same time serves to reconsecrate the boundaries of the holy. Just as the ritual will provide a safe passage for the leper back into the land of the living and thus back into society, thereby restoring the normal societal boundaries, so will there be the restoration of the structure of the holy, disrupted because of the leper's impurity. Again it is seen that a rupture in the societal boundaries is accompanied by a rupture in the sacred boundaries. This acts as a threat both to society and the sacred. The עלה serves to avert the wrath of Yahweh and serves as a gift to Yahweh to secure the peaceful (whole) bond between the offerer (and even the whole society) and Yahweh. Thus, the leper is brought back into society and the normal structures of existence, both societal and cultic, are restored to a whole and normal state.

Conclusion

Leprosy was a social concern. It was seen as a threat to the integrity of society. As such, the one who was pronounced 'leprous' was expulsed from the camp, a symbol of their expulsion from society. Thus, the ritual for the recovered leper is concerned with more than passage from an unclean state to a clean state. It is designed to bring the recovered leper back into right standing within the community.

A deeper concern is present in this ritual. The leper was seen as one who had evidenced signs of corruption and death. The leper was viewed as one who had already, to some extent, passed over the boundary separating life and death. Thus, the ritual must function at a deeper level to effect passage for the recovered leper back to the realm of life. This passage to life is reflected in the ritual through spatial categories as the one being cleansed moves back into the camp and then back to his own tent. The movement of the recovered leper back inside the camp reflects the passage back into life. The camp, the social body, was seen as the place of life—wholeness, blessing, well-being. Life could only be fully realized and experienced within the context of the community, 'inside the camp'.

The blood of the slaughtered bird is placed on the bird that is then set free 'into the open field'. It was suggested that this reflects the idea that the 'leprosy', the cause of the leper's expulsion, was sent to a place of judgment and death. The blood of the slaughtered bird is then sprinkled seven times on the one to be cleansed. The blood of the bird serves to bring the recovered leper back into the camp. Thus, this blood serves to cleanse the individual, while, at the same time, communicating life to the individual. It thus serves to effect the passage from death to life.

The passage, however, is not yet complete. On the eighth day, sacrifices and offerings must be presented at the tent, 'inside' the camp. The blood of the bird, placed on the recovered leper 'outside the camp', allows the individual to return to the camp, but not to his own tent. This will only be allowed after the sacrifices of the eighth day. On this day, the blood of the אשם is placed on the extremities of the recovered leper. This blood functions to give full and final passage into 'the realm of life'. Thus, blood functions not only as a cleansing agent, but also as a means to effect restoration. The one who is defiled is made clean *and* restored to full standing within the social body.

Excursus II

THE ROLE OF BLOOD IN THE *KIPPER*-ACT:
BLOOD AS SYMBOL OF LIFE AND DEATH

There are three significant texts in the Priestly traditions
where the phrase 'the life of the flesh is in the blood' is found:
Gen. 9.4; Lev. 17.11, 14.[1] In Gen. 9.4 the phrase is incorporated
into Elohim's 'blessing' of Noah and his sons after the flood
(Gen. 9.1-7).[2] The vegetarian ordinance of the original creation (Gen. 1.29-30) is now set aside by God in allowing human
beings to eat meat. There is, however, a qualification: 'Only,
flesh with its life, that is its blood, you shall not eat' (Gen. 9.4).[3]
Verse 5 further defines and qualifies the eating of meat:
'Indeed, I will demand your blood for your life. I will demand it
from any living thing—from the human being, from the
brother. I will demand the life of the man'. In the larger context of the passage it is clear that two issues have been brought
together: (1) the killing of animals for food and (2) the taking
of human life. Animals may be killed for food, but the blood is to

1 Outside of P, see Deut. 12.23; Jer. 2.34.
2 The actual form of Gen. 9.4 is that of prohibitive law. See Westermann,
  Genesis, p. 464.
3 Westermann (*Genesis*, pp. 464-65) reivews the various understandings of
  this phrase. He concludes (p. 465) that נפש is not identical with the substance of blood, but only with the rhythmic, pulsating blood'.

be poured from them before their consumption. Human life taken in murder carries with it the demand for return payment. Violence is recognized as a part of human existence at this point.

This connection should not be overlooked. In the Priestly strata the cause of the flood is violence (חמס)[1]—'brutal, killing attacks on the body and the very life which takes place between man and beast (sometimes in the search for food), but more especially between man and man'.[2] Indeed, this is the one fact of human existence that P recognizes to have taken shape between the initial creation and the flood. In light of this it may be stated that the Priestly writers are offering the killing of animals as a channel for violence. Violence is a recognized fact of human existence. Is there some way that it can be channeled and controlled so that it remains within prescribed bounds? The answer of the Priestly writers is that the killing of animals is one means by which violence can be structured.

A second means for such violence to be structured and controlled is through ritual.[3] Indeed, it has been suggested that sacrifice is *the* means by which human aggression and violence is given control. Girard sees the purpose of sacrifice, as ordered and sacred violence, to be the restoration of harmony to the community in order 'to reinforce the social fabric'.[4] In this way, the connection between the violence of human beings against other human beings and 'prescribed' violence against animals, for the obtaining of food, is clear. The sacrificial element, however, is not yet apparent. It must be remembered that for the Priestly writers there can be no mention of sacrifice at this point in the narrative because the sacrificial system will only be revealed at the time of Moses.

---

1 The result of this violence is corruption (שחת). Gen. 6.12b reads, 'because (כי) all flesh had corrupted its way on the earth'. In the context, this corruption is primarily understood in terms of violence.
2 See Steck, *World and Environment*, p. 93. See also his *Schöpfungsbericht*, pp. 145-46.
3 At this point the broad definition of 'ritual' is being used. This is social ritual, prescribed actions for social relationship, that need not, necessarily, be religious or sacred.
4 R. Girard, *Violence and the Sacred* (Baltimore: Johns Hopkins University Press, 1977), p. 8, see the whole discussion, pp. 1-38.

The use of the phrase, however, in Lev. 17.11 and 14 brings prescribed sacrifice at the sanctuary into the discussion.

Lev. 17.11 refers to the use of sacrificial blood on the altar.[1] The precise translation of this verse is a problem. R. de Vaux renders the verse as 'the life of the flesh is in the blood. This blood I have given it to you, [I have done this] so that you may on the altar perform the rite of expiation for your lives; for it is the blood which expiates by the life which is in it'.[2] The ב of בנפש is taken instrumentally and is understood to be the means by which expiation is performed.[3] Milgrom translates the verse as follows: 'For the life of the flesh is the blood, and it is I who have assigned it to you upon the altar to expiate for your lives, for it is the blood, as life, that expiates'.[4] Milgrom understands the ב of בדם and בנפש to be the '[ב] essentiae', thereby forming an exact inclusion at the beginning and end of the verse. He further argues that the use of כפר in this verse is related to *kôpher* and is best understood as 'expiate' or 'ransom'.[5] Levine offers the following translation: 'For the life of the flesh is in the blood, and I have assigned it to you to serve as expiation (*kôpher*) for your lives (*lᵉkappēr 'al napšôtêkem*) on the altar; for the blood may expiate according to the value of life'.[6] Levine argues that the ב of בנפש is the 'ב pretii', the ב of price. The blood is able to serve as a substitute for the life, *pars pro*

---

1 On Lev. 17.11, see the following: A. Metzinger, 'Die Substitutionstheorie und das alttestament. Opfer mit besonderer Berücksichtigung von Lev. 17,11', *Bib* 21 (1940), pp. 159-87, 247-72, 353-77; Elliger, *Leviticus*, pp. 218-29; Milgrom, 'A Prolegomenon to Leviticus 17.11' *JBL* 90 (1971), pp. 149-56; J.M. Grintz, '"Do Not Eat on the Blood": Reconsiderations in setting and dating of the Priestly Code', *ASTI* 8 (1972), pp. 78-105; Levine, *In the Presence*, pp. 67-68; H.C. Brichto, 'On Slaughter and Sacrifice, Blood and Atonement', *HUCA* 47 (1976), pp. 22-28; N. Füglister, 'Sühne durch Blut— Zur Bedeutung von Leviticus 17,11', *Studien zum Pentateuch* (ed. G. Braulik; Wien–Freiburg–Basel: Herder, 1977), pp. 143-64; Wenham, *Leviticus*, pp. 240-46.
2 *Studies*, p. 93.
3 This is also the view of Metzinger, 'Die Substitutionstheorie', pp. 257-72. See also J.E. Steinmueller, 'Sacrificial Blood in the Bible', *Bib* 40 (1959), pp. 556-67.
4 'Prolegomena to Lev. 17.11', p. 156.
5 *Ibid.*, pp. 149, 151 (n. 15). He maintains the use of 'expiate' in the article even though he notes (p. 151, n. 15) that 'ransom' is to be preferred.
6 *In the Presence*, p. 68.

toto, and is thus able to provide the 'ransom' necessary to redeem the life of the one who killed the animal.[1] Brichto translates the verse as '. . . the life-essence of flesh is in the blood and I for my part have on your behalf designated it (to be put) on the altar to serve to *kipper* for your lives, for it is the blood which serves to *kipper* in exchange for the life [taken]'.[2] Brichto understands the ב of בנפש to be the ב pretii, in agreement with Levine, and understands the *kipper* in the legal sense of 'composition'. The blood thus serves as *kôpher*, compository payment, for the life that is taken from the animal.[3]

The last three writers agree that the use of כפר in this verse is related to *kôpher* and the idea of 'ransom'.[4] Milgrom argues further, and in this he is followed by Brichto, that v. 11 refers *only* to the שלמים sacrifices discussed in vv. 3-7.[5] Milgrom argues that the reference to the altar and the eating of blood must refer to a sacrifice eaten by the laity, i.e., the שלמים. Since the שלמים sacrifices are discussed in the preceding context, this verse must continue that discussion. Milgrom then notes the problem of such an interpretation in light of the 'expiatory' (כפר) nature of the blood. The שלמים are not said to *kipper* in P. Thus, the use of כפר here must be related to the noun *kôpher* and be understood as 'ransom'. Such a 'ranson' is required, Milgrom suggests, because human life is in jeopardy when (animal) life has been taken. 'Lev. 17.11 implies that human life is in jeopardy unless the stipulated ritual is carried out'.[6] Thus, Lev. 17.11 is not a general statement about the role of blood, but only about the blood of the שלמים.

Before addressing this argument directly, it will be helpful to look at the structure of the whole chapter. Verses 1-2 serve as the standard introduction to Priestly instructions delivered by

1 *Ibid.*
2 'On Slaughter and Sacrifice', p. 23.
3 *Ibid.*, pp. 27-28.
4 An older view saw in this verse the basis for a sustitutionary theory of sacrifice in P. See, for example, Elliger, *Leviticus*, p. 228.
5 'Prolegomena to Lev. 17.11', pp. 152-56: Brichto, 'On Slaughter and Sacrifice', p. 27.
6 'Prolegomena to Lev. 17.11', p. 150.

Yahweh to Moses. Verses 3-16 present four sections introduced by the formula: איש איש מביה/מבני ישראל (vv. 3, 8, 10, 13).[1]

Verses 3-9

Verses 3-9 constitute the first section and are concerned with the death of sacrificial animals. Verses 3-4 read:

> If any man of the house of Israel kills (ישחט) an ox (שור), or a lamb (כשב), or a goat (עז) within the camp or kills (ישחט) it outside the camp, *but* does not bring it (הביאו) to present (להקריב) it as an offering (קרבן) to Yahweh, bloodguilt (דם)[2] shall be imputed (יחשב) to that man; he has shed blood. That man shall be cut off from the midst of his people.

The focus continues through v. 7 on the animals of the שלמים sacrifices and their appropriate offering to Yahweh. It should be noted that the animals mentioned in v. 3 are the animals associated with the three catagories of animals of the שלמים sacrifices as described in Leviticus 3: בקר (v. 1), צאן (v. 6), עז (v. 12). It is important to note that these are the primary catagories of *domestic* animals. This demonstrates that domestic animals are the *only* animals appropriate for the שלמים sacrifices. The slaughter of one of these animals must incorporate its offering at the door of the tent of meeting (v. 4).[3] The slaughter of a domestic animal, when it is to be used for food, and it is probable that they are to be slaughtered for that reason alone, must be placed in the context of a sacred offering at the door of the tent of meeting. Thus, in order to use the 'home-animals' as food, they must be presented and offered at the sanctuary in the context of the sacred.[4]

---

1 For similar formulations in the Priestly material, see Lev. 15.2; 18.5; 20.2, 9; 22.4, 18; 24.15; Num. 5.19; 9.10.

2 For this meaning, see Wolff, *Anthropology*, pp. 61-62. These concluding clauses, incorporating the *kareth* penalty, demonstrate the seriousness of this issue and underscore the demand for payment for such acts. This is the force of the statement in Gen. 9.4-5.

3 It must be noted that the LXX and Samaritan Pentateuch do not limit the concern of v. 4 to the שלמים, but include the עלה as well.

4 Verses 3-9 are also concerned with the appropriate *place* of sacrifice, in an attempt to prohibit sacrifices to gods other than Yahweh. Indeed, it is the slaughter of the animal and the manipulation of its blood at the door of the tent of meeting that constitute the act as sacred. This suggests that the

Verses 8-9
Verses 8-9 form the second set of instructions in this chapter
and are clearly directed at the appropriate place for sacrifice.
In this section, the Hebrew text broadens its concern and
includes the עלה sacrifice.[1] This creates a problem for the view
that v. 11 refers only to שלמים sacrifices. The primary concern
of this section is found in v. 9—the sacrifices are to be brought
to the door of the tent of meeting to be sacrificed before
Yahweh. The *kareth* penalty is added and indicates the importance of this ritual prescription regarding sacrificial space.

Verses 10-12
Verses 10-12 are clearly marked off as a unit. Verse 10 begins
with the phrase איש איש מבית ישראל. The same introductory
formula in v. 13 indicates the beginning of a new unit, demonstrating that v. 12 marks the close of the unit begun in v. 10.
The structure of vv. 10-12 is clearly defined by the syntax.
Verse 10 provides the primary statement: 'If any man from
the house of Israel or from the sojourner who sojourns in your
midst eats *any blood* (כל־דם), I will set my face against the life
that eats the blood; and I will cut it [the נפש] off from the midst
of its people.' Verse 11 opens with כי stating the reason for the
statement of v.10. Verse 12 begins with על־כן and restates the
position of v.10 in prohibitive form: 'Therefore I have said to
the sons of Israel, 'Not one of you shall eat blood nor shall the
sojourner who sojourns in your midst eat blood'. The basic
structure of this section then consists of a statement of
conduct, the reason such conduct is required, and a restate-
ment, in prohibitive form, of the original statement of conduct.
 It is important to note that the original statement prohibits
the eating of *any* blood. This is a general statement that

sacrifice is only effective if performed at the ritually prescribed area. It is
clear, then, that for the ritual to be effective, there must be a convergence
of performance and place. The mere performance of the rite is not enough
to insure its effectiveness. The rite must be preformed in the prescribed
place.
1 Thus, v. 8 refers to עלה או־זבח and the verb is יעלה. Verses 3-7, while
generally concerned with the שלמים sacrifices (v. 5), also speak of the זבח
(vv. 5, 7) and use the verb (יזבח) (vv. 5, 7). As noted above, there are textual
traditions which include the עלה in v. 4.

excludes 'all blood' from human consumption. There is no
indication that this is only the blood of the שלמים, as suggested by
Milgrom. Verse 11 gives two reasons for why the eating of
blood is prohibited. First, the eating of blood is prohibited
because (כי) the life of the flesh is blood. This is in agreement
with the statement in Gen. 9.4. The life is sacred, outside of the
prescribed human bounds, hence, bounded and set apart, and
cannot be consumed by humans. Second, the eating of blood is
prohibited because Yahweh has given the blood to be used on
the altar—to perform *kipper*. Indeed, the blood performs its
kipper-function because (כי) the life is in the blood. The blood is
once again placed outside bounds of human consumption by
being marked for its use in sacred ritual. Before continuing
the discussion of these verses, it will be helpful to examine the
rest of the chapter.

Verses 13-16
Verse 13 clearly marks a new section with its introductory
ואיש איש מבני ישראל. There are actually two distinct units within
these verses. Verse 15 begins with וכל-נפש אשר, an indication
that a new element of instruction has begun. Verses 15-16 are
concerned with defilement that occurs when someone eats
what dies of itself or what is torn by beasts (cf. Lev. 11.39-40).
These verses follow the instructions of vv. 13-14 which deal
with the proper ritual actions for *game animals* killed for food.
Verses 15-16 thus provide instruction concerning animals of
the field obtained for food. It is clear that vv. 15-16 have some
connections with the rules concerning corpse-contamination
since the issue in these twelve verses shifts to *defilement*. An
animal that dies of natural causes or an animal that is torn by
beasts defile because their ritual/sacred slaughter cannot be
performed and their blood cannot be properly manipulated. It
should be noted that these two elements are combined in
normal sacrificial rituals because the slaughter is performed
in a way that allows the blood to be used. The act of slaughter
itself becomes a sacred act, but controlled by ritual structures.
    Verses 13-14 form a unit, clearly indicated by the use of כי at
the beginning of v. 14. These verses are concerned with game
animals—beast and bird. Verse 13 gives instructions for the

proper disposal of the blood of a game animal that is killed for food:[1] 'he will pour out (וְשָׁפַךְ) its blood and cover it with dust'. These verses show a clear recognition of the difference between slaughter for sacrifice and slaughter for food. Even when the slaughter concerns a game animal and is done in order to obtain food, the act of killing must be placed in a ritual context by the manipulation of the blood. It cannot be consumed, but must be poured out in the dirt and covered. Verse 14 states the reason for this requirement: 'Because (כִּי) the life of *all flesh* is its blood, it is its life, and I have said to the sons of Israel, "You shall not eat the blood of *any flesh*, because the life of *all flesh* is its blood. Everyone who eats it will be cut off."'[2]

Again, it is the relation of the blood of an animal to its life that demands that the blood not be eaten. The slaughter of these animals does not require that they be brought before Yahweh and, hence, there is no requirement that their blood be brought to the altar. Still, the blood must be poured out on the ground and covered. In that this is a prescribed act that rests on the prohibition of the human consumption of blood, it can be referred to as a sacred act; it establishes boundaries that cannot be crossed over by human beings. It recognizes and maintains the boundaries placed on human action which prohibit the human use of blood because it is the life of the animal.

This discussion suggests that vv. 10-12 are best understood as a transitional bridge between vv. 3-9 and vv.13-16. Verses 3-9 deal with the sacrificial animals and the presentation of the animal at the door of the tent of meeting and the use of their blood on the altar. Verses 13-16 are concerned with animals of the field and how they are to be eaten. Their blood is to be poured out and not eaten. Verses 10-12 form a bridge between these two units of text and serve as a *general statement* about the blood of animals. It is removed from human consumption for two reasons. It contains the life of the animal

---

1 The phrase 'an animal or bird which may be eaten' shows recognition of the distinction between animals which may be eaten and animals that may not be eaten, i.e., the difference between clean and unclean animals. Thus, there is indication that this verse is aware of some type of system of animal classification such as is found in Lev. 11.

2 The reading of the LXX is generally followed at this point.

which is prohibited as food, and, in this way, placed into the sacred realm. At the same time, the blood is removed from human consumption because it has been given by Yahweh to perform the *kipper*-function on the altar. Thus, *all* blood is prohibited from human consumption. This last reason, however, can only be stated by the Priestly writers after Moses has recieved the divine instructions from Yahweh for the structure and operation of the cult.

Verse 11 may, then, be translated as follows: 'For the life of the flesh is in the blood. And I have assigned it to you [to put] on the altar in order to *kipper* on behalf of your lives. For it is the blood, with the life, that *kippers*.' Such a rendering, in light of the above discussion, points to the bi-polar value of blood as a symbol for life *and* death. The נפש of the flesh is in the blood which has been assigned to the altar to *kipper* for the נפש of the people. The life of the people is 'ransomed' by the life of the animal when its blood is properly manipulated.[1] This recognizes the requirement of a 'reckoning' by Yahweh when the life is taken as indicated in Gen. 9.4-6. This blood can only be obtained, however, when the animal is killed. Death is the prerequiste, but, at the same time, the necessary reason for the ritual manipulation of the blood. The blood, with the life of the animal in it, effects life for and communicates life to the human, but it requires the death of the animal in order to obtain the blood. In this way, blood serves as the agent for cleansing defilement from contact with death and for effecting passage from the realm of death to the realm of life.

---

1 While 'ransom' seems to be the key idea of *kipper* in this verse, caution must be exercised. As seen throughout this study, *kipper* has a broad range of functions in the cult. Thus, the *kipper*-act involves blood and is concerned with the ritual elimination of sin, and more importantly, the effects of sin. Hence, *kipper* must be recognized as a word carrying a broad range of meanings which must be identified specifically according to the specific function it has in any given ritual.

Chapter 6

NUMBERS 19

Introduction

The basic purpose of the ritual activity of Numbers 19 is the preparation of waters which are then to be used for the cleansing of one who has become unclean (טמא) through contact with a corpse. In Israel, as in many other cultures, corpse-contamination was considered a severe and dangerous form of defilement.[1] The boundary between life and death separates basic forms of existence, absolutely separated categories, which must be kept distinct. In Israel, death represents a break with life, understood as the created norm for human existence. As such, it represents a severe disruption of the order of creation.

The importance of undergoing the necessary cleansing rites for corpse-contamination and the consequences of failure to do so are emphasized in Num. 19.13, 20. The one who fails to undergo the cleansing defiles (טמא) the tabernacle of Yahweh and is to be cut off (כרת) from the people. The *kareth* penalty serves as an ominous threat against the failure to keep separate the sacred and the profane, the clean and the unclean, and involves not only the transgressor but includes the extermination of the lineage as well.[2] In that the *kareth*

---

1 See G.B. Gray, *Numbers* (ICC; 1903; rpt. Edinburgh: Clark, 1965), pp. 243-45; Pedersen, *Israel*, I, pp. 490-96.
2 See D.J. Wold, 'The *KARETH* Penalty in P: Rationale and Cases' (SBLSP 1; ed. P.J. Achtemeier; Missoula, Montana: Scholars Press, 1979), p. 1025.

penalty is concerned with the most basic categorical distinctions of Israelite cosmology,[1] its presence in reference to corpse-contamination suggests that such defilement is of a severe type—confusion of the boundaries between life and death. Numbers 19 is a clear example of how ritual serves to guard, maintain, and, when necessary, restore the categories of Yahweh's created order.

Numbers 19 is a ritual designed for the cleansing of a defiled individual, a cleansing that includes a passage from one state of existence to another, from one status to another. It is clear, however, that the concern for the cleansing of the individual is placed in the context of the order, wholeness, and wellbeing of the community—failure to enact the cleansing ritual defiles the tabernacle which would have consequences for the community. Thus, Numbers 19 presents a ritual for an individual which has as its concern the restoration of right social and cultic order.

This chapter will present arguments in support of the following theses:

1. The spatial categories operative in Numbers 19 reflect a complex order in which the categories of holy/profane must be carefully distinguished from the categories of clean/unclean. While these sets of categories must be kept distinct, there5 are important points of intersection between them.
2. The concern for cleansing from corpse-contamination must be situated within and understood in terms of the Priestly traditionists' concern for right social and cultic order.

See also Frymer-Kensky, 'Pollution', pp. 403-405. Frymer-Kensky states, 'The deeds that entail the *karet* sanction are acts against the fundamental principles of Israelite cosmology; in particular, acts that blur the most vital distinction in the Israelite classificatory system, the separation of sacred and profane' (p. 404).

1 Wold ('The *KARETH* Penalty in P', pp. 3-24) divides *kareth* cases into the following types of violations: (1) against sacred time; (2) against sacred substance; (3) against failure to perform purification rituals; (4) illicit worship; (5) illicit sexual relations.

3. The blood in the 'waters of impurity', derived from the red cow, which is termed a חטאת, functions to cleanse *and* restore to life the corpse-contaminated.

Type of Material
The chapter is made up of different types of material.[1] Verses 1-10 are instructions on how to prepare the ashes of the red heifer which will then be used for making water with which the contaminated person will be cleansed. Verses 17-19 continue these instructions and detail how the ashes are combined with water to form the cleansing mixture and then how the mixture is to be applied to the contaminated person or object. Thus, vv. 1-10 and vv. 17-19 may be understood as ritual instructions for effecting the cleansing of a corpse-contaminated person or object.

Verses 11-16 are of a different character. Verses 11-13 present two possible results that might occur when one has come into contact with a corpse. Verses 11-12 state the first possibility. Verse 11 presents the situation (or case): 'The one who touches the dead body of any person shall be unclean for seven days'.[2] The correct response to the situation is detailed in v. 12a: 'he shall cleanse himself with it [the mixture] on the third day and on the seventh day he will be clean'. Verse 12b presents the alternative possibility: 'but if he does not cleanse himself on the third day, he will not be clean'. Thus, v. 12 details two possible responses to the unclean state with two results—clean or unclean.

Verse 13 presents the same case—'anyone who touches the dead body of a person who has died'[3]—but further clarifies the results of failure to undertake the cleansing ritual—'and does

---

1 See Rendtorff, *Gesetze*, pp. 64-66; S. Wefing, 'Beobachtungen zum Ritual mit der roten Kuh (Num 19, 1-10a)', *ZAW* 93 (1981), pp. 342-59.
2 This is a nominal formulation (see M.J. Buss, 'The Distinction Between Civil and Criminal Law in Ancient Israel', *Proceedings of the Sixth World Congress of Jewish Studies* I [Jerusalem: Academic Press, 1977], pp. 59-60) and is here presented as (priestly) instruction which defines an unclean state (see Lev. 10.10). Cf. Lev. 11.24 for a similar formulation with a concluding temporal notice.
3 The parallel to v. 11 is clear in spite of the minor differences in formulation.

not cleanse himself, defiles the tabernacle of Yahweh, and that person shall be cut off from Israel.[1] Because the waters of impurity were not sprinkled upon him, he will be unclean, his uncleanness is still upon him'. These instructions concerning corpse-contamination define the unclean state brought about by contact with a corpse, describe the means for a return to a clean state, and provide a reason, through the *kareth* penalty, for undertaking the cleansing ritual.

Verses 14-16 further define persons and objects that may be defiled by a corpse; they define further cases of such defilement. There are two distinct situations presented in these verses. Verses 14-15 concern persons and objects that are found within a tent in which a person has died.[2] Verse 14 concerns persons: 'Everyone who comes into the tent and everyone who is in the tent will be unclean for seven days'. Verse 15 concerns objects: 'And every open vessel which does not have a cover fastened on it is unclean'. It is clear in both cases that the uncleanness of the corpse can defile by proximity within an enclosed area. Verse 16 shifts the focus away from a tent and defines the situation when someone touches a corpse in an open field: 'And everyone in an open field who touches one slain with a sword, or a dead body, or a bone of a man, or a grave, will be unclean for seven days'.[3] Defilement from a corpse can be contracted by direct contact or by proximity within an enclosed area. In all cases, the unclean state lasts for seven days and requires the waters of impurity to effect cleansing.

The chapter does not narrate the actual performance of the ritual, but rather gives instructions for how the ritual is to be

---

1 The dominant formulation of the situation that entails the *kareth* penalty is a noun followed by אֲשֶׁר (e.g., Num. 9.13; Lev. 23.29; 7.27; Exod. 30.33). It is also found, however, with a participle formulation as here (cf. Exod. 12.15; Lev. 7.25; Exod. 31.14).

2 The introductory formula of v. 14 has two basic formulations: one using the absolute תּוֹרָה and one using the construct תּוֹרַת. The forumla serves both as an introduction to instructions and as a conclusion to a series of instructions, and all the cases are concerned either with (1) ritual matters of sacrifices and/or offerings or (2) ritual matters of clean and unclean. See J. Begrich, 'Die priesterliche Tora', in *Werden und Wesen des Alten Testaments* (BZAW 66; Berlin: Töpelmann, 1936), pp. 63-88.

3 This case is formulated with אֲשֶׁר.

performed when it does take place. This may account for the
insertion of the instructions regarding the cases of corpse-
contamination and the alternative possibilities resulting from
this contact. In this way, the text presents instructions for the
ritual *and* the cases that will give rise to its enactment.

History of the Text
It is generally held that the ritual of Numbers 19 reflects a
very old practice that has been adapted by Israel for its own
use. The chapter is often considered to be a secondary addition
to the Priestly strata.[1] Additions to an original text are found
particularly in the opening verse which directs the instructions to Moses and Aaron, the ascription of the enactment of
the ritual preparations of the ashes to Eleazer (v. 3), and in the
case instructions of vv. 11-16.[2]

Milgrom has argued that the ritual of Numbers 19 reflects
a pre-Israelite rite of exorcism which 'has been transformed
by the Israelite values inherent in its sacrificial procedure'.
Through this transformation, 'the priestly legislators have
reduced the degree of corpse-contamination from the severest
of the severe impurities to the least of them'.[3] According to
Milgrom, the transformation can be seen in three ways in
particular.[4] First, the ritual of Numbers 19, unlike the rituals
of Leviticus 16 and Leviticus 14, does not include a rite of
elimination of the dangerous contagion. Second, the severity of
corpse-contamination is reduced because Numbers 19 does
not expulse the corpse-contaminated person from the camp as
is called for in the older law of Num. 5.2. Nowhere does the
text of Numbers 19 state that the individual is to be expelled
nor is the statement found that after the cleansing the
individual may return to the camp. Indeed, the text clearly
states that failure to undergo the cleansing ritual will result in
the defilement of the tabernacle (v. 13), a situation only

1 Milgrom, 'The Red Cow', 72; Wefing, 'Beobachtungen zum Ritual mit der
  roten Kuh', pp. 362-63.
2 See Gray, *Numbers*, pp. 241-56; Noth, *Numbers*, pp. 139-43; Rendtorff,
  Gesetze, pp. 64-66.
3 'The Red Cow', pp. 71-72.
4 *Ibid.*, pp. 70-71.

possible if the defiled is within the camp boundaries. Finally,
the corpse-contaminated does not undergo bathings on the
first day and brings no sacrifices at the end of the cleansing
process. Thus, the ritual reflects a situation in which the
severity of corpse-contamination has been greatly reduced.

Two problems remain, however, which suggest that the
transformation of the ritual has not been entirely successful.
(1) If the corpse-contaminated is not expelled from the camp,
why does the preparation of the ashes have to take place
outside the camp? This problem is compounded when the text
clearly states that this is a sacrificial act. If the sprinkling of
the waters is to take place inside the camp, why does their
preparation not take place inside the camp, at the tent, as is
normal for a חטאת? (2) The text reflects a clear concern for the
defiling nature of the ashes (vv. 9-10) and the waters of
impurity/cleansing (v. 21). Why, then, are the potentially
defiling waters of impurity/cleansing brought inside the
camp? Would this not present a threatening and dangerous
situation?

The Elements of the Ritual

Materials and Objects
This ritual calls for no special ritual clothing, but it does
employ clothing in its larger structure. Verse 7 instructs that
the priest is to wash his clothes and bathe his body after he has
sprinkled some of the red cow's blood toward the tent of meeting and the cow has been burned. The reason for this washing
will be discussed below, but it is clear that this washing of the
clothes is part of a purification ritual for the priest. The same is
true for the instructions in v. 19 which state that the one who
performs the sprinkling act is to wash his clothes and bathe his
body in order to become clean.

Verse 18 details those objects which receive ritual action.
These are unclean objects that are sprinkled with the מי נדה—a
tent and its furnishings. This list, including unclean persons as
well, refers to the instructions in vv. 14-16. The purpose of this
action is to effect cleansing.

The materials used in this ritual are of a limited number,
the majority being involved in the preparation of the מי נדה, and

the preparation and use of the מי נדה dominate the ritual instructions of Numbers 19. נדה generally means 'impurity' and quite often refers to a woman's impurity during her menstruation (e.g., Lev. 12.2; 15.20, 24, 25, 26, 33). In translating the phrase as 'waters for impurity', the meaning is 'the waters that cleanse impurity'.[1]

In preparing these waters, the major ingredient is a red cow, without blemish, in which there is no defect, on which a yoke has never been placed. While the requirement of a 'red' cow might have some connection with the color's association with blood,[2] caution must be exercised because of the difficulty in knowing the exact color designations of ancient Israel, and the obvious problem of finding a 'red' cow.[3] It is probable, however, that a symbolic association with 'blood' is intended by the fact that the color is specified at all. Some of the blood of the cow is sprinkled toward the front of the tent of meeting and then the whole cow is burned—skin, flesh, blood, and dung (v. 5). Into this fire is thrown cedar wood, hyssop, and scarlet string. The ashes that remain after this burning are then mixed with running water (מים חיים) in a vessel to form the cleansing solution to be sprinkled on the unclean (vv. 17-19). It is further noted that hyssop is to be used for the purpose of the sprinkling (v. 18). Beyond this, the only other material used in the ritual is water. The priest who officiates must wash his

1 The phrase is found elsewhere in Num. 31.23 with instructions for booty taken in war. What passes through the fire will be clean but must also be sprinkled with the מי נדה. A similar phrase is found in Num. 8.7 in the ritual for the establishment of the Levites. The Levites are to be sprinkled with the מי חטאת. Whether a parallel should be drawn between the ritual of Num. 19 and Num. 5.11-22 (see Wefing, 'Beobachtungen', pp. 362-63) is doubtful in light of the different purposes of the rituals, the different functions of the water in the two rituals, and the different manner in which the water is used.

2 See Milgrom, 'The Red Cow', 65; Feldman (*Biblical and Post-Biblical Defilement and Mourning*, pp. 153-55, n. 27) notes the association of red (blood) and death and the connection of blood with life in many cultures. McCarthy ('The Symbolism of Blood and Sacrifice', pp. 166-76; and 'Further Notes', pp. 205-10) argues that the association of blood with life was peculiar to Israel. Turner (*The Forest of Symbols*, pp. 59-92) notes that red has a dual significance of life and death in Ndembu ritual.

3 See A. Brenner, *Colour Terms in the Old Testament* (JSOTS 21; Sheffield: JSOT, 1982), pp. 58-80.

clothes and bathe his body in water before returning to the camp (v. 7); the one who burns the cow is to do likewise (v. 8); the one who deposits the ashes is to wash his clothes (v. 10); and the one who performs the sprinkling must wash his clothes and bathe his body after the sprinkling ceremony (v. 19).

Ritual Roles

Several distinct roles are exhibited in the ritual of Numbers 19. The most obvious is the person who has become contaminated by a corpse. The ritual serves as a means of passage for this individual from an unclean state to a clean state. A second important role is filled by the priest, identified in v. 3 as Eleazer. The primary role of the priest is the act of blood sprinkling toward the front of the tent of meeting (v. 4). This is consistent with the Priestly viewpoint that the priests are the only ones who should perform sacred rites with blood. This action is normally concentrated on the altar, or in the holy place, and is, therefore, limited to the priests.

Four other roles are suggested in the text. Verse 3b suggests a third party who actually burns the red cow. This is evident from the לפניו. Someone is to slaughter the cow before Eleazer. Similarly, v. 5a implies that someone burns the cow before Eleazer (in this case לעיניו). That the one who burns the cow is distinct from the priest is clearly indicated by v. 8 where it is stated that the one who burns the cow must wash his clothes and bathe his body. These instructions were already given for the priest in v. 7.[1] It is possible, although not stated, that the same person who slaughters the cow also burns it. Verse 9 states that a clean man is to gather the ashes and deposit them in a clean place outside the camp. This is certainly a person distinct from the one who burns the cow in that the instructions of v. 8 state that the one who burns the cow is unclean.

---

1 The fact that no cleansing instructions are given for the one who slaughters the cow is probably due to the fact that the slaughtering takes place before the sprinkling of the blood toward the tent. This act constitutes the moment when the animal becomes dedicated to its ritual purpose. It is only after this act that the animal can make unclean. See Milgrom, 'The Red Cow', p. 66.

This is further shown by the instructions of v. 10 for the one who gathers and deposits the ashes. Finally, a clean person is instructed to perform the actual sprinkling of the mixture on the corpse-contaminated person (vv. 18-19).

Spatial Categories
Three spatial categories are specified in the text. First, the ritual of the burning cow is to take place *outside* the camp (אל-מחוץ למחנה, v. 3). The fact that the Priestly writers stipulate that a חטאת sacrifice is to take place away from the altar suggests that a dangerous situation is being addressed. Second, the priest is to sprinkle some of the blood of the cow toward *the front of the tent of meeting* (אל-נכח פני אהל-מועד, v. 4). It can be seen here that even when taking place outside the camp, Priestly ritual takes the tent as the focal point of blood ritual. A final spatial category indicated in Numbers 19 is the place where the ashes of the red cow are to be deposited. This is specified as a 'clean place outside the camp' (v. 9). It is clear from this that 'cleanness' as a conceptual category is not limited to the *inside* of the Israelite camp. As will be seen, these spatial categories provide significant clues in understanding the ritual of Numbers 19.

Temporal Categories
Two temporal specifications are stated in Numbers 19 with regard to the period of uncleanness. The first concerns the time of uncleanness for the priest (v. 7), the one who burns the cow (v. 8), the one who deposits the ashes of the cow (v. 10), and the one who actually sprinkles the mixture (v. 19). All four of these must undertake a washing of their clothes and a bathing of their bodies (although not specified for the depositor) and are then said to be unclean until evening.[1]

The primary temporal category is the seven-day period necessary to effect the cleansing and passage of the corpse-contaminated person. This seven-day period is also found in rituals designed to cleanse major pollution. Numbers 19 states that the unclean person is to be sprinkled on the third and

1 See Frymer-Kensky, 'Pollution', p. 402.

seventh days. As already noted, the seven day period is associated with rituals that effect a dangerous passage in ritual processes.

Ritual Actions

  I. *Preparations* (vv. 2b-3b): Tell (דבר) the sons of Israel to bring (ויקחו) to you a red cow, without defect, in which there is no blemish, and upon which no yoke has come. And they will give (ונתחם) it to Eleazer the priest, and he will bring (הוציא) it outside of the camp.

 II. *Ritual Preparation of the Ashes* (3bβ-6):
    A. Blood manipulation (3bβ-4): And it will be slaughtered (ושחט) before him. And Eleazer the priest shall take (ולקח) some of its blood with his finger and he shall sprinkle (והזה) some of the blood toward the front of the tent of meeting seven times.
    B. The burning (vv. 5-6): And the cow will be burned (ושרף) before his eyes—its skin, flesh, blood, and dung will be burned (ושרף). Then the priest will take (ולקח) the cedar wood, the hyssop, and the scarlet string and will throw (והשליך) them into the midst of the burning cow.

III. *Instructions for those involved in the preparation of the ashes* (vv. 7-10):
    A. The priest (v. 7): Then the priest will wash (וכבס) his clothes and bathe (ורחץ) his body in water and, afterward, he will come (יבא) into the camp. The priest will be unclean (וטמא) until evening.
    B. The one who burns the cow (v. 8): And the one who burns (והשרף) it shall wash (וכבס) his clothes in water and bathe (ורחץ) his body in water. And he will be unclean (וטמא) until evening.
    C. The one who gathers and deposits the ashes (vv. 9-10): And a man who is clean shall gather (ואסף) the ashes of the cow and deposit (והניח) them outside the camp in a clean place. And it will be kept (והיתה למשמרת) for the congregation of the sons of Israel for the waters of impurity; it is a חטאת. And the one who gathers the ashes of the cow shall wash (וכבס) his clothes. And he will be unclean (וטמא) until evening. And this will be for the sons of Israel and for the sojourner who sojourns in their midst a perpetual statute.

IV. *The Use of the Ashes* (vv. 17-19): And they will take (ולקחו)
for the unclean some of the ashes of the burned חטאת and
running water will be placed (ונתן) in a vessel. Then a
clean person shall take (ולקח) hyssop and dip (וטבל) it in the
water and sprinkle (והזה) it on the tent and all the
furnishings, and upon the persons who were there, and
upon the one who touched the bone, or the slain, or the
dead, or the grave. Then the clean shall sprinkle (והזה) on
the unclean on the third day and upon the seventh day.
Thus shall he cleanse (וחטאו) him on the seventh day. And
he shall wash (וכבס) his clothes and bathe (ורחץ) in water
and be clean (וטהר) at evening.[1]

The Meaning of the Ritual and its Enactment

It is clear that the ritual described in Numbers 19 may be
divided into two major segments. The first is concerned with
the preparation of the ashes of the red cow and the deposit of
these ashes in an appropriate place outside the camp (vv. 2-
10). The second segment is concerned with the actual use of
the ashes in sprinkling the contaminated individual (vv. 17-
19). It should be noted that while the primary purpose of the
ritual is the sprinkling of the waters for impurity on the
corpse-contaminated person or object, the preparation of these
ashes receives more attention in the text and is itself perceived
to be a ritual enactment.

The Preparation of the Ashes: vv. 2-10
The first act of the ritual is the obtaining of an appropriate
animal from which the ashes will be gained. This is to be a red
cow without defect, which has no blemish, and which has
never had a yoke upon it. A female animal is appropriate for a

---

1 The last washings and the declaration of uncleanness are understood to
refer to the one who does the sprinkling. There are three reasons for this.
First, the seven days have already been stated as the time of the corpse-
contamination. Second, the one contaminated by a corpse has already
received a 'washing' with the waters of impurity in the sprinkling ceremony. Finally, v. 21 states that the clean person who comes into contact
with the waters of impurity becomes unclean until evening. This is
precisely not the case for the corpse-contaminated who is *cleansed by* these
waters.

חטאת for the individual (Num. 6.14; Lev. 4.27; 5.6; 14.10),
although it is normally prescribed as a female from the flock.
While פרה is sometimes taken to mean a young cow or a cow
that has not given birth,[1] there is no real evidence to support
such a viewpoint.[2] Milgrom suggests that a female was
chosen because the animal was viewed as a חטאת, and a bovine
was chosen in this instance to obtain the maximum amount of
ashes.[3]

The requirements that the animal be without defect and
without blemish serve to place it within the context of a
sacrifice in that these requirements are also prescribed for
sacrificial animals (see Lev. 1.3, 10; 3.1, 6; 4.3; 22.20, 21, 25). It
is, therefore, appropriate to say that this animal is being
described in terms of traditional sacrificial categories and
should be understood as a sacrifice.[4]

It is precisely because the animal is perceived as a sacrifice
that the prescription that it be a 'red' cow may be important.
While it certainly must be recognized that אדמה reflects a
broad range of colors that would be seen as 'reddish brown' or
'brown' today,[5] the connection that אדמה has with the color for
blood cannot be completely overlooked.[6] It is not necessary to
have a 'bright red' cow intended in order to make this connection. If the 'red cow' is specified on the basis of its relationship to the color of blood, as seems probable, then the traditionists have placed the ritual in the context of the symbolic values
of blood. Blood is used to effect dangerous passage from death
to life precisely because it holds together images of death and

---

1 P.J. Budd, *Numbers* (WBC 5; Waco: Word Books, 1984), p. 212.
2 See Gray, *Numbers*, p. 249.
3 'The Red Cow', p. 65. Firth ('Offering and Sacrifice', pp. 12-23) discusses
   the economic and pragmatic nature of choosing sacrificial animals. Such
   considerations may very well be at work in this ritual. It should be noted
   that a female cow is also prescribed for the ritual of Deut. 21.1-9.
4 Contra Gray, *Numbers*, pp. 249-50.
5 Brenner, *Colour Terms*, pp. 62-65; Snaith, *Leviticus*, p. 166.
6 See 2 Kgs 3.22 where the morning sun shines on the water and it is said to
   be 'red as blood' (אדמים כדם). Elsewhere the word is used to describe the
   stain of grapes (Isa. 63.2), lentils (Gen. 25.30), the color of a horse (Zech.
   1.8; 6.2), and human skin (Cant. 5.10). The fact that the traditionists felt a
   need to specify the color suggests that the color was indeed of significance.

life. As a tensive symbol, it has the power to effect passage from death to life because it partakes of both of these states.

The cow is to be presented to Eleazer the priest by 'the people of Israel'. This suggests that a ritual is under consideration that has the larger social order as its concern. The community is responsible to bring the sacrificial animal and give it to the priest. This not only means that the ashes are available for anyone in the community, but also that this cleansing ritual is understood as a community concern—it is designed to protect the social order.

The priest takes the animal outside the camp where it is slaughtered (שחט) before Eleazer. This word is typically used in P for the *ritual* slaughter of an animal, i.e., for the slaughter of a sacrificial animal.[1] Indeed, the slaughter of an animal in the context of the sacred is an essential characteristic of sacrifice.[2] That this slaughter takes place in the context of the sacred is indicated by the presence of the priest, the sprinkling of the blood toward the tent of meeting, and the use of the animal's ashes for the purpose of cleansing a defiled individual. These elements all serve to indicate that the text understands the slaughter of the red cow as a sacrifice.

The text clearly identifies the ritual as a sacrificial ritual. In v. 17 the cow is specifically identified as a burnt חטאת. In addition, v. 9 identifies the ashes as a חטאת.[3] This suggests one transformation of the חטאת necessitated by this ritual. Normally, the remains of a חטאת are disposed of by burning and/or eating. The ashes in Num. 19, however, function as an *ongoing* חטאת. A second transformation of the חטאת in this ritual is seen in the fact that the חטאת mixture, composed of the ashes

---

1 See N.H. Snaith, 'The Verbs ZĀBAH and ŠĀHAT', *VT* 25 (1975), pp. 242-46; Milgrom, 'Profane Slaughter and a Formulaic Key to the Composition of Deuteronomy', *HUCA* 47 (1976), pp. 13-14. Both writers suggest that שחט means to slaughter by cutting the throat.

2 This is argued by the following: Hubert and Mauss, *Sacrifice*, p. 9; Evans-Pritchard, 'The Meaning of Sacrifice', p. 21; Middleton, *Lugbara Religion*, p. 88; Firth, 'Offering and Sacrifice', pp. 12-13; van Baaren, 'Theoretical Speculations on Sacrifice', p. 9; van Baal, 'Offering, Sacrifice and Gift', p. 11; Turner, 'Sacrifice as Quintessential Process', p. 189.

3 Milgrom ('Paradox of the Red Cow', p. 67) argues that the *ketib* is to be followed so that the phrase 'it is a חטאת' refers to the ashes and not the cow.

of the red cow and running water, is placed on a person. Normally, the blood of the חטאת is not placed on a person.

After the slaughter of the cow, the priest undertakes a rite involving the blood of the cow. He takes some of the blood on his finger and sprinkles it seven times toward the front of the tent of meeting (v. 4). The text offers no specific explanation for this act. As discussed above, the ritual act of sprinkling has four distinct purposes: (1) preparation, (2) consecration, (3) purification, and (4) purgation.[1] As discussed there, consecration, purification, and purgation were involved as the anointing substance was placed on an object or person. It is clear, since the blood of the red cow is not sprinkled on anything in Numbers 19, that this act must be understood in terms of preparation.

In agreement with Milgrom, this act of preparation is best understood as the moment when the blood itself is consecrated and thereby made effective for its use in the larger ritual. As such, this sprinkling is parallel to the sprinkling of the blood of the חטאת sprinkled before the veil when the blood is brought inside the tent. It serves to present the blood to Yahweh, to make known its purpose, and to place the blood in a sacrificial state. It is through this ritual presentation and preparation that the blood is placed into a 'safe' ritual category—it is sacrificial blood that has been placed into a specific ritual situation for a specific ritual use. This is of particular importance in this ritual because the ashes will continue to function as an ongoing חטאת. The act of presentation and preparation serves to place the blood and the ashes in a specific and ritually guarded state.

The blood of the cow is sprinkled toward the front of the tent of meeting. Milgrom argues that this is best understood as toward the altar and that the sprinkling is equivalent to placing the blood on the altar.[2] This situation is demanded because the ritual takes place outside the camp. There are two problems with this proposal. First, the writers chose to say 'toward the front of the tent of meeting' and not 'toward the altar'. It would seem that if the altar had been intended, the

1 See above, pp. 82-85.
2 'The Red Cow', p. 66.

writers would have stated this. Second, Milgrom argues that the purpose of the placing of the blood on the altar in the חטאת was for the purpose of purgation of the altar. This purgation takes place as the blood absorbs the impurity of the altar on which it is placed. This is clearly distinct from sprinkling the blood for the purpose of consecrating the blood to prepare it for purgation of an individual, as he argues for the sprinkling rite in Numbers 19.

The front of the tent of meeting is a spatial designation in P that indicates a focal point of ritual activity[1] and is distinct from the altar. Specific types of ritual activity are associated with the altar, but the front of the tent of meeting/tabernacle is a broader category which indicates a place of sacred, ritual activity. Indeed, it is often described as the place of presenta-tion of sacrifices. Thus, the fact that the blood of a חטאת is sprinkled toward the front of the tent in order to prepare it for further ritual use indicates another transformation of the חטאת in this ritual. This is, in part, required because the ritual takes place outside the camp. It is also required, however, because of the nature of the ritual. This חטאת is not designed for purgation of some part of the tabernacle structure, but to provide ritual passage from a defiled state brought about by contact with a corpse to a state of purity.

Thus, there are three distinct transformations of the חטאת found in the ritual of Numbers 19. (1) The ashes of the red cow function as an on-going, continual חטאת. This is a shift from the normal חטאת in which the animal is slaughtered and its blood used at that moment. (2) The blood is sprinkled toward the front of the tent of meeting, from *outside* the camp boundaries, to prepare it for further ritual use. The sprinkling act of preparation is distinct from the regular חטאת. (3) The blood of the חטאת of the red cow and ashes is placed on a person for the purposes of purification and passage. This is distinct from normal use of the חטאת blood which is placed on sacred objects to purge and restore them.

Verses 5-6 give the instructions for the burning of the cow along with cedar wood, hyssop, and scarlet string. In this case,

---

1 See above, p. 56.

the burning is not intended as an עלה,[1] but is simply the necessary procedure for obtaining the ashes to be mixed with the water. The whole animal is burned, but it is the blood that endows the ashes with their special purificatory powers. It is just at this point that this ritual demonstrates its close conceptual relationship to the ritual for the purification of the recovered leper. Blood is the necessary purificatory agent for purification from contact with death. It is especially effective for this because it not only purifies but also communicates life to the individual. This would help explain the application of the blood of the חטאת upon the person. It is necessary because, in these instances, purification is only fully realized by the communication of life to the individual. This is a case not only of passage from an unclean state to a clean state, but from 'death' to 'life'. The exact significance of the other elements, the cedar wood, hyssop, and scarlet thread, remains unexplained. It is clear that they were perceived to play an important role in the process of cleansing, but precisely what that importance was is not stated.

A detailed list of instructions follow in vv. 7-10 concerning those who are involved in the preparation of the ashes. The primary focus of these instructions is the uncleanness contracted by those who come into contact with the red cow or its ashes. Verse 7 addresses the priest. The priest must wash his clothes and bathe his body and then is unclean until evening. Verse 8 details the same instructions for the one who burns the cow.[2] Finally, v. 10 offers the same instructions for the one

---

1 But see Wefing ('Ritual mit der roten Kuh', pp. 360-61) who sees behind this ritual a pre-P form of a burnt offering. It is extremely difficult to so interpret it in its present form, however, because there is no indication given of the sacrificial purpose of the burning. The cow is burned simply to obtain its ashes. This is supported further by the fact that the עלה is not understood to effect purification or purgation of any type. There is no evidence to support that the עלה in Israel was ever employed for purposes of purification.

2 The instructions for the priest include the statement that after his washings he may enter into the camp. It is probable that this applies to the other participants as well and, although not specifically stated, is assumed for them.

who gathers the ashes.[1] These cases have in common their contact with the presented cow or its ashes. The fact that it is termed a חטאת explains the uncleanness contracted by contact with it.

An important issue that needs attention is the prescription in v. 9 that the ashes of the cow be deposited 'outside the camp in a clean place'. The same formula is found in Lev. 4.12 with reference to the refuse of the חטאת and in Lev. 6.4b with reference to the deposit of the ashes from the altar of the עלה. These phrases must be seen in conjunction with the similar phrase that speaks of 'an unclean place outside the city' which occurs in Lev. 14.40, 41, 45 with regard to the refuse of a house declared to be 'leprous'. This is important in light of the emphasis that has been placed on the camp boundaries and the need to protect these boundaries from impurity.

The discussion of these spatial categories must begin with the recognition that there is no simple one to one correlation between holy and clean, on the one hand, and profane and unclean, on the other.[2] Thus, Lev 10.10 distinguishes two distinct, although not unrelated, categories of priestly judgments—to make known the distinction, to separate, between the holy (הקדש) and the profane (החל) and between the impure (הטמא) and the pure (הטהר).

The most basic categorical distinction made by the Priestly writers is that between the holy and the profane. This basic categorical distinction is defined by the paradigmatic division between the holy of holies, set apart by the כפרת, and all other spaces. Within the context of this basic division, however, a further refinement may be seen in the grades of holiness reflected in the tabernacle complex.[3] The whole tabernacle complex is holy in relation to other spaces, but with less and

---

1 It is not specifically stated that the gatherer is to bathe, although it is probably assumed.
2 On the categories of 'clean' and 'unclean', see J. Döller, *Die Reinheits- und Speisergesetze des Alten Testaments in religionsgeschichtlicher Beleuchtung* (Münster: Aschendorffsche Verlagsbuchhandlung, 1917); W.H. Gispen, 'The Distinction between Clean and Unclean', *OTS* 5 (1948), pp. 190-96; H. Cazelles, 'Pureté et impureté: Ancien Testament', *DBSup* 9 (1979), pp. 491-508.
3 See Milgrom, 'Israel's Sanctuary', pp. 390-99 and his 'The Compass of Biblical Sancta', *JQR* 65 (1974), pp. 205-16.

less degrees of holiness found as one moves away from the holy of holies.

In light of this system of holiness, it may be said that the Israelite camp itself is thought to be holy to some degree in relation to the area outside of the camp. The camp boundaries form a basic division between those areas affected by the holiness radiating from the holy of holies and those areas outside the camp. The camp boundaries thereby establish a basic line of demarcation between the realm of the holy and the realm of the profane.

It is precisely because of the basic spatial boundary of the camp that the distinction between clean and unclean becomes so important. The extended realm of the holy must be protected from anything that is 'unclean' or 'defiled'. Thus, those things that partake of major defilement must be expulsed from the camp to protect the holy. The operative principle in this case is that the threatening realm of contagion is the area 'inside of the camp'. The camp boundaries form the dividing line between the area within which pollution can threaten the extended realm of the holy, ultimately posing a threat to the sanctuary and society, and the area outside the camp from which uncleanness may not pose a threat.[1] The area outside the camp, then, comes to be viewed as a neutral area which may have spaces designated as 'clean' and 'unclean'.[2] It is clear, however, that these designations have a different force in the context of 'outside the camp' than they do in the context of 'inside the camp'.

It is in the context of the Priestly writers' understanding of holiness that the intersection of cosmic, social, and cultic order may be seen. The holiness of the tabernacle complex is an ongoing state, although a state that must be ritually protected. The Priestly traditions speak of the origin of this holiness in two ways. First, the holiness is said to derive from the presence of Yahweh in the holy of holies. 'There [at the door of the tent

---

1 See Milgrom, 'Two Kinds of *hatta't*', pp. 334-35; Wenham, *Leviticus*, pp. 18-25.

2 Thus, Milgrom's argument ('Two Kinds of *hatta't*', p. 334) that the area inside the camp and the area outside the camp are both neutral areas (חל) holds true only in terms of the clean/unclean system but not with reference to the holy/not-holy system. The two are related but not coterminous.

of meeting] I will meet with the people of Israel, and it shall be sanctified [ונקדש] by my glory; I will consecrate [וקדשתי] the tent of meeting and the altar; Aaron also and his sons I will consecrate [אקדש], to serve me as priests. And I will dwell among the people of Israel, and will be their God' (Exod. 29.43-45). It is Yahweh, the holy one, whose presence in the tent makes the area holy. The holiness of the sanctuary is derived from the presence of Yahweh in the sanctuary.

At the same time, however, the tabernacle complex and the Aaronide priesthood are consecrated, made holy, through the founding and anointing ritual of Leviticus 8. It is clear, however, that these two means of consecration are insepar-able in the Priestly traditions. The statement that Yahweh will consecrate the tabernacle area is found at the conclusion of the instructions for the anointing and founding ritual (Exod. 29). The glory of Yahweh is seen by all Israel at the conclusion of the offering of sacrifices by Aaron for the first time (Lev. 9). The ritual makes possible the reality of Yahweh's dwelling in the holy of holies, but, at the same time, through the enact-ment of the ritual, the reality of Yahweh's presence is brought into existence. The existence of the holy area—inner sanctum, tabernacle, camp—is a state of being which is understood as part of the larger created order. The distinctions between the various grades of holiness, the 'separation' of categories, are brought into being through the ritual enactment of that state in accordance with the instructions of Yahweh. Holiness is a state of being ultimately related to the presence and being of Yahweh and ritually founded as part of the created order.

The socio-cultic categories of clean and unclean are related to human existence and human situations. Holiness is context; clean/unclean are situational. The distinctions between clean and unclean are formulated in the context of the holiness of the camp. The holiness of the tabernacle and camp is a qualitative state founded in the on-going created order. Clean and unclean are socio-cultic states related to situations that arise in the everyday flow of human existence.

At the same time, however, these two sets of categories intersect. The holiness of the tabernacle and camp can be disrupted and profaned by the presence of defilement within the camp boundaries. The unclean person defiles the taber-

nacle of Yahweh and thereby disrupts the established socio-
cultic order of holiness. The sacred can be desecrated if defilement is left unattended in the camp. Thus, the situational
states of clean and unclean can disrupt the context of holiness.
Both states, however, are subject to ritual manipulation.
Defilement must be purged and eliminated. More than this,
however, the order of holiness which has been disrupted must
be restored, restructured, reconsecrated. The חטאת serves to
accomplish purgation of the holy area and reconsecration—it
re-establishes the order of holiness and cleanness in the socio-
cultic context.

Thus, the concern for the distinction between clean and
unclean is focused on the issue of the camp boundaries.
Outside the camp boundaries space is neutral and can be
designated, or interpreted and given meaning, as is necessary
or desirable. It is possible, then, to have 'a clean place' and 'an
unclean place' outside the camp. In looking at texts which
distinguish specific spaces outside the camp, a basic division is
apparent. In Lev. 4.12, 6.4, and Num. 19.9, the ashes of sacrificial animals, animals slaughtered for ritual purposes, are
deposited in 'a clean place outside the camp'. In Lev. 4.12, the
refuse of the חטאת bull is carried outside the camp and burned
in the place where the ashes are poured out. There is no
statement indicating that the one who performs this task is
made unclean.[1] In Lev. 6.4, a priest is to take off his priestly
clothes and carry the ashes of the עלה to a clean place outside
the camp. There is no indication that this priest becomes
unclean in undertaking this duty. Finally, Num. 19.9 states
that the ashes of the cow are to be deposited in a clean place
outside the camp.

In the three references to 'an unclean place outside the
camp', the concern is with the disposal of refuse from a house
declared 'leprous'. In this case it is evident that the 'diseased'

1 On the basis of Lev. 16.27-28, Milgrom argues ('Two Kinds of *hatta't*',
p. 335) that the one who comes into contact with the remains of an animal
offered as a חטאת is defiled. It must be noted, however, that Lev. 16.28 does
not say that contact causes uncleanness; rather, it is the one who burns
the remains who must wash his clothes and bathe his body. This is also
what Num. 19.8 states. This suggests that it is not contact with the animal
remains that causes uncleanness, but the burning and the smoke.

elements are removed from the camp and placed in an area that is off-limits. It is a dumping site for unclean materials and is to be avoided. It is clear that the unclean debris of the leprous house remains unclean and capable of defiling regardless of its location. This material continues to hold the ability to defile and, thus, is cast into a place declared unclean.

The situation is different with regard to the ashes of sacrificial animals. The animals were presented to Yahweh and slaughtered in the context of the sacred. These animals, and by extension, their remains have been qualitatively changed by their use in a sacrificial and, therefore, sacred context. They are holy. Thus, they cannot be cast into an 'unclean' area. This is true even though they are capable of 'defiling', a 'defilement' brought about because they have been removed from the profane context through their presentation and dedication to the sacred. Their danger is limited to the area inside the camp where their potential for defiling could be realized. Thus, the removal of the ashes to a clean place outside the camp functions not only as a means of disposal of refuse, but also as a means of safeguarding life within the camp.

The Use of the Ashes: vv. 17-19
The actual use of the ashes in bringing about cleansing is detailed in vv. 17-19. The first step is the mixing of the ashes with running water (מים חיים). As in the ritual for purification of the recovered leper, the call for 'living water' serves as a symbol of the effectiveness of the ritual in cleansing and communicating life to the defiled individual. This mixture makes up the 'waters for impurity'.

A clean person is then to take some hyssop, dip it in the mixture, and sprinkle it on the objects or persons needing cleansing. Verse 18 lists such objects with an obvious view toward the instructions concerning cases of uncleanness found in vv. 14-16. Verse 19 details the procedure for a contaminated person. The clean person shall sprinkle the unclean on the third day and on the seventh day. Thus, the clean shall cleanse the unclean on the seventh day. The final prescription of v. 19 refers to the person who performed the sprinkling. He will wash his clothes and bathe in water and be unclean until evening.

The sprinkling rite of Num. 19.17-19 functions to effect the cleansing of a corpse-contaminated person and to pass that person from contact with 'death' to a state of 'life'. It is not, however, the act of sprinkling in and of itself that effects the cleansing and passage; rather, it is the act of sprinkling the *waters of impurity*. The waters of impurity are effective for this because they contain the blood of the חטאת. In that the cow and its ashes are termed a חטאת, it may be said that the waters cleanse by absorbing the impurity of death. At the same time, however, this blood serves to communicate life to the individual. Thus, it both cleanses and restores in the same way that the normal חטאת cleanses and reconsecrates the altar or holy place.

The ritual sprinkling of the corpse-contaminated person involves a temporal process. He is to be sprinkled on the third and seventh days, and the cleansing is not complete until the seventh day. Again, it is clear that extreme defilement can only be cleansed over a period of time, in this case seven days. The eighth day, which normally serves as the day for offering sacrifices and offerings, is precluded in this instance because there are no sacrifices or offerings to be brought by the person who has been cleansed.

Conclusion

The ritual of the red cow is another rite of passage. It is designed to effect the safe passage of one contaminated by a corpse to a state of cleanness. In this case, however, blood is the required detergent for effecting passage. This is so because, in conjunction with Leviticus 8 and Leviticus 14, blood is the necessary ritual agent for effecting passage from the realm of death to the realm of life. In this case, the blood is found in the ashes of the burned red cow, termed a חטאת. This designation is appropriate because the normal function of the sacrifice was to effect purgation.

A few remarks on the structural relationship of the rituals of Leviticus 8; 14; and Numbers 19 will indicate the different nuances in these similar rituals. It has been argued that the application of blood to the individual is common to these three rituals. This act is necessary because all three rituals are concerned with the passage of the individual or individuals from contact with the category of death to a state of life. Blood is peculiarly effective for this passage in that it is capable of communicating life to the individual to whom it is applied.

In the ritual of the recovered leper and the corpse-contaminated, the ritual process begins outside the camp and makes it possible for those so defiled to return to the camp. In both cases, the concern is the restoration of the individual to a normal place within the societal order from which the individual had been expulsed. For the leper, the application of the blood takes place after re-entry into the camp, but prior to a return to his own tent. In the case of the corpse-contaminated, the blood application serves to effect the return to the camp. The ritual for the ordination of the priests, however, takes place entirely inside the camp. The passage of the priests is not from outside society to inside society, but is a psssage from status to status within society. In this case, however, there is an inverse structural element in relation to the other two rituals. In the latter two cases, there is a seven-day period of cleansing that takes place as the individual is excluded from a full and open standing within society that concludes with the individual's return to an open social standing. In the case of the priests, there is a seven-day period of exclusion that serves to limit their standing and locate them in a particular institutional status. They are being located in a particular category of social existence, so that their ritual concludes in a closed status within society.

The priests and the recovered leper have the blood placed on their extremities directly, while the corpse-contaminated has the blood sprinkled on him indirectly through the mixture of the ashes and water. Two things could account for this difference. First is the notice that the mixture sprinkled on the corpse-contaminated is made up of חטאת materials so that the Priestly traditionists would be reluctant to have that material, especially the blood, placed directly on an individual. It is a mediated form of the חטאת that is sprinkled on the person, but nonetheless, it is חטאת material. A second possibility is the nature of the final state achieved by the ritual. Both the priests and the recovered leper have an outward material sign of their changed status—the priests in their special priestly clothing and the leper in a changed skin condition. The corpse-contaminated has no outward sign of his changed status. The placing of the blood directly on the first two cases reflects this actual, observable change in outward appearance.

Chapter 7

NUMBERS 28–29

Introduction

The argument of this chapter is three-fold: (1) Numbers 28–
29 serves to give social and ritual order to the Israelite year by
prescribing certain ritual activity for specific times and, thus,
separates the year into distinct types of time; (2) the temporal
order established in Numbers 28–29 must be understood in
the larger context of Priestly creation theology; (3) the Priestly
material reflects several distinct kinds of time which must be
understood not simply in terms of the dichotomy between
linear and cyclical time, but in terms of the modalities of time.
The concern is not with the historical question of the development of the calendar in Israel; rather, the concern is with the
way in which the Priestly traditionists have brought together
ritual and temporal categories in order to impose order on
Israelite life.

Basic Structure of the Ritual

The following outline is included in order to indicate the basic
ritual moments specified in the text. Each prescribed moment
has specific ritual activity indicated for it. The present concern
is with the ritual moments as temporal categories of order and
not with the specifics of the ritual activity called for in those
moments.

   I. Introduction (28.1-2)
  II. Daily sacrifices: one in the morning and one in the
       evening (28.3-8)
 III. Additional sacrifices for the Sabbath (28.9-10)
  IV. Sacrifices for the beginning of the months (28.11-15)
   V. Passover: the 14th day of the first month (28.16)
  VI. Feast of Unleavened Bread: 15th to 21st days of the first
       month (28.17-25)
       First day: 'a holy convocation'
       Seventh day: 'a holy convocation'
 VII. First Fruits: 'a holy convocation' (28.26-31)
VIII. First day of the seventh month: 'a holy convocation' (29.1-6)
  IX. Seventh day of the seventh month: 'a holy convocation'
       (29.7-11)
   X. 15th day of the seventh month begins a seven day feast
       (29.12-38)
       First day: 'a holy convocation'

Liturgical Order-Social Order

Numbers 28–29 does not present a calendar primarily designed to mark time; rather, it serves to mark recurring ritual moments in the year. It does this by coordinating certain regularly prescribed sacrifices and offerings (ritual activity) with certain days and times (moments).[1] This is indicated in Num. 28.2 in which the Israelites are instructed to be certain to offer the correct sacrifice/offering in its appointed (correct, prescribed, or ordered) time (במועדו). Numbers 28–29 indicates the appointed and established times when the people are to present certain prescribed sacrifices and offerings to Yahweh.[2] Organization and order are given to the year because regularly recurring ritual moments are prescribed for the ever-recurring cycle of the year.

---

1 D.F. Morgan, 'The So-Called Cultic Calendars in the Pentateuch [Ex 23.10-19; 34.18-26; Lev 23; Num 28–29; Dt 16.1-17]: A Morphological and Typological Study', PhD Dissertation, Claremont Graduate School, Claremont, CA, 1974, pp. 215-19.
2 Morgan, 'So-Called Cultic Calendars', p. 196; N.H. Snaith, 'Time in the Old Testament', in *Promise and Fulfilment* (ed. F.F. Bruce; Edinburgh: Clark, 1963), p. 175.

As such, Numbers 28–29 presents a liturgical order.[1] The text presents the divine order (as directive) for a regularly recurring socio-cultural order.[2] This liturgical order provides organization, form, and regularity in time and thereby pro-- vides a means for maintaining orderliness in contrast to disorder and chaos. This order comes about not only through disjunctions, but also through conjunctions. Rappaport states:

> While it may be that festivals distinguish the seasons one from another, it is also the case that they join them into the circle of the year. The intervals between the rituals in protracted liturgical orders become, in part because they are set apart by rituals, not simply durations during which there has been more growth or the weather has grown warmer, but distinctive periods... Bound together by the rituals distinguishing them, they form significant wholes: lives and histories, and the years that set lives into histories and histories into cosmos.[3]

Rappaport's statement recognizes that there can be a conjunction of cyclical, liturgical temporal categories and progressive, chronological, linear temporal categories. Historical development can be understood to take place in the context of a recurring ritual framework that reflects a cyclical understanding of time.

A liturgical order of this type is one means of structuring social life. At the same time, it is a means for supporting the structure and processes of society. A liturgical order not only provides a structural pattern for society, it also provides a means by which that pattern can be realized.[4] Numbers 28–29 is concerned not only with the cultic life of the people, it is

---

1 Rappaport (*Ecology, Meaning, and Religion*, p. 192) uses 'liturgical order' to refer to 'the more or less invariant sequences of formal acts and utter-ances that comprise single rituals, and to the sequences of rituals that make up ritual cycles and series'. He notes the usefulness of the idea of 'order' because of its various senses of meaning beyond that of sequence. Liturgical orders 'are also orders in the sense of organization, form, or regularity... As such, they constitute order, or maintain orderliness, in contrast to disorder, entropy, or chaos. They are, further, orders in that they are in some sense imperatives or directives' (p. 192).
2 *Ibid.*, p. 192.
3 *Ibid.*, p. 187.
4 See Geertz, *The Interpretation of Cultures*, pp. 92-95.

also concerned with the non-cultic social order of the people.[1]
In this way, time is given a stable and recurring meaning.[2]
Time as a product of society serves not only to provide
sequence, it also serves to mark boundaries of social processes.[3]
Thus, not only the cultic life of the people is given structure,
but also the non-cultic life between the ritual moments is given
structure.[4]

Creation and the Liturgical Order

The liturgical order of Numbers 28–29 reflects several important conceptual relationships to the Priestly creation account
in Gen. 1.1-2.4a. On the fourth day God said, 'Let there be
lights in the firmament of the heavens to separate (להבדיל) the
day from the night. And let them be for signs and for (the
appointed) times (ולמועדים), for days and for years'. Time is
clearly considered part of the created order.[5] Temporal categories are one means in which cultures divide up the natural
order and thereby impose a culturally meaningful order on
the natural order. Two kinds of time are indicated in this text:
progressive, chronological time and regularly, recurring
ritual times.

The Priestly traditionists here affirm that the appointed
times of the liturgical order (the מועדים) prescribed in Numbers
28–29 (see Num. 28.2) have been built into the very structure
of the created order. The lights of the firmament—the sun,
moon, and stars—serve not only to mark the forward movement of time, they also serve to mark those moments in the
yearly cycle when specified types of ritual activity are to take

---

1 On time as social product of order, see Pepper, 'The Order of Time', pp. 18-
   19; Sorokin and Merton, 'Social Time', pp. 625-27; Moore, *Man, Time, and
   Society*, pp. 8-9; Sorokin, *Sociocultural Causality, Space, Time*; Lynch,
   What Time is This Place?, pp. 119-26; Gurevich, 'Time as a Problem of
   Cultural History', p. 229.
2 P. Ricoeur, 'The History of Religions and the Phenomenology of Time
   Consciousness', in *History of Religions*, p. 21.
3 Moore, *Man, Time, and Society*, pp. 8-9.
4 Rappaport, *Ecology, Meaning, and Religion*, p. 187; Turner, *The Ritual
   Process*, pp. 168-70.
5 O.H. Steck, *World and Environment* p. 94.

place.[1] The natural order has structure, order, and meaning given to it, placed upon it, in the construction of the yearly liturgical order. Thus, the appointed ritual moments become one means in which society participates in, gives support to, and helps to realize the ongoing existence, structure, and meaning of the divinely created order. This relationship between created order and liturgical order is a clear demonstration of Geertz's notion of cultural patterns of meaning which provide a model *of* and a model *for* society.[2] The pattern of order established in creation is given a means of realization in the liturgical order. This view reflects one means of dealing with the problem of whether culture is to be found in a static pattern or in the social processes. The pattern is given a means of realization in ritual processes.

A second way in which the liturgical order is related to the creation account of Gen. 1.1–2.4a is found in the prescriptions for the daily sacrifices and offerings. One lamb is to be offered in the morning and one lamb is to be offered in the evening (28.3-8). In the Priestly creation account, the first act of God is the separation of light and darkness, called 'the day' and 'the night' respectively ('and God separated (ויבדל) the light from the dark'). This original act of the ordering of creation is marked by the ritual offering of sacrifices. The morning and evening sacrifices point to the divinely established order of creation and serve to impose a ritual order on it. The sacrifices thus serve to sustain the division of day and night at creation and, thus, to sustain the order established at creation. The recurring cycle of day and night become signs of the order of creation; the daily sacrifices are one means of sustaining that order in that they are prescribed ritual moments designed to mark the division of day and night.

Two brief notes will be useful before proceeding. As argued in Chapter 2, basic to the Priestly traditionists' understanding of order is the idea that order is achieved through divisions and separations. Creation in Gen. 1.1–2.4a is constructed primarily through the separation of things created into basic

1 Snaith, 'Time in the Old Testament', p. 175.
2 *The Interpretation of Cultures*, pp. 92-95.

categories.[1] Order is brought about through divisions, separations, and distinctions between one thing and another. It is only as these lines of demarcation, or boundaries, are established, observed, and maintained that order is realized. This is true not only of the created order, but also of the social and cultic orders of creation. The priests are instructed 'to distinguish (להבדיל = 'separate') between the holy and the not-holy, and between the unclean and the clean' (Lev. 10.10). The cultic order of the Priests consists primarily of a concern for the separation, the proper division, of certain categories (clean, holy) from other categories (not-clean, not-holy).

Secondly, Num. 28.6 relates the daily offerings to a prescription established at Mt Sinai. This prescription is found in Exod. 29.38-46 and is there related to Yahweh's presence in the midst of Israel. The daily sacrifices are to be offered at the door of the tent of meeting.

> There I will meet with the people of Israel, and it shall be sanctified by my glory. I will consecrate the tent of meeting and the altar; Aaron also and his sons I will consecrate, to serve me as priests. And I will dwell among the people of Israel, and will be their God. And they shall know that I am Yahweh their God, who brought them forth out of the land of Egypt that I might dwell among them; I am Yahweh their God (Exod. 29.43-46).

The cultic, liturgical order of the Priests is concerned with the ongoing presence of Yahweh in the midst of the nation. It is being argued here that the liturgical order of Numbers 28–29 is significantly related to Gen. 1.1–2.4a. The relationship between the Priestly creation account and the texts dealing with the construction of the tabernacle has already been discussed.[2] Ritual order is intimately related to cultic order for the Priests. By observing the liturgical order, Israel participates in the sustaining and maintaining of the divinely constructed order of creation. Cult and creation are thus placed in a tensive, mutually supportive relationship in Numbers 28–29.

---

1 See Soler, 'The Dietary Prohibitions of the Hebrews', pp. 28-30; Fishbane, *Text and Texture*, p. 10; Westermann, *Genesis*, p. 88; Beauchamp, *Création et séparation* (BSR; Paris: Desclée de Brouwer, 1969), pp. 17-148.
2 See above, pp. 42-44.

The daily morning and evening sacrifices thus serve to provide a bipartite structure for the day. The sacrifices clearly mark out and separate the 'day-time' from the 'night-time'. The sacrifices also serve to separate two kinds of time in the day: ritual time and non-ritual time. There are at least two ritually prescribed moments in the day and these moments are distinct from the other non-ritually prescribed moments in the day.

This bipartite structure is further reflected in the separation of two kinds of days in the week according to the Priestly creation account.

> On the seventh day God finished the work which he had done, and he rested on the seventh day from all the work which he had done. And God blessed the seventh day and made it holy [ויקדש = 'set it apart' or separated it from all the other days] because on it God rested from all the work which he had done in the work of creating (Gen. 2.2-3).

The Sabbath[1] is marked off and made distinct from all other days by its being made holy. There is thus reflected in the structure of the week, so ordered at creation, a basic division between the two types of days. Westermann in noting the 'set apart' nature of the Sabbath states,

> when he arranged the works of creation in the seven-day pattern, P intended to structure a unit of time which consists of two parts: it would not be a whole without the seventh day, which is something different from the six days. Creation is set out on a time scheme comprising days of work and rest.[2]

The seven-day week, with the Sabbath being set apart from the other days, reflects the bipartite structure of the day—it is ordered both as creative act and prescribed ritual.

The Sabbath is clearly set apart in the ritual calendar of Numbers 28–29 in that additional sacrifices and offerings are prescribed for the Sabbath (Num. 28.9-10). The additional ritual activity serves to mark this day as a day distinct from all

---

1 See M. Tsevat, 'The Basic Meaning of the Biblical Sabbath', *ZAW* 84 (1972), pp. 447-59; H.W. Wolff, 'The Day of Rest in the Old Testament', *LTQ* 7 (1972), pp. 65-76; N.-E.A. Andreasen, 'Recent Studies of the Old Testament Sabbath', *ZAW* 86 (1974), pp. 453-69.
2 *Genesis*, p. 171.

other days. This becomes even more significant when it is seen in light of Yahweh's concluding instructions to Moses on Mt Sinai.

> And Yahweh said to Moses, 'Speak to the people of Israel, 'You shall keep my Sabbaths, for this is a sign between me and you throughout your generations, that you may know that I, Yahweh, sanctify you [מקדשכם]. You shall keep the Sabbath, because it is holy for you; every one who profanes it shall be put to death; whoever does any work on it, that person shall be cut off from among his people. Six days shall work be done, but the seventh day is a Sabbath of solemn rest, holy to Yahweh; whoever does any work on the Sabbath day shall be put to death. Therefore, the people of Israel shall keep the Sabbath, observing the Sabbath throughout their generations, as a perpetual covenant. It is a sign forever between me and the people of Israel that in six days Yahweh made heaven and earth, and on the seventh day he rested, and was refreshed (Exod. 31.12-17).

The Sabbath is not only a day set apart from the other days, it is a day when Israel, in ceasing from its normal everyday work, celebrates the creation of heaven and earth. By observing the Sabbath, Israel actualizes the order of creation and realizes that order. It may be said, then, that the Sabbath is a day in which the divinely created order is not only observed but also actualized.

In addition to this, the emphasis on the Sabbath as a day 'set apart', 'made holy', provides the foundational act of setting apart for time. Just as in the tabernacle the Priests present a 'set apart' spatial category, and just as in the priesthood they present a 'set apart' category of status, so in the Sabbath they present a 'set apart' temporal category. All three of these 'set apart' and 'holy' categories are founded in an act of Yahweh. Thus, it may be said that just as the tabernacle was founded in ritual and just as the priesthood was founded in ritual, so also the Sabbath was founded in ritual—Yahweh's creation of the heaven and earth was a ritual of founding by the divine creator.

The bipartite structure present in the day and week is also present in the structure of the liturgical year. This structure may be depicted as follows:

FIRST HALF
    1st Month   *Months 2-6*
    14th: Passover
    15th-21st: Unleavened Bread
    Seven-day observance
        Day 1: מקרא קדש
        Day 2: מקרא קדש

                                First Fruits: מקרא קדש

SECOND HALF
    7th Month   *Months 8-12*
    1st: מקרא קדש
    10th: יום הכפרים
            מקרא קדש
    15th-21st: Seven-day festival
        Day 1: מקרא קדש
    22nd: (מקרא קדש עצרה) עצרה

While the structure does not reflect a perfect balance, and there need not be perfect balance for significance, the year is divided into two basic halves with a similar ritual structure. Each half is marked out by a beginning month heavy in ritual occasions. It should also be clear that these months not only mark the beginning of a segment of the liturgical year, but also serve to join together the two halves of the year. This reflects the structure of the day and the week. Thus, the dualistic structure of the day with its recurring cycle of light and dark, each begun with a ritual moment, is reflected in the recurring cycle of the year.[1] This means that the year not only has its sacred, appointed times, as does the day, but it also has the periods between these appointed times, as does the day. The regularly appointed times, then, serve not only to designate the sacred and ritual moments, but also the times in between these moments. In this way, order is imposed on the year and society is given a regulated order within which to live its collective life.

Finally, the number seven plays a significant role in the order of the week and in the annual liturgical order. In the liturgical order of the year, there are seven distinct ritual occasions called for, excluding the daily rituals, sabbaths, and

1 On bipartite divisions of time, see M.P. Nilsson, *Primitive Time-Reckoning* (Lund: Gleerup, 1920), pp. 71-72.

new moons, and there are within these seven ritual occasions, seven days designated as a מקרא קדש. The structuring function of the number seven is further evidenced by the fact that both halves of the year have a seven-day ritual occasion prescribed for them. Finally, by keeping count of the sacrifices called for in the seven-day festival of the seventh month, it can be seen that the number of animals sacrificed is significantly related to the number seven.[1]

It has often been argued that the number seven indicates 'wholeness' or 'completeness'. This is suggested by the Priestly creation account in which God *completes* the creation process in seven days. The wholeness of the created order came into being in seven days. This idea is further supported by the prominence of the number seven in rituals of cleansing and purification. For example, the cleansing ritual for the recovered leper involves a seven-day process (Lev. 14.8-9). Corpse-contamination requires a seven-day period of cleansing (Num. 19.11, 12, 14, 16, 19). Lev. 15.13, 19, 24, 28 require a seven-day period of cleansing for various types of impurity relating to bodily discharge. Finally, a seven-day process is prescribed for the ordination of the priesthood (Exod. 29.35) and for the consecration of the altar (Exod. 29.37).

It is clear that the number seven plays a prominent role in the movement from not-complete to complete, from not-clean to clean, from not-holy to holy, from not-ordered to ordered. In all of these cases, the movement is from an improper state to a proper, whole state. Cleansing rituals may provide the basis for a proper understanding of the number seven as a symbol for wholeness and order.[2] If defilement is viewed as a dis-

---

1 G.B. Gray, *Numbers* (ICC. 1903; rpt. Edinburgh: Clark, 1965), pp. 406-407.
2 Lev. 26 (H) may reflect, in part, an interpretation of history based on restorative cleansing rituals. In the list of punishments, it is stated no less than four times (vv. 18, 21, 24, 28) that they are the result of Yahweh's chastisement of Israel because of Israel's sin (חטא). The final result is the desolation of the land and the removal of Israel so the land can enjoy its rest (Lev. 26.34-39). This time of rest for the land will be followed by the restoration of Israel to its former position (based on the covenant with the patriarchs) before God. Such a ritual interpretation of history in this context is further supported by Lev. 18.24-30 which warns the people not to defile themselves (טמא) lest they are vomited out by the land. On the Priestly

ruption of proper order (wholeness), then the cleansing process may be seen as a ritual of restoration of the proper order (wholeness). Seen in this light, the liturgical order of Numbers 28–29 may be said to be a recurring process designed to maintain wholeness and a state of cleanness. It serves to give order to the life of the community, but also provides a ritual process for maintaining that order, i.e., keeping it from falling into disorder (= not whole, defiled). Thus, as Israel enacts the prescribed rituals at the prescribed moments, it is a means by which the nation participates in and actualizes the world of the divine order.

Thus far the following points have been made:

1. The liturgical order is a social construction in which meaningful order is imposed on the natural order in such a way that it gives regularized organization to the life of the community. It does this through disjunctions (distinct kinds of time) and conjunctions (the times fit together to make a whole).

2. The liturgical order of Numbers 28–29 is to be seen as a model *of* order—what order is—and a model *for* order —how that order can be realized.

3. Numbers 28–29 reflects Priestly creation theology in its conceptualization of time in bipartite categories: the day (= day and night) and the week (holy day and not-holy days) of Gen. 1.1–2.4a parallels the division of the year into two basic liturgical parts.

4. The liturgical order of Numbers 28–29 is part of the larger Priestly cultic order (which includes, for example, the sacrificial order, the dietary order, and the cleanliness order) which is integrally related to the created order—creation, society, and cult are ordered.

5. The liturgical order of Numbers 28–29 is one means by which the Priestly traditionists sought to realize order and, thus, hold back the threat of disorder. This is accomplished by seeing the liturgical order as a regularly recurring process of creating wholeness and purity in the life of the community.

interpretation of history in terms of purification processes, particularly the flood story, see Frymer-Kensky, 'Pollution'.

The Modalities of Time in P

Numbers 28–29 reflect, at least in their attempt to establish a temporal order, a cyclical view of time.[1] The yearly cycle of rituals is an ever-recurring process. The same may be said for Gen. 1.1–2.4a in which time is presented in its basic structure as the endless cycle of day and night and the endless cycle of the week. Both of these texts mark off regular ritual moments and, at the same time, regular non-ritual moments. Both texts thus serve to distinguish two distinct kinds of time: ritual time and non-ritual time.

The matter is more complex than this, however, in that the non-ritual moments, as defined in Numbers 28–29, may themselves become 'ritual' moments through the need for the occasional rituals, e.g., the חטאת, the עלה, or the נדר.[2] These are ritual moments that arise as a result of a situation caused by an individual's actions or circumstances. These non-recurring ritual moments which take place within the non-ritual times of Numbers 28–29 must be understood differently than the regularly recurring and prescribed ritual moments in those chapters. These are different kinds of times because they arise from distinct situations.

Another temporal category operative in the Priestly ritual material is found in the cleansing rituals which involve a seven-day temporal process. On the face of it, such rituals seem to reflect a linear conception of time. Time is understood as a succession of units which move toward a goal, a conclusion. The goal toward which cleansing rituals move is a changed status for an individual (e.g., the leper, the corpse-contaminated). It should be seen, however, that the true goal of such ritual processes is a return to a pre-defiled state of existence. Such 'linear' processes are designed to create a return to a previous state. Cleansing rituals are restorative

---

1 J. Barr (*Biblical Words for Time* [SBT 33; rev. edn; Naperville: Alec R. Allenson, 1969], pp. 143-49) argues for at least six distinct ways in which 'cyclical' may be understood in terms of temporal processes. See also, Ricoeur, 'Time Consciousness', p. 19.

2 G. Dumezil ('Temps et mythes', *RP* 5 [1935/1936], pp. 235-51) distinguishes three types of models by which ritual repetition may be viewed: continuous (taboos), occasional (defilement, funerals, births, initiations), and periodical (related to the calendar).

rituals designed to restore a proper order. They, thus, exhibit a 'cyclical' nuance, a return to a pre-defiled state, as well as a 'linear' nuance, a temporal process that moves toward a goal.

It is necessary, then, to distinguish at least four kinds of times in the Priestly ritual material:

1. the regularly recurring and prescribed ritual moments of Numbers 28–29;
2. the regularly recurring non-ritual moments of Numbers 28–29;
3. the occasional ritual sacrifices that take place in the non-ritual moments of Numbers 28–29;
4. the temporal process of cleansing or restorative rituals which take seven days.

Each of these 'kinds of time' will have its own nuance, its own texture, its own concerns. Each of these times will serve to give order and meaning in its own way to the people participating in the moment.

This suggests that the dichotomy often made between 'cyclical' views of time and 'linear' views of time is too simplistic to account for the *views* of time in the Priestly ritual material. The conceptual categories of time in the Priestly ritual material cannot be reduced to an either/or proposition where cyclical time is opposed to linear time; rather, time must be seen to express various modalities and nuances which are determined, in part, by the ritual situation within which the temporal categories are operative. This suggests that time should not be graphically spoken of or depicted as a line, either a straight line or a circle, but should be understood in terms of qualitative tone or texture.

CONCLUSION

Introduction

The Priestly traditionists lived in a world of meaning and significance. In the Priestly ritual texts we have their reflections on that world. These texts present, through their description of rituals, the results of these reflections. The texts thus stand as theological statements by the Priests. The rituals depicted in the texts, however, present a means by which the Preists thought their world of meaning and significance could be enacted, actualized, and realized. The Priestly ritual texts, thus, embody the Priests' thinking 'theologically'; the rituals proper present ways of 'doing' theology.

The Priestly World View and Ritual

At the heart of Priestly ritual theology is the Priestly world view. Their world view is a complex system of relationships and meaning and provides a means by which they locate, orient, and situate themselves in the world. The basic framework of that world view may be seen in the following.

A system of identification. The Priests saw the cosmos as a constructed order. God constructed the cosmic order through a series of separations by which chaos, the darkness and deeps, were ordered and placed in their appropriate places. The divine order will only continue to exist so long as the categories of creation are maintained and continued. Ongoing order, then, is only realized as these categories are kept intact. It is also affirmed that this cosmic order is 'very good'. That is, within the context of the construction of the cosmos, God evaluates the order as proper, good, correct.

The process of the creation of the divine order, however, is not fully complete at the end of the creation account in Gen. 1.1–2.4a. For the Priestly traditionists, the order of creation is not fully finished until Israelite society and the tabernacle cult are constructed. That is, the Priests think of creation as made up of cosmos, society, and cult. All three of these acts of creation are presented as the result of the word of Yahweh. Yahweh spoke and they came into existence. These three elements of the created order, cosmos, society, and cult, are interactive. Each provides context for the other. At the same time, each derives context from the other. Just as cosmic order was achieved through a series of separations that must be maintained if cosmic order is to continue, so also, society and cult are created with categories and separations that must be maintained if order is to continue. This brings the discussion to the second element of the Priestly world view.

A system of meaning and identification. The meaning of human existence is placed by the Priestly traditionists within the context of a created order. In that this order is understood to be based on the idea of 'order through separations', it follows that human beings are called upon to maintain that order of creation—cosmic, social, and cultic. Thus, human existence must be understood in the context of the call to find a means of maintaining and continuing the created order. They must find a means of maintenance and, when necessary, a means of restoration.

In this way it may be said that human beings are called to become participants in the continual renewal and maintenance of the created order. The meaning of human existence is realized and actualized precisely when humans become participants in the process of constructing the created order. Thus, while the Priests recognize a moment when the divine order came into being—creation of cosmos, the instructions for society, the founding of cult—they also recognize the possibility of a collapse of that order. Chaos has only been placed, it has not been eliminated. Thus, human meaning is found through those acts that serve to support and restore the created order.

This idea is clearly expressed in the Priestly account of the creation of human beings. Human beings are created in the image and likeness of God. In that capacity they are given dominion over the created order. If one looks at the 'image' of God presented in Gen. 1.1–2.4a, it is clear that the dominant characteristic is that of God as creator. Thus, if humans are made in the image and likeness of God, it seems reasonable to say that they are understood as 'creators'. This is, in part, made clear by the 'blessing' that they be fruitful and multiply. It would seem, however, in light of the emphasis on creation, that they are being called upon to be participants in the process of creation. That is, the dominion of humans over the created order in conjunction with the idea that they are made in the image and likeness of the creator, suggests that they are called on to watch over, maintain, and, when necessary, restore the order of creation. It is precisely as humans, acting as the representatives of God in the created order, act so as to continue the order of creation, that they realize the meaning and significance of their existence—they are participants with God in the ongoing actualization of creation. The question must now be asked: How do humans act out their role in creation?

Praxis. The Priestly traditionists answer this question with ritual. The Priestly writers, faced with the need to hold back chaos and maintain the order of creation, look to ritual as the means to accomplish this. Ritual, thus, becomes a means by which humans participate in the ongoing order of creation. Their existence is made meaningful as they participate in the never-ending drama of creation in ritual. This is why ritual must function as a means of 'manipulating' the orders of creation. It is the means by which the categories of 'order' and 'chaos' can be negotiated. Ritual, thus, must be seen as the enactment of world—it is the bringing into being and the continuation of the order of creation.

Ritual becomes a means of interaction with the world and cosmos. 'Religion' for the Priests is not simply an ethical issue,

nor is it simply a ritualistic issue; rather, it is a vision of the
world held in conjunction with a means of situating oneself in
that world. Ritual is a way of enacting meaning in one's existence in this world. It is a way of construing, actualizing, realiz-
ing, and bringing into being a world of meaning and ordered
existence. Ritual is, thus, seen as a means of enacting one's
theology.

The Categories Operative in Priestly Ritual

It has been argued that there are four sets of categories
operative in Priestly rituals: clean/unclean, holy/not-holy, life/
death, order/chaos. These four sets of categories interact and
intersect in various configurations which provide the context
for Priestly ritual. Different rituals focus on different aspects
of this system of concern and, thus, will be nuanced according
to the particular configuration present in the situation calling
forth a particular ritual.

The Role of Blood in the Priestly Ritual System

At the heart of the Priestly ritual system is sacrificial blood. It
has a twofold function: it purifies and restores. In the context
of the חטאת, it was argued that the blood placed on the altar
functions to cleanse it, while the blood poured out at the base of
the altar functions to reconsecrate, or restore, it. The same
holds true for the blood which is sprinkled on the כפרת and
before it. The חטאת blood, in this way, operates within the
context of the categories of holy/not-holy and clean/unclean.

This dual function of the חטאת blood is also operative in the
ritual for the corpse-contaminated. The חטאת blood, found in
the מי נדה, is placed on the corpse-contaminated to purify and
restore. In this case, the restoration is to a full standing within
the community as the individual is passed from contact with
'the realm of death' to 'the realm of life'. Thus, the ritual for
the corpse-contaminated operates within the context of the
categories clean/not-clean and death/life.

These categories are also operative in the ritual for the
recovered leper. The leper was seen as one who had come into
contact with 'the realm of death'. Thus, the individual not only
needed to be purified, but also restored to 'the realm of life'.

There are two primary differences, however, between this ritual and the ritual for the corpse-contaminated. The leper's passage is reflected in a return to the camp and tent. This is necessary because the leper was expelled from the camp. Thus, the blood of the slaughtered bird, slaughtered over running water outside the camp, was sprinkled on the recovered leper to allow a return to the camp. The blood in this case, even though not termed a sacrifice, functions to restore the individual to the camp, hence, to the social body. The blood served as an effective ritual symbol for this because it holds together the bi-polar values of death and life. Death is reflected in the slaughter of the bird used to obtain the blood; life is reflected in the belief that the life of an animal was in its blood. Thus, the blood served to communicate life to the recovered leper and allow a return to the camp, itself a symbol of life.

Both of these rituals are restorative rituals and the blood functions to restore an individual to a right social status. The ritual for the ordination of the priesthood is a founding ritual, but, within this ritual, the blood functions to effect passage through 'the realm of death' to 'the realm of life'. The priests are daubed on their right ear, thumb, and big toe, with the blood of the איל המלאים. This blood serves to pass them through 'the realm of death' to 'the realm of life'. This passage is necessary because of the nature of the work of the priesthood. They are placed in an institutional status within society, but this status reflects a dangerous situation. They perform their priestly duties in the holy place, a categorically distinct area from all other areas. At the same time, their duties are concerned with the maintenance and restoration of holiness and purity. Hence, they come into contact with the profane and impure within the context of the holy and the sacred. They are mediators between two categorically distinct spheres, the sacred and the profane as well as the pure and the impure. This is seen as a dangerous place; it is 'betwixt and between'. Thus, the blood of the איל המלאים effects their passage through 'the realm of death' back to 'the realm of life' so that they might perform their duties within the context of the tension between death and life, a crucial concern of the Priestly cult.

The Categories of the Priestly Ritual System

Thus, in the Priestly ritual system, there are four sets of categories addressed in the rituals: order/chaos, holy/profane, clean/unclean, and death/life. The tabernacle cult functions to address these sets of categories, each one reflecting a dangerous and contagious quality, and, through ritual, enact and bring into being a world characterized by order, holiness, purity, and life.

These concerns are operative throughout the Priestly ritual system in varying degrees. Through all three types of rituals—foundational, maintenance, and restorative—the concern of the Priestly traditionists is to create a world that reflects the original good order of God. This means that ritual must address the structure of cosmos, society, and cult so as to enact a world of order.

This ritual manipulation or 'creation' of world is seen most clearly in the way that the conceptual categories of space, time, and status are understood in Priestly rituals. Each of these foundational categories has a moment of founding—'set apart' temporal categories in the founding of the Sabbath; 'set apart' spatial categories in the founding of the tabernacle; and 'set apart' status in the founding of the priesthood. In the founding of these categories, the basic structure of the Priestly system is established. Categories of space, time, and status serve to give an ordered structure to the Priestly world, a structure of meaning. Priestly rituals function to make statements about these categories and the world of creation and, when necessary, to change them.

Thus, Priestly ritual must be seen as a complex, interactive system of three distinct elements: the world view in which the created order is seen to be made up of cosmos, society, and cult; a concern for the categories of order/chaos, holy/profane, clean/unclean, and life/death; and, finally, the categories of space, time, and status. It is as these three elements of meaning and concern interact in ritual that the theology of the Priests can be seen and understood. Ritual was not only a way of acting, it was also a way of thinking, speaking, and creating.

BIBLIOGRAPHY

Abrahams, I. 'Tabernacle', *EJ* 15 (1972), pp. 679-87.

Anderson, B.W. *Creation in the Old Testament*. IRT 6. Philadelphia/London: Fortress Press/SPCK, 1984.

Andreasen, N.-E.A. 'Recent Studies of the Old Testament Sabbath', *ZAW* (1974), pp. 453-69.

Arinze, F.A. *Sacrifice in Ibo Religion*. Ed. J.S. Boston. Ibadan, Nigeria: Ibadan University, 1970.

Baal, J. van. 'Offering, Sacrifice and Gift', *Numen* 23 (1976), pp. 161-78.

Baaren, Th.P. van. 'Theoretical Speculations on Sacrifice', *Numen* 11 (1964), pp. 1-12.

Bailey, L.R. 'Horns of Moses', *IDBSup* (1976), pp. 419-20.

Barbour, I.G. *Myths, Models, and Paradigms: A Comparative Study in Science and Religion*. New York/Hagerstown/San Francisco/London: Harper & Row, 1974.

Barr, J. *Biblical Words for Time*. SBT 33 (1st series). Rev. edn. Naperville: Alec R. Allenson, 1969.

Bean, S.S. 'Toward a Semiotics of "Purity" and "Pollution" in India', *AA* 8 (1981), pp. 575-95.

Beauchamp, P. *Création et séparation. Étude exégétique du chapitre premier de la Genèse*. BSR. Paris: Desclée de Brouwer, 1969.

Begrich, J. 'Die priesterliche Tora', in *Werden und Wesen des Alten Testaments*. BZAW 66. Ed. P. Volv et al. Berlin: A. Töpelmann, 1936, pp. 63-88.

Berger, P. and T. Luckmann. *The Social Construction of Reality: A Treatise in the Sociology of Knowledge*. Garden City, New York: Doubleday, 1966.

Beyerlin, W. *Origins and History of the Oldest Sinaitic Traditions*. Trans. S. Rudman. Oxford: Basil Blackwell, 1961.

Blenkinsopp, J. 'The Structure of P', *CBQ* 38 (1976), pp. 275-92.

Bollnow, O. 'Lived-Space', in *Readings in Existential Phenomenology*. Ed. N. Lawrence and D. O'Connor. Englewood Cliffs, New Jersey: Prentice-Hall, 1967, pp. 178-86.

Brenner, A. *Colour Terms in the Old Testament.* JSOT Supp. 21. Ed. D.J.A. Clines and D.M. Gunn. Sheffield: JSOT Press, 1982.

Brichto, H.C. 'On Slaughter and Sacrifice, Blood and Atonement', *HUCA* 47 (1976), pp. 19-55.

Brown, J.P. 'The Sacrificial Cult and its Critique in Greek and Hebrew (I)', *JSS* 24 (1979), pp. 159-77.

Browne, S.G. *Leprosy in the Bible.* London: Christian Medical Fellowship, 1970.

Brueggemann, W. 'Weariness, Exile and Chaos (A Motif in Royal Theology)', *CBQ* 34 (1972), pp. 19-38.

Budd, P.J. *Numbers.* WBC 5. Ed. D.A. Hubbard and G.W. Barker. Waco, Texas: Word Books, 1984.

Buss, M.J. 'The Distinction Between Civil and Criminal Law in Ancient Israel', *Proceedings of the Sixth World Congress of Jewish Studies I.* Jerusalem: Academic Press, 1977, pp. 51-62.

—'Understanding Communication', in *Encounter with the Text: Form and History in the Hebrew Bible.* Ed. M.J. Buss. Philadelphia/Missoula: Fortress Press/Scholars Press, 1979, pp. 3-44.

Carney, T.F. *The Shape of the Past: Models and Antiquity.* Lawrence, KS: Coronado Press, 1975.

Carroll, R.P. 'Rebellion and Dissent in Ancient Israelite Society', *ZAW* 89 (1977), pp. 176-204.

Casalis, M. 'The Dry and the Wet: A Semiological Analysis of Creation and Flood Myths', *Semiotica* 17 (1976), pp. 35-67.

Cazelles, H. 'Pureté et impureté: Ancien Testament', *DBSup* (1979), pp. 491-508.

Childs, B.S. *The Book of Exodus: A Critical, Theological Commentary.* OTL. Philadelphia: Westminster Press, 1974.

Clements, R.E. *God and Temple.* Philadelphia: Fortress Press, 1965.

Clifford, R.J. *The Cosmic Mountain in Canaan and the Old Testament.* Cambridge, Mass.: Harvard University Press, 1977.

Coats, G.W. 'The King's Loyal Opposition: Obedience and Authority in Exodus 32-34', in *Canon and Authority: Essays in Old Testament Religion and Theology.* Ed. G.W. Coats and B.O. Long. Philadelphia: Fortress Press, 1977, pp. 91-109.

Cohn, R.L. *The Shape of Sacred Space: Four Biblical Studies.* AARSR 23. Chico, CA: Scholars Press, 1981.

Colby, B.N., J.W. Fernandez, and D.B. Kornfeld, 'Toward a Convergence of Cognitive and Symbolic Anthropology', *AA* 8 (1981), pp. 422-450.

Comstock, W.R. 'A Behavioral Approach to the Sacred: Category Formation in Religious Studies', *JAAR* 49 (1981), pp. 625-43.

Crites, S. 'The Narrative Quality of Experience', *JAAR* 39 (1971), pp. 291-311.

Cross, F.M. 'The Priestly Tabernacle', *BAR* 1. Ed. G.E. Wright and D.N. Freedman. Garden City: Doubleday, 1961, pp. 201-28.

—*Canaanite Myth and Hebrew Epic: Essays in the History of the Religion of Israel.* Cambridge/London: Harvard University Press, 1975.

Daniel, S. *Recherches sur le Vocabulaire du Culte dans la Septante.* EC 61. Paris: Librairie C. Klincksieck, 1966.

Davies, D. 'An Interpretation of Sacrifice in Leviticus', *ZAW* 91 (1979), pp. 387-98.

Dilthey, W. *Dilthey's Philosophy of Existence: Introduction to Weltanschauungslehre.* Trans. W. Kluback and M. Weinbaum. London: Vision Press, 1957.

Döller, J. *Die Reinheits- und Speisegesetze des Alten Testaments in religionsgeschichtlicher Beleuchtung.* Münster: Aschendorffsche Verlagsbuchhandlung, 1917.

Dougherty, J.W.D. and J.W. Fernandez, 'Introduction', *AA* 8 (1981), pp. 413-21.

Douglas, M. *Implicit Meanings: Essays in Anthropology.* London/Boston/Henley: Routledge & Kegan Paul, 1975.

—*Natural Symbols: Explorations in Cosmology.* 2nd edn. London: Barrie & Jenkins, 1973.

—'Pollution', *IESS* 12 (1968), pp. 336-42.

—*Purity and Danger: An Analysis of the Concepts of Pollution and Taboo.* 1966; rpt London/Boston/Henley: Routledge & Kegan Paul, 1979.

Driver, G.R. 'Three Technical Terms in the Pentateuch', *JSS* 1 (1956), pp. 97-105.

Dumezil, G. 'Temps et mythes', *RP* 5 (1935/1936), pp. 235-51.

Dummermuth, F. 'Moses strahlendes Gesicht', *ThZ* 17 (1961), pp. 241-48.

Durkheim, E. *The Elementary Forms of the Religious Life.* Trans. J.W. Swain. 1915; rpt New York/London: The Free Press/Collier Macmillan, 1965.

Durkheim E. and M. Mauss. *Primitive Classification.* Trans. R. Needham. Chicago: University of Chicago Press, 1963.

Dussaud, R. *Les origines cananéenes du sacrifice israélite.* Paris: Ernest Leroux, 1921.

Eaton, J.H. 'Some Questions of Philology and Exegesis in the Psalms', *JThSt* 19 (n.s.), (1968), pp. 603-609.

Eisenbeis, W. *Die Wurzel š-l-m im Alten Testament.* BZAW 113. Berlin: A. Töpelmann, 1969.

Eliade, M. *The Myth of the Eternal Return or Cosmos and History.* Trans. W.R. Trask. Bollingen Series XLVI. Princeton: Princeton University Press, 1954.

—*The Sacred and the Profane: The Nature of Religion.* Trans. W.R. Trask. New York/London: Harcourt Brace Jovanovich, 1959.

Elliger, K. *Leviticus.* HAT 4. Tübingen: J.C.B. Mohr [Paul Siebeck], 1966.

—'Sinn und Ursprung der priesterlichen Geschichtserzählung', *ZThK* 49 (1952), pp. 121-43.

Emerton, J.A. 'The Meaning of אבני־קדש in Lamentations 4,1', *ZAW* 79 (1967), pp. 233-36.

Evans-Pritchard, E.E. 'The Meaning of Sacrifice among the Nuer', *JRAI* 84 (1954), pp. 21-33.

Feldman, E. *Biblical and Post-Biblical Defilement and Mourning: Law as Theology*. LJLE. New York: Yeshiva University Press, KTAV Publishing House, 1977.

Firth, R. 'Offering and Sacrifice: Problems of Organization', *JRAI* 93 (1963), pp. 12-24.

—*Symbols: Public and Private*. SMRit. Ithaca: Cornell University Press, 1973.

Fishbane, M. *Text and Texture: Close Readings of Selected Biblical Texts*. New York: Schocken Books, 1979.

Fraine, J. de. 'Moses 'cornuta facies' (Ex 34.29-35)', *BTFT* 20 (1959), pp. 28-38.

Fretheim, T.E. 'The Theology of the Major Traditions in Genesis-Numbers', *RevExp* 74 (1977), pp. 301-20.

Fritz, V. *Tempel und Zelt: Studien zum Tempelbau in Israel und zu dem Zeltheiligtum der Priesterschrift*. WMANT 47. Neukirchen: Neukirchener Verlag, 1977.

Frymer-Kensky, T. 'Pollution, Purification, and Purgation in Biblical Israel', in *The Word of the Lord Shall Go Forth*. Ed. C.L. Meyers and M. O'Connor. Winona Lake, ID: Eisenbrauns, 1983, pp. 399-414.

Füglister, N. 'Sühne durch Blut—Zur Bedeutung von Leviticus 17,11' in *Studien zum Pentateuch*. Ed. G. Braulik. Wien/Freiburg/Basel: Herder, 1977, pp. 143-64.

Gedo, J.E. and A. Goldberg. *Models of the Mind: A Psychoanalytic Theory*. Chicago/London: University of Chicago Press, 1973.

Geertz, C. 'Blurred Genres: The Refiguration of Social Thought', *AmerSch* 49 (1980), pp. 165-79.

—*The Interpretation of Cultures*. New York: Basic Books/Harper Colophon, 1973.

Gennep, A. van. *The Rites of Passage*. Trans. M.B. Vizedom and G. L. Caffee. Chicago: University of Chicago Press, 1960.

Gerleman, G. *Studien zur alttestamentlichen Theologie*. Heidelberg: Lambert Schneider, 1080.

Girard, R. *Violence and the Sacred*. Trans. P. Gregory. Baltimore/London: Johns Hopkins University Press, 1977.

Gispen, W.H. 'The Distinction between Clean and Unclean', *OTS* 5 (1948), pp. 190-96.

Goody, J. 'Against Ritual', in *Secular Ritual*. Ed. S.F. Moore and B.G. Myerhoff. Amsterdam: van Gorcum, 1977, pp. 25-35.

Görg, M. *Das Zelt der Begegnung: Untersuchung zur Gestalt der sakralen Zelttraditionen Altisraels*. BBB 27. Bonn: Peter Hanstein, 1967.

Gradwohl, R. 'Das 'fremde Feuer' von Nadab und Abihu', *ZAW* 75 (1963), pp. 288-96.

Grainger, R. *The Language of the Rite*. London: Darton, Longman & Todd, 1974.

Gray, G.B. *Numbers*. ICC. 1903; rpt Edinburgh: T.&T. Clark, 1965.

Gressmann, H. *Mose und seine Zeit*. Göttingen: Vandenhoeck und Ruprecht, 1913.

Grimes, R.L. *Beginnings in Ritual Studies*. Lanham/New York/ London: University Press of America, 1982.

Grintz, J.M. '"Do Not Eat on the Blood": Reconsiderations in Setting and Dating of the Priestly Code', *ASTI* 8 (1972), pp. 78-105.

Gurevich, A.J. 'Time as a Problem of Cultural History', in *Cultures and Time*. Ed. L. Gordet et al. Paris: Unesco Press, 1976, pp. 229-45.

Gurvitch, G. *The Spectrum of Social Time*. Dordrecht: D. Reidel, 1964.

Haran, M. 'The Complex of Ritual Acts Performed Inside the Tabernacle', *SH* 8. Ed. C. Rabin. Jerusalem: Magnes Press, 1961, pp. 272-302.

—*Temples and Temple-Service in Ancient Israel: An Inquiry into the Character of Cult Phenomena and the Historical Setting of the Priestly School*. Oxford: Clarendon Press, 1978.

Hayes, J.H. and F. Prussner. *Old Testament Theology: Its History and Development*. Atlanta: John Knox Press, 1985.

Hentschke, R. *Satzung und Setzender. Ein Beitrag zur israelitischen Rechtsterminologie*. BWANT 83. Stuttgart: W. Kolhammer, 1963.

Hermisson, H.-J. *Sprache und Ritus im altisraelitischen Kult. Zur 'Spiritualisierung' der Kultbegriffe im Alten Testament*. WMANT 19. Neukirchen-Vluyn: Neukirchener, 1965.

Hillers, D.R. 'Delocutive Verbs in Biblical Hebrew', *JBL* 86 (1967), pp. 320-24.

Hoffmann, D. *Das Buch Leviticus*. 2 vols. Berlin: M. Poppelauer, 1905-1906.

Horn, H. 'Traditionsschichten in Ex 23,10-33 und Ex 34,10-36', *BZ* (n.s.) 15 (1971), pp. 203-22.

Hubert, H. and M. Mauss. *Sacrifice: Its Nature and Function*. Trans. W.D. Halls. Chicago: University of Chicago Press, 1964.

Hulse, E.V. 'The Nature of Biblical 'Leprosy' and the Use of Alternative Medical Terms in Modern Translations of the Bible', *PEQ* 107 (1975), pp. 87-105.

Hutton, R.R. 'Declaratory Formulae: Forms of Authroitative Pronouncement in Ancient Israel', Ph.D. Dissertation, Claremont Graduate School, Claremont, CA, 1983.

Janowski, B. *Sühne als Heilsgeschehen. Studien zur Sühnetheologie der Priesterschrift und Wurzel KPR im Alten Orient und im Alten Testament*. WMANT 55. Neukirchen-Vluyn: Neukirchener Verlag, 1982.

Jaroš, J. 'Des Mose 'strahlende Haut'. Eine Notiz zu Ex. 34:29,30,35', *ZAW* 88 (1976), pp. 275-80.

Jenkins, I. *Social Order and the Limits of Law*. Princeton: Princeton University Press, 1980.

240   *The Ideology of Ritual*

Jennings, T.W. 'On Ritual Knowledge', *JR* 62 (1982), pp. 111-27.

Jirku, A. 'Die Gesichtsmaske des Mose', *ZDPV* 67 (1944/1945), pp. 43-45.

Kapferer, B. 'Performance and the Structuring of Meaning and Experience', in *The Anthropoloogy of Experience*. Ed. V. Turner and E.M. Bruner. Chicago: University of Illinois, 1986, pp. 188-203.

Kapelrud, A.S. 'Die Theologie der Schöpfung im Alten Testament', *ZAW* 91 (1979), pp. 159-70.

Kaufmann, Y. *The Religion of Israel: From its Beginnings to the Babylonian Exile*. Trans. M. Greenberg. Chicago: University of Chicago Press, 1960.

Kearney, P.J. 'Creation and Liturgy: The P Redaction of Ex 25-40', *ZAW* 89 (1977), pp. 375-87.

Keil, C.F. *Manual of Biblical Archaeology*. 2 vols. Trans. P. Christie. Edinburgh: T. & T. Clark, 1887-1888.

Kiuchi, N. *The Purification Offering in the Priestly Literature: Its Meaning and Function*. JSOTS 5; Sheffield: JSOT, 1987.

Klapp, O.E. *Models of Social Order. An Introduction to Sociological Theory*. Palo Alto, CA: National Press, 1973.

Kliever, L. 'Fictive Religion: Rhetoric and Play', *JAAR* 49 (1981), pp. 657-69.

Knierim, R. *Die Hauptbegriffe für Sünde im Alten Testament*. Gütersloh: Gerd Mohn, 1965.

—'The Messianic Concept in the First Book of Samuel', in *Jesus and the Historian*. Ed. F.T. Trotter. Philadelphia: Westminster, 1968, pp. 20-51.

Koch, K. *Die Priesterschrift von Exodus 25 bis Leviticus 16*. FRLANT (n.s.) 53. Göttingen: Vandenhoeck und Ruprecht, 1959.

Kristensen, W.B. *The Meaning of Religion*. Trans. J.B. Carman. The Hague: Martinus Nijhoff, 1960.

Kroeber, A.L. and T. Parsons, 'The Concepts of Culture and of Social System', *ASR* 23 (1958), pp. 582-83.

Kuschke, A. 'Die Lagervorstellung der priesterschriftlichen Erzählung. Eine überlieferungsgeschichtliche Studie', *ZAW* 63 (1951), pp. 74-105.

Kutsch, E. *Salbung als Rechtsakt im Alten Testament und im alten Orient*. BZAW87. Berlin: A. Töpelmann, 1963.

Labuschagne, C.J. 'The Pattern of the Divine Speech Formulas in the Pentateuch', *VT* 32 (1982), pp. 268-96.

Langer, S.K. *Philosophy in a New Key: A Study in the Symbolism of Reason, Rite, and Art*. 3rd edn. Cambridge, Mass.: Harvard University Press, 1980.

Laughlin, J.C.H. 'The 'Strange Fire' of Nadab and Abihu', *JBL* 95 (1976), pp. 559-65.

Leach, E.R. *Culture and Communication: The Logic by which Symbols are Communicated*. 1976; rpt Cambridge/London/New York: Cambridge University Press, 1982.

—*Genesis as Myth and Other Essays*. London: Jonathan Cape, 1969.

—'Ritual', *IESS* 13 (1968), pp. 520-26.

Leeuw, G. van der. *Religion in Essence and Manifestation: A Study in Phenomenology*. 2 vols. Trans. J.E. Turner. 1938; rpt New York/ Evanston: Harper & Row, 1963.

Levenson, J.D. 'The Theologies of Commandment in Biblical Israel', *HTR* 73 (1980), pp. 17-33.

—*Creation and the Persistence of Evil*. San Francisco: Harper & Row, 1988.

—'The Descriptive Ritual Texts from Ugarit: Some Formal and Functional Features of the Genre', in *The Word of the Lord Shall Go Forth*. Ed. C.L. Meyers and M. O'Connor. Winona Lake, ID: Eisenbrauns, 1983, pp. 467-75.

—'The Descriptive Tabernacle Texts of the Pentateuch', *JOAS* 85 (1965), pp. 307-18.

—*In the Presence of the Lord: A Study of Cult and Some Cultic Terms in Ancient Israel*. SJLA 5. Leiden: E.J. Brill, 1974.

—'On the Presence of God in Biblical Religion', in *Religions in Antiquity*. Ed. J. Neusner. *Numen* Sup. 14. Leiden: E.J. Brill, 1968, pp. 71-87.

Lévi-Strauss, C. *Structural Anthropology*. Trans. C. Jacobson and B.G. Schoepf. New York: Basic Books, 1963.

Lohfink, N. 'Creation and Salvation in Priestly Theology', *TD* 30 (1982), pp. 3-6.

—'Die Priesterschrift und die Geschichte', *VTSup* 29 (1978), pp. 189-225.

—'Die Ursünden in der priesterlichen Geschichtserzählung', in *Die Zeit Jesu*. Ed. G. Bornkamm and K. Rahner. Freiburg: Herder, 1970, pp. 38-57.

Luckmann, T. *The Invisible Religion: The Problem of Religion in Modern Society*. London: Collier-Macmillan, 1967.

Lynch, K. *What Time is This Place?* Cambridge, Mass./London: MIT Press, 1972.

Maass, F. כפר *kpr* pi. sühnen', *THAT* 1 (1971), pp. 842-57.

Maertens, J.T. 'Un Rite de pouvoir: l'imposition des mains, 1', *SR* 6 (1976-1977), pp. 637-49.

Malina, B.J. 'The Individual and the Community Personality in the Social World of Early Christianity', *BTB* 9 (1979), pp. 126-38.

—*The New Testament World: Insights from Cultural Anthropology*. Atlanta: John Knox Press, 1981.

—'The Social Sciences and Biblical Interpretation', *Int* 36 (1982), pp. 229-42.

Mann, T.W. *Divine Presence and Guidance in Israelite Tradition: The Typology of Exaltation*. JHNES. Baltimore/London: Johns Hopkins University Press, 1977.

McCarthy, D.J. 'Further Notes on the Symbolism of Blood and Sacrifice', *JBL* 92 (1973), pp. 205-10.

—'The Symbolism of Blood and Sacrifice', *JBL* 88 (1969), pp. 166-76.

Meeks, W.A. 'Moses as God and King', in *Religions in Antiquity*. Ed. J. Neusner. *Numen* Sup. 14. Leiden: E.J. Brill, 1968, pp. 354-71.

Mettinger, T.N.D. *The Dethronement of Sabaoth. Studies in the Shem and Kabod Theologies*. Trans. F.H. Cryer. CB OT Series 18. Lund: CWK Gleerup, 1982.

Metzinger, A. 'Die Substitutionstheorie und das alttestamentl. Opfer mit besonderer Berücksichtigung von Lev 17,11', *Bib* 21 (1940), pp. 159-87, 247-72, 353-77.

Middleton, J. *Lugbara Religion: Ritual Authority among an East African Tribe*. London: Oxford University Press, 1960.

Milgrom, J. 'The Alleged Wave Offering in Israel and the Ancient Near East', *IEJ* 22 (1972), pp. 33-38.

—'Atonement, Day of', *IDBSup* (1976), pp. 82-83.

—'Atonement in the OT', *IDBSup* (1976), pp. 78-82.

—'The Compass of Biblical Sancta [Lev. 5:15]', *JQR* 65 (1975), pp. 205-16.

—'The Concept of Ma'al in the Bible and the Ancient Near East', *JAOS* 96 (1976), pp. 236-47.

—*Cult and Conscience. The Ashem and the Priestly Doctrine of Repentance*. SJLA 18. Leiden: E.J. Brill, 1976.

—'Cultic שׁגגה and its Influence in Psalms and Job', *JQR* 58 (1967), pp. 115-25.

—'Day of Atonement as Annual Day of Purgation in Biblical Times', *EncJud* 5 (1971), pp. 1385-86.

—'The Graduated *Hatta't* of Lev. 5:1-13', *JAOS* 103 (1983), pp. 249-54.

—'Israel's Sanctuary: The Priestly Picture of Dorian Gray', *RB* 83 (1976), pp. 390-99.

—'Leviticus', *IDBSup* (1976), pp. 541-45.

—'The Paradox of the Red Cow (Num xix)', *VT* 31 (1981), pp. 67-72.

—'Priestly Doctrine of Repentance [Lev. 5:20-26; 6:1-7]', *RB* (1975), pp. 186-205.

—'A Prolegomena to Leviticus 17:11', *JBL* 90 (1971), pp. 149-56.

—'Profane Slaughter and a Formulaic Key to the Composition of Deuteronomy', *HUCA* 47 (1976), pp. 1-17.

—Review of G.J. Wenham, *The Book of Leviticus. JBL* 100 (1981), p. 628.

—'Sacrifices and Offerings, OT', *IDBSup* (1976), pp. 763-771.

—'The Shared Custody of the Tabernacle and a Hittite Analogy', *JAOS* 90 (1970), pp. 204-209.

—*Studies in Cultic Theology and Terminology*. SJLA 36. Leiden: E.J. Brill, 1983.

—*Studies in Levitical Terminology I*. Berkeley: University of California Press, 1970.

—'Two Kinds of *Hatta't*', *VT* 26 (1976), pp. 333-37.

Moberly, R.W.L. *At the Mountain of God: Story and Theology in Exodus 32-34*. JSOT Supp 22. Sheffield: JSOT Press, 1983.

Moerman, D.E. 'Anthropology of Symbolic Healing', *CurAnt* 20 (1979), pp. 59-66.

Moore, S.F. 'Epilogue: Uncertainties in Situations, Indeterminancies in Culture', in *Symbols and Politics in Communal Ideology*. Ed. S.F. Moore and B.G. Myerhoff. Ithaca/London: Cornell University Press, 1975, pp. 210-39.

Moore, S.F. and B.G. Myerhoff, 'Introduction: Secular Ritual: Forms and Meanings', in *Secular Ritual*. Ed. S.F. Moore and B. G. Myerhoff. Amsterdam: van Gorcum, 1977, pp. 3-24.

Moore, W.E. *Man, Time, and Society*. New York/London: John Wiley & Sons, 1963.

Morgan, D.F. 'The So-Called Cultic Calendars in the Pentateuch [Ex 23:10-19; 34:18-26; Lev 23; Num 28-29; Dt 16:1-17]: A Morphological and Typological Study', Ph.D. Dissertation, Claremont Graduate School, Claremont, CA, 1974.

Morgenstern, J. 'Biblical Theophanies', *ZAW* 25 (1911), pp. 139-93.

—'Moses with the Shining Face', *HUCA* 2 (1925), pp. 1-27.

—'The Tent of Meeting', *JAOS* 38 (1918), pp. 125-39.

Napier, B.D. 'Community under Law: On Hebrew Law and its Theological Presuppositions', *Int* 7 (1953), pp. 404-17.

Newing, E.G. 'A Rhetorical and Theological Analysis of the Hexateuch', *SEAJT* 22 (1981), pp. 1-15.

Nilsson, M.P. *Primitive Time-Reckoning*. Lund: J.C.B. Mohr [Paul Siebeck], 1953.

Noth, M. *Exodus*. Trans. J.S. Bowden. OTL. Philadelphia: Westminster, 1962.

—*A History of Pentateuchal Traditions*. Trans. B.W. Anderson. Englewood Cliffs, NJ: Prentice-Hall, 1972.

—*The Laws of the Pentateuch and Other Essays*. Trans. D.R. Ap-Thomas. Philadelphia: Fortress Press, 1966.

—*Leviticus*. Trans. J.E. Anderson. OTL. Rev. edn. Philadelphia: Westminster Press, 1977.

—*Überlieferungsgeschichtliche Studien I. Die sammelnden und bearbeitenden Geschichtswerke im Alten Testament*. Tübingen: Max Niemeyer Verlag, 1943.

Oknuki-Tierney, E. 'Phases in Human Perception/Conception/ Symbolization Processes: Cognitive Anthropology and Symbolic Classification', *AA* 8 (1981), pp. 451-67.

Otto, E. and T. Schramm. *Festival and Joy*. Trans. J.L. Blevins. BES. Nashville: Abingdon, 1980.

Park, R.E. 'Behind Our Masks', *Survey* 56 (1926), pp. 135-39.

Parsons, T. and E. Shils. *Toward a General Theory of Action*. Cambridge, Mass.: Harvard University Press, 1961.

Paschen, W. *Rein und Unrein. Untersuchung zur biblischen Wortgeschichte*. StANT 25. Münich: Kösel-Verlag, 1970.

Pedersen, J. *Israel: Its Life and Culture*. 4 vols. in 2. 1926; rpt London/ Copenhagen: Oxford University Press/Banner Og Korch, 1946.

Pepper, S.C. 'The Order of Time', in *The Problem of Time*. Ed. G.P. Adams, J. Loewenberg, S.C. Pepper. UCPP 18. Berkeley: University of California Press, 1935, p. 3-20.

—*World Hypotheses: A Study in Evidence*. Berkeley: University of California Press, 1961.

Péter, R. 'L'imposition des mains dans l'A.T.', *VT* 27 (1977), pp. 48-55.

Pilch, J.J. 'Biblical Leprosy and Body Symbolism', *BTB* 11 (1981), pp. 108-13.

Plastaras, J. *The God of Exodus: The Theology of the Exodus Narratives*. Milwaukee: Bruce, 1966.

Postal, S.K. 'Body-Image and Identity: A Comparison of Kwakiutl and Hopi', *AA* 67 (1965), pp. 455-62.

Rad, G. von. 'δoξα: כבד in the OT', *TDNT* 2 (1964), pp. 238-42.

—*Genesis*. Trans. J.H. Marks. OTL. Rev. edn. Philadelphia: Westminster, 1972.

—*Old Testament Theology*. 2 vols. Trans. D.M.G. Stalker. New York/ Evanston: Harper & Row, 1962/1965.

Rainey, A.F. 'The Order of Sacrifices in Old Testament Rituals', *Bib* 51 (1970), pp. 485-98.

Rappaport, R.A. *Ecology, Meaning, and Religion*. Richmond, CA: North Atlantic Books, 1979.

Rendtorff, R. 'The Concept of Revelation in Ancient Israel', in *Revelation as History*. Trans. D. Granskou. Ed. W. Pannenberg. London: Collier-Macmillan, 1968, pp. 25-53.

—*Die Gesetze in der Priesterschrift. Eine gattungsgeschichtliche Untersuchung*. FRLANT (n.s.) 48. Göttingen: Vandenhoeck & Ruprecht, 1954.

—*Studien zur Geschichte des Opfers im Alten Testament*. WMANT 24. Neukirchen-Vluyn: Neukirchener Verlag, 1967.

Ricoeur, P. 'The History of Religions and the Phenomenology of Time Consciousness', in *The History of Religions: Retrospect and Prospect*. Ed. J.M. Kitagawa. New York/London: Macmillan/ Collier Macmillan, 1985, pp. 13-30.

—*Interpretation Theory: Discourse and the Surplus of Meaning*. Fort Worth: Texas Christian University Press, 1976.

—'Introduction', in *Culture and Time*. Ed. L. Gordet et al. Paris: Unesco Press, 1976, pp. 13-33.

—'The Narrative Function', *Semeia* 13 (1978), pp. 177-202.

—*The Symbolism of Evil*. Trans. E. Buchanan. Boston: Beacon Press, 1967.

Rigby, P. 'Some Gogo Rituals of 'Purification': An Essay on Social and Moral Categories', in *Dialectic in Practical Religion*. Ed. E.R. Leach. Cambridge: Cambridge University Press, 1968, pp. 153-78.

Rogerson, J.W. 'Sacrifice in the Old Testament: Problems of Method and Approach', in *Sacrifice*. Ed. M.F.C. Bourdillon and M. Fortes. New York: Academic Press, 1980, pp. 45-59.

Rost, L. *Die Vorstufen von Kirche und Synagoge im Alten Testament. Eine wortgeschichtliche Untersuchung*. BWANT 76. Stuttgart: W. Kohlhammer, 1938.

Rowley, H.H. *Worship in Ancient Israel: Its Forms and Meanings.* 1967; rpt London: SPCK, 1976.

Sarna, N.M. 'The Psalm Superscriptions and the Guilds', in *Studies in Jewish Religious and Intellectual History.* Ed. S. Stein and R. Loewe. University, Alabama: University of Alabama Press, 1979, pp. 281-300.

Sasson, J.M. 'Bovine Symbolism in the Exodus Narrative', *VT* 18 (1968), pp. 380-87.

Schechner, R. *Essays on Performance Theory, 1970-1976.* New York: Drama Books, 1977.

Schmid, H.H. *Altorientalische Welt in der alttestamentlichen Theologie.* Zurich: Theologischer Verlag, 1974.

—'Schöpfung, Gerechtigkeit und Heil', *ZThK* 70 (1973), pp. 1-19.

Schmid, R. *Das Bundesopfer in Israel. Wesen, Ursprung, und Bedeutung der alttestamentlichen Schelamim.* Munich: Kösel-Verlag, 1964.

Schmitt, R. *Zelt und Lade als Thema altestamentlicher Wissenschaft. Eine kritische forschungsgeschichtliche Darstellung.* Gerd Mohn: Gutersloher Verlagshaus, 1972.

Schneider, D.M. 'Notes toward a Theory of Culture', in *Meaning in Anthropology.* Ed. K.H. Basso and H.A. Selby. Albuquerque: University of New Mexico Press, 1976, pp. 197-220.

Schötz, P.D. *Schuld- und Sündopfer im alten Testament.* BSHT 18. Breslau: Müller & Seiffert, 1930.

Skorupski, J. *Symbol and Theory: A Philosophical Study of Theories of Religion in Social Anthropology.* Cambridge: Cambridge University Press, 1976.

Smith, J.Z. 'Earth and Gods', *JR* 49 (1969), pp. 103-27.

—*Map is Not Territory: Studies in the History of Religions.* SJLA 23. Leiden: E.J. Brill, 1978.

Smith P. 'Aspects of the Organization of Rites', in *Between Belief and Transgression: Structuralist Essays in Religion, History, and Myth.* Ed. M. Izard and P. Smith. Chicago/London: University of Chicago Press, 1982, pp. 103-28.

Snaith, N.H. *Leviticus and Numbers.* NCB. 1969; rpt Greenwood, S.C.: Attic Press, 1977.

—'Time in the Old Testament', in *Promise and Fulfillment.* Ed. F.F. Bruce. Edinburgh: T.&T. Clark, 1963, pp. 175-86.

—'The Verbs ZABAH and SAHAT', *VT* 25 (1975), pp. 242-46.

Soler, J. 'The Dietary Prohibitions of the Hebrews', *New York Review of Books* 26 (June, 1979), pp. 24-30.

Sorokin, P.A. *Sociocultural Causality, Space, Time: A Study of Referential Principles of Sociology and Social Science.* New York: Russell & Russell, 1964.

Sorokin, P.A. and R.K. Merton, 'Social Time, a Methodological and Functional Analysis', *AJSoc* 42 (1937), pp. 615-29.

Stamm, J.J. *Erlösen und Vergeben im alten Testament. Eine begriffsgeschichtliche Untersuchung.* Bern: A. Franke, 1940.

—'Zur Frage der Imago Dei im Alten Testament [Gen 1:26f.; Ps. 8:6-9]', in *Humanität und Glaube. Gedenkschrift für Kurt Guggisberg*. Ed. U. Neuenschwander and R. Dellspergen. Bern/Stuttgart: Paul Haupt, 1973, pp. 243-53.

Steck, O.H. *Der Schöpfungsbericht der Priesterschrift. Studien zur literarkritischen und überlieferungsgeschichtlichen Problematik von Genesis 1,1–2,4a*. FRLANT 115. Göttingen: Vandenhoeck und Ruprecht, 1975.

—*World and Environment*. BES. Nashville: Abingdon Press, 1980.

Steinmueller, J.E. 'Sacrificial Blood in the Bible', *Bib* 40 (1959), pp. 556-67.

Stuhlmueller, C. 'Leviticus: The Teeth of Divine Will into the Smallest Expectations of Human Courtesy', *BibT* 88 (1977), pp. 1082-88.

Suhr, E. 'The Horned Moses', *Folklore* 74 (1963), pp. 387-95.

Sullivan, H.P. 'Ritual: Attending to the World', *ATR* 57, supp. 5 (1975), pp. 9-32.

Sullivan, L.E. 'Sound and Senses: Toward a Hermeneutics of Performance', *HR* 26 (1986), pp. 1-33.

Talmon, S. 'The 'Desert Motif', in *Biblical Motifs: Origins and Transformations*. Ed. A. Altmann. Cambridge, Mass.: Harvard University Press, 1966, pp. 31-63.

—'Wilderness', *IDBSup* (1976), pp. 946-48.

Tawil, H. ''Azazel the Prince of the Steepe: A Comparative Study', *ZAW* 92 (1980), pp. 43-59.

Thompson, L.T. 'The Jordan Crossing: *Sidqot* Yahweh and World Building', *JBL* 100 (1981), pp. 343-58.

Tsevat, M. 'The Basic Meaning of the Biblical Sabbath', *ZAW* 84 (1972), pp. 447-59.

Turner, T.S. 'Transformation, Hierarchy and Transcendence: A Reformulation of van Gennep's Model of the Structure of Rites de Passage', in *Secular Ritual*. Ed. S.F. Moore and B.G. Myerhoff. Assen: van Gorcum, 1977, pp. 53-70.

Turner, V. 'The Anthropology of Performance', in *Process, Performance, and Pilgrimage: A Study in Comparative Symbology*. RAS 1. New Delhi: Concept, 1979, pp. 60-93.

—*Dramas, Fields, and Metaphors*. SMRit. Ithaca/London: Cornell University Press, 1974.

—*The Forest of Symbols: Aspects of Ndembu Ritual*. Ithaca/London: Cornell University Press, 1967.

—*The Ritual Process: Structure and Antistructure*. SMRit. 1969; rpt Ithaca: Cornell University Press, 1979.

—*From Ritual to Theatre: The Human Seriousness of Play*. New York: Performing Arts Journal Publications, 1982.

—'Sacrifice as Quintessential Process: Prophylazis or Abandonment?' *HR* 16 (1977), pp. 189-215.

—'The Waters of Life: Some Reflections on Zionist Water Symbolism', in *Religions in Antiquity*. Ed. J. Neusner. *Numen* Sup 14. Leiden: E.J. Brill, 1968, pp. 506-20.

Vaux, R. de. *Studies in Old Testament Sacrifice*. Cardiff: University of Wales Press, 1964.

Vriezen, Th. C. 'The Term *hizza*: Lustration and Consecration', *OTS* 7 (1950), pp. 201-35.

Wefing, S. 'Beobachtung zum Ritual mit der roten Kuh (Num 19,1-10a)', *ZAW* 93 (1981), pp. 342-59.

Weinfeld, M. *Deuteronomy and the Deuteronomic School*. Oxford: Oxford University Press, 1972.

Wellhausen, J. *Prolegomena to the History of Israel*. Trans. J.S. Black and A. Menzies. Gloucester, Mass.: Peter Smith, 1973.

Wenham, G.J. *The Book of Leviticus*. NICOT. Grand Rapids: Eerdmans, 1979.

—'Why Does Sexual Intercourse Defile (Lev 15.18)?' *ZAW* 95 (1983), pp. 432-34.

Westermann, C. *Genesis 1–11*. Trans. J.J. Scullion. Minneapolis: Augsburg, 1984.

—'Die Herrlichkeit Gottes in der Priesterschrift', in *Wort–Gebot–Glaube. Beiträge zur Theologie des Alten Testaments*. Ed. H.J. Stoebe, J.J. Stamm, and E. Jenni. Zurich: Zwingli Verlag, 1970, pp. 227-45.

Wheelock, T.W. 'The Problem of Ritual Language: From Interpretation to Situation', *JAAR* 50 (1982), pp. 49-71.

Wildberger, H. 'צלם *saelem* Abbild', *THAT* 2 (1976), pp. 556-63.

Wilkinson, J. 'Leprosy and Leviticus: The Problem of Description and Identification', *SJT* 30 (1977), pp. 153-69.

—'Leprosy and Leviticus: A Problem of Semantics and Translation', *SJT* 31 (1978), pp. 153-66.

Wold, D.J. 'The KARETH Penalty in P: Rationale and Cases', in *SBLSP* 1979, vol. 1. Ed. P.J. Achtemeier. Missoula: Scholars Press, 1979, pp. 1-25.

Wolff, H.W. *Anthropology of the Old Testament*. Trans. M. Kohl. Philadelphia: Fortress Press, 1974.

—'The Day of Rest in the Old Testament', *LTQ* 7 (1972), pp. 65-76.

Wright, D.P. 'The Disposal of Impurity in the Priestly Writings of the Bible with Reference to Similar Phenomena in Hittite and Mesopotamian Cultures', Ph.D. Dissertation. University of California, Berkeley, CA, 1984.

Würthwein, E. 'Chaos und Schöpfung im mythischen Denken und in der biblischen Urgeschichte', in *Zeit und Geschichte*. Ed. E. Dinkler. Tübingen: J.C.B. Mohr [Paul Siebeck], 1964, pp. 317-27.

Wuthnow, R. *Meaning and Moral Order: Explorations in Cultural Analysis*. Berkeley: University of California Press, 1987.

Zuesse, E.M. 'Meditation on Ritual', *JAAR* 43 (1975), pp. 517-30.

—'Taboo and the Divine Order', *JAAR* 42 (1974), pp. 482-504.

INDEXES

INDEX OF BIBLICAL REFERENCES

Genesis		*Exodus*			
1.1–2.4a	39, 43, 47, 49, 112, 138, 138n1, 147n1, 218, 219, 220, 225, 226, 230,231	4.11	57	28.2	118n3
		4.42	57	28.4	67n2, 108, 118n3
		12.14	66n1		
		12.15	194n1		
		12.17	66n1	28.5-39	107
		12.37– Num. 25.18	98	28.38	125n1
				28.39-40	108
				28.41	128
				28.42	67, 108
				28.43	66n1
1.1	44n1	16.7	145	29	104, 105, 106, 209
1.2	99	16.10	145		
1.4	40, 138n1	23:38	145	29.2-3	110
1.6-7	138n1	24.15-18	46, 145	29.10	96
1.7	40	24.15	45	29.21	84
1.9	40	25-31	43, 46, 47, 50	29.23	110
1.14	41, 138n1	25.1	47	29.28	129
1.18	41, 138n1	25.6	174n3	29.9	66n1, 128
1.29-30	181	25.8-9	47, 48	29.32	110
2	44n1	25.8	145	29.35-37	112
2.2-3	221	25.9	47n1, 144	29.35	58, 224
2.2	48	25.16	68n2	29.37	224
6.12b	182n1	25.21-22	144	29.38-46	47, 220
8.11-13	126n1	25.22	47, 56, 68n2	29.38-42	127n3, 137
8.13	112	25.40	47n1, 144		
9.1-7	181	26.30	47n1	29.42	43
9.4-6	189	26.31-33	56	29.43-46	42, 220
9.4-5	185n2	26.33	56	29.43-45	209
9.4	181, 181n2, 187	26.34	56	29.45	48
		27.8	47n1	30.1-10	70
		27.20	107, 174n3	30.6-9	70
9.5	181	27.21	66n1	30.7-8	56, 107
25.30	202n6	28	67, 91	30.11	47
48.14	96			30.17-21	69n3

30.17	47	40.23	48	4.7	49, 57, 88
30.18-21	116	40.25	48	4.11-12	81n2
30.22-33	118	40.26-27	70	4.12	207, 210
30.22	47	40.27	48	4.16-18	80, 122
30.23-33	109	40.29	48, 57	4.17-18	85, 86
30.25	109	40.30-32	116	4.17	83, 85
30.26-28	109	40.32	48	4.18	57, 88
30.29	109	40.33	44n1, 48	4.21	81n2
30.30	109, 118	40.34-38	48	4.22-26	122
30.31	118	40.34-35	145	4.24	96
30.33	194n1			4.25	80, 85, 88
30.34-38	70	*Leviticus*		4.27-31	122, 156
31.1	47	1–7	46, 48, 50, 123n2, 154	4.27	202
31.12-17	222			4.29	96
31.12	47			4.30	80, 85, 88
31.14	194n1			4.33-34	122
32-34	146	1–5	46	4.33	96
32.25-29	128	1.1-13	156	4.34	85, 88
32.29	128	1.1-2	49	5.5	91
33.1-17	46	1.3-17	46	5.6	202
33.7-11	143n3	1.3	49, 57, 125n1, 202	5.9	86
34	47			5.11	174n3
34.27-28	143n1			5.14-26	46, 176
34.29-35	141-49	1.4	96, 124, 125n1	5.14	44
34.29-33	143			5.17-19	176
34.29	142, 142n6, 143n6	1.5-9	35n1	5.20-26	176
		1.5	49	6-7	46
		1.10	202	6.1-6	46
34.30	142	1.11	49	6.1	49
34.31	143n6	1.15	86	6.4	210
34.33-35	142	2	155	6.4b	207
34.34-35	143, 144	2.1-16	46	6.7-11	46, 155
34.32	143n6	2.1	70, 174n3	6.8	49, 70
34.33	143n6	2.6	174n3	6.12-16	46
34.34	143, 143n2, 143n6	2.15	70, 174n3	6.17-23	46
		3.1-17	46	6.19	49
		3.1	185, 202	6.21	165
34.35	142, 143n6	3.2	49, 96	6.23	81
		3.6	49, 185, 202	6.24	49
35-40	46, 48, 144			7.1-10	46
35-39	106	3.8	96	7.1-7	176
35.14	174n3	3.12	49, 185	7.11-18	46, 136
39.1-31	107	3.13	96	7.12-17	129n2
39.28	108	3.16-17	124	7.18	125n1
39.32	44n1	3.17	66n1	7.19-38	46
39.37	174n3	4.1-5.13	46	7.22-27	124
40.2	112	4.2-7	122	7.22	49
40.17-33	48, 50	4.3	202	7.25	194n1
40.19	48	4.4	49, 85, 96	7.27	194n1
40.20	68n2	4.5-7	80	7.28-36	124
40.21	48	4.6-7	85, 86	7.28	49
		4.6	83	7.36	66n1

Reference	Pages	Reference	Pages	Reference	Pages
7.37-38	49	8.17	49, 104, 111, 124	10	46, 50
8–9	46, 48, 49	8.18-21	110, 114, 121, 124	10.1-3	64, 65
8	10, 49, 50, 54, 80, 84, 100, 103-39, 141, 163, 174, 175, 177n2, 178, 209, 212	8.18	125	10.1	70
		8.19	108, 110, 125	10.2	64
		8.20-21	109, 110	10.6	126n1, 132, 162
		8.20	125	10.7	50, 120n1
		8.21	49, 104, 109, 125	10.8-11	51
		8.22-29	114, 121, 128, 129	10.9	66n1
8.1-4	49, 115	8.22-26	110	10.10-11	138n1
8.1-2	115	8.23-24	110	10.10	44, 161, 193n2, 207, 220
8.2-4	113	8.23	173		
8.2	107, 110	8.24	108, 111n1, 173	11–15	47, 51, 153
8.3	21, 49, 111	8.25-28	110	11	47, 164, 188n1
8.4	21, 49, 104, 111	8.25-27	110	11.24	193n2
8.5-12	117-18	8.25-26	109	11.33	165
8.5-6	113	8.26	110, 174n3	11.39-40	187
8.6	109, 111n1, 116-17	8.28	109	11.44	126n2
8.7-9	107, 109, 113	8.29	49, 104, 110, 124	12	47
8.9	49, 104	8.30	84, 108, 115, 135, 174	12.2	58, 112n1, 137, 197
8.10-12	109, 113, 135	8.31-36	115, 136	12.3	159
8.10	83, 108, 109, 119	8.31-32	136	13-14	47, 162
8.11	83, 84, 108, 109, 119, 119n1, 120	8.31	110, 111	13	47, 152, 156n2, 162
		8.33-35	58, 158	13.6	156n2
		8.33	49, 111, 112, 122, 128, 136	13.13	156n2
8.12	109, 119, 119n1, 120	8.34-35	136	13.17	156n2
		8.34	137	13.23	156n2
		8.35	111, 136	13.28	156n2
8.13	13, 49, 104, 108, 120	8.36	49, 104, 50, 54, 123n2, 209	13.34	156n2
		9		13.45-46	151
8.14-17	110, 113, 121	9.1	159	13.45	132, 162
8.14-15	86, 87	9.4	50	13.46	131, 157
8.14	96, 121	9.5-6	145	13.59	156n2
8.15	85, 87, 108, 110, 122	9.6	50	14	47, 83, 84, 131, 151-79, 195, 212
		9.7	124	14.1-20	10, 26, 32, 35, 152, 153, 154
		9.22-24	64n3		
8.15b	87	9.23-24	50, 145	14.1-9	163-172
8.16	109	9.24	64n3	14.1	153
				14.1b	156n1
				14.2-9	154

Reference	Pages
14.2b-4	159
14.2	152
14.2b	161, 162
14.3	157, 161
14.3b	156
14.4	155
14.5-8	159
14.5	154, 165, 166n4
14.6-7	155, 156
14.6	154
14.7	84, 85, 155, 156, 169, 170
14.7b	158
14.8-14	131
14.8-9	224
14.8	58, 112n1, 116, 137, 154, 156, 157, 158
14.9	58, 116, 154, 156, 160
14.10-20	154, 172-78
14.10	155, 160, 172, 202
14.11-20	160
14.11	57, 156n3, 160, 172
14.11b	158
14.12-18	160-61
14.12	155, 160, 172
14.13	154, 160
14.14-18	135, 173
14.14	85, 156, 160
14.15-18	131, 155, 173
14.15-18a	160-161
14.15	85
14.16	83, 84
14.17	155
14.18b	161
14.19-20a	161
14.19	173
14.19a	155
14.20	124, 156, 173
14.20b	161
14.23	57
14.27	83, 84
14.40	32, 207
14.41	207
14.44	35
14.45	207
14.49	155n1
14.50	165
14.51	84, 84, 85, 155n1, 166n4
14.52	155n1
14.53	170
15	47, 166n2, 67n2
15.2-3	185n1
15.2	116
15.5	116
15.6	116
15.7	67n2, 116
15.8	116
15.10	116
15.11	116
15.12	165
15.13	58, 112n1, 116, 137, 165, 224
15.14	57, 159
15.16	116
15.17	165
15.18	41n4, 116
15.19	58, 112n1, 137, 224
15.20	197
15.21	116
15.22	116
15.24	58, 112n1, 137, 197, 224
15.25	197
15.26	197
15.27	116
15.28	58, 137, 224
15.29	159
15.31	50, 79
15.33	197
16	10, 36, 36n1, 47, 51, 56, 57, 61-102, 106, 109, 111, 116, 117, 121, 137, 162, 164, 166n3, 169, 170, 171, 195
16.1-28	65, 67, 72
16.1-3a	63, 74
16.1-2	64, 65
16.1	64, 65
16.2	56, 68, 73, 92
16.3b-5	74
16.4	67, 69, 116, 117
16.5	97
16.6	74
16.7-10	74
16.7-8	95
16.7	57, 74
16.8	74
16.9	74
16.10	74, 95, 97
16.11-19	69, 74
16.11-14	74
16.11a	74
16.11b	74
16.12-13	64, 74
16.12	70, 74
16.13	68n2, 70, 74
16.13b	89
16.14-16a	87
16.14	74, 83, 84, 87, 88, 90
16.15-16a	74
16.15	74, 84, 87
16.16	51, 69, 81, 82
16.16a	74, 87
16.16b-19	75
16.16b	75, 87
16.18-19	69, 87
16.18a	87
16.18b-19	87

16.18	75		186n1	22.27	125n1,
16.19	75, 84,	17.5	170,		159n1
	85, 86, 87		186n1	22.29-30	129n2
16.19b	87	17.7	66n1, 97,	22.29	125n1
16.20-22	75, 95		185,	23.11	125n1
16.20	69, 75		186n1	23.14	66n1
16.21	35n1, 75,	17.8-9	186	23.21	66n1
	91, 94,	17.8	185,	23.29	194n1
	96, 121		186n1	23.31	66n1
16.21b	95	17.10-12	186-88	23.36	159n1
16.23-24	75, 90	17.10	185, 186	23.38	125n1
16.23	75	17.11	181, 183,	23.39	159n1
16.24	69, 75,		183n1,	23.41	66n1
	100, 116,		184, 186,	24.2	107
	117, 124		187, 189	24.3	66n1
16.25-28	75	17.12	186	24.5-9	108
16.25	71, 75	17.13-16	187-89	24.15	185n1
16.26-28	100	17.13-14	187	26	224n2
16.26	70, 75,	17.13	185, 186,	26.18	224n2
	100, 116		187	26.21	224n2
16.27-28	210n1	17.14	181, 183,	26.24	224n2
16.27	70, 75,		187, 188	26.28	224n2
	101	17.15-16	187	26.34-39	224n2
16.28	75, 116,	17.15	116, 187	26.40	91
	210n1	17.16	116	27-28	72
16.29-34	52, 63,	17.18	125n1		
	66, 71	18.5	185n1	*Numbers*	
16.29-31	91	18.11-12	118	1.53	126n1
16.29-30	63	18.24-30	224n2	3.3	128
16.29	63, 66n1,	19	166n2	4.4	56
	72, 73	19.5	125n1	4.19	56
16.30	52	19.7	125n1	5.2	195
16.31	63, 66n1,	20.2	185n1	5.3b	126n2
	72, 73	20.3	51, 79	5.7	91
16.32	63, 71,	20.9	185n1	5.11-22	197n1
	128	21.10-12	120n1	5.17	165
16.33-34	63	21.10-11	132	5.19	185n1
16.33	52, 63	21.10	128	6.9-12	176n4
16.34	45, 63,	21.11	120n1	6.9-10	58
	66n1, 73	21.12	120n1	6.10	159
16.34b	66	22.4	185n1	6.14	156, 202
17.1-2	184	22.6	116	6.15	110
17.3-16	184	22.18	185n1	6.17	110
17.3-9	185,	22.19	125n1	6.19	110
	185n4,	22.20	125n1,	7.89	56
	188		202	8.7	85, 197n1
17.3-7	184,	22.21-23	129n2	8.10	96
	186n1	22.21	125n1,	8.12	96
17.3-4	185		202	9.10	185n1
17.3	185	22.23	125n1	9.13	194n1
17.4	185,	22.25	125n1,	10	56
	185n3,		202	10.8	66n1

12.10-12	132	19.9-10	196, 200	27.11	66n1
12.10	132	19.9	32, 167,	27.18	96
12.12	132		198, 199,	27.23	96
14.10	145		203, 207,	28-29	10, 34,
15.15	66n1		210		55,
16-18	133	19.10	66n1,		127n3,
16.5	133		198, 199,		155, 215-
16.6	70		206		27
16.19	145	19.11-16	193, 195	28.1-2	216
16.22	126n1	19.11-13	193	28.2	216, 218
17.5	133	10.11-12	193	28.3-8	216, 219
17.6-15	133	19.11	58, 112,	28.6	220
17.11-12	70		137, 193,	28.9-10	216, 221
17.11	126n1,		224	28.11-15	216
	134	19.12	58, 193,	28.16	216
17.13	134		224	28.17-25	216
17.16-28	134	19.12a	193	28.26-31	216
17.27-28	134	19.12b	193	29.7-11	216
18	134	19.13	191, 193,	29.12-38	216
18.5	126n1		195	31.9	58
18.7	134	19.14-16	194, 196,	31.23	197n1
18.9	56		211	35.29	66n1
18.10	56	19.14-15	194		
18.23	66n1	19.14	58,	*Deuteronomy*	
19	10, 155,		112n1,	12.23	181n1
	162, 163,		194, 224	21.1-9	202n3
	166n2,	19.15	194	34.9	96
	167, 191-	19.16	58,		
	214		112n1,	*Joshua*	
19.1-10	193		194, 224	19.51	44n1
19.1-6	216	19.17-19	193, 197,	13.19	155
19.2-10	201-11		201, 211-		
19.2b-3b	200		14	*Judges*	
19.3	195, 198,	19.17	162, 166,	13.23	155
	199		203		
19.3bβ-6	200	19.18-19	199	*1 Samuel*	
19.3bβ-4	200	19.18	85, 169,	10.1	174
19.3b	198		196, 197,	16.13	174
19.4	84, 198,		211		
	199, 204	19.19	85, 116,	*2 Samuel*	
19.5-6	200, 205		196, 198,	14.2	174
19.5	197		199, 211,		
19.5a	198		224	*1 Kings*	
19.6	162	19.20	51, 79,	1.39	174
19.7-10	200, 206		191	8.64	155
19.7	116, 196,	19.21	66n1,		
	198, 199,		196,	*2 Kings*	
	200, 206		201n1	3.22	202n6
19.8	116, 198,	20.4	98	9.3	174
	199, 200,	20.5	98	9.6	174
	206,	20.13	79	16.13	155
	210n1	24.14	96	16.15	155

2 Chronicles
26.16-19   177

Psalms
23.5   174
45.8   174
51.9   155n1
104.15   174
133.2   174

Proverbs
27.9   174

Ecclesiastes
9.8   174

Canticles
5.10   202n6

Isaiah
34.9-16   98
61.3   174
63.2   202n6

Jeremiah
2.34   181n1
4.23-26   99

Ezekiel
16.5   170
16.26   67n2

23.20   67n2
29.5   170
32.4   170
33.27   170
39.5   170

Habakkuk
3.4   146

Zechariah
1.8   202n6
6.2   202n6

INDEX OF AUTHORS

Abrahams, I. 32n3
Andreasen, N.-E.A. 221n1
Arinze, F.A. 78n2

Baal, J. van 97n5, 203n2
Baaren, T.P. van 67n1, 78n1, 97n5, 203n2
Bailey, L.R. 142n1
Barbour, I.G. 30n1
Barr, J. 226n1
Bean, S.S. 10n1, 151n1
Beauchamp, P. 220n1
Begrich, J. 194n2
Berger, P.L. 32n2, 33n2
Beyerlin, W. 141n2
Blenkinsopp, J. 42n1, 44n1, 48n1, 112, 144n2
Bollnow, O.F. 32n1,n2
Brenner, A. 197n3, 202n5
Brichto, H.C. 183n1, 184
Brown, J.P. 146n5
Browne, S.G. 153n3
Brueggemann, W. 40n1
Budd, P.J. 202n1
Buss, M.J. 21n1, 193n2

Carney, T.F. 30n1
Carroll, R.P. 82n1
Casalis, M. 40n4
Cazalles, H. 207n2
Childs, B.S. 128n4, 141-42n4, 142n2, 145n1
Clements, R.E. 145n1
Clifford, R.J. 144n1
Coats, G.W. 146n2
Cody, A. 128
Cohn, R.L. 71n1, 98, 105n3, 148
Colby, B.N. 16n4
Comstock, W.R. 20n1, 65n1
Crites, S. 15n2
Cross, F.M. 145n1

Daniel, S. 130n1

Davies, D. 91n2, 99n3
Dilthey, W. 16n2
Döller, J. 207n2
Dougherty, J.W.D. 16n4
Douglas, M. 9, 10n1, 27n2, 40n3, 41n2,n4, 65n1, 79n2, 90n1, 92, 151n2, 167n1
Driver, G.R. 97n1
Dumezil, G. 226n2
Dummermuth, F. 141n3,n4
Durkheim, E. 14n2, 40n3
Dussaud, R. 130n4

Eaton, J.H. 156n4
Eisenbeis, W. 130n4
Eliade, M. 32n1, 33n4, 62n1, 134n3
Elliger, K. 8n3, 63n1, 64n1, 66n2, 106, 153n2, 154n2, 162n1, 183n1, 184n4
Emerton, J.A. 156n4
Evans-Pritchard, E.E. 78n1, 96n2, 121n5, 203n2

Feldman, E. 132, 197n2
Fernandez, J.W. 16n4
Firth, R. 23n1, 97n5, 202n3, 203n2
Fishbane, M. 40n2, 42n1,n2, 220n1
Fraine, J. de 142n1
Fretheim, T.E. 106n1
Fritz, V. 69n2
Frymer-Kensky, T. 126n3, 132n1, 137n1, 164n1, 191-92n2, 199n1, 224-25n2
Füglister, N. 183n1

Gedo, J.E. 22n3
Geertz, C. 9,15n1, 16n1, 17, 19n2, 22n4, 23, 25n1, 29, 31n2, 41n5, 217n4, 219
Gennep, A.van 53, 90nn1,2, 134n3
Gerleman, G. 77n1
Girard, R. 182
Gispen, W.H. 207n2
Goldberg, A. 22n3
Goody, J. 18n4

Gorg, M. 69n2
Gradwohl, G. 64n4
Grainger, R. 21n1, 22nn1,2, 33n4
Gray, G.B. 191n1, 195n2, 202nn2,4, 224n1
Gressmann, H. 141n4, 142n1
Grimes, R.L. 18n4, 19n2, 20nn1,4, 25n3, 27n4, 31n3, 34n2, 118n2
Grintz, J.M. 183n1
Gurevich, A.J. 33n2, 218n1
Gurvitch, G. 33n2

Haran, M. 8, 32n3, 56nn1,2, 65n2, 67n3, 68n2, 70, 107-108, 145n1
Hayes, J.H. 8n1
Hentschke, R. 66n1
Hermisson, H.-J. 156-57n4
Hillers, D.R. 156-57
Hoffmann, D. 97n3
Horn, H. 141n4
Hubert, H. 122n1, 203n2
Hulse, G.V. 153n3
Hurowitz, V. 42n1
Hutton, R.R. 82, 126n2, 176n5

Janowski, B. 76n1
Jaroš, K. 141n4, 146n2
Jenkins, I. 26n2
Jennings, T.W. 15n1, 27n3
Jirku, A. 141n4

Kapelrud, A.S. 42n2
Kapferer, B. 20n4
Kaufmann, Y. 36n2
Kearney, P.J. 42n1, 47
Keil, C.F. 118n1
Kiuchi, N. 73n1
Klapp, D.E. 16n1
Kliever, L. 15n2
Knierim, R. 82, 118n4
Koch, K. 105n1, 106n2, 154n1
Kornfeld, D.B. 16n4
Kristensen, B.W. 27n5
Kroeber, A.L. 23n1
Kuschke 145n1
Kutsch, E. 118n4

Labuschagne, C.J. 47n1
Langer, S.K. 23n1
Laughlin, J.C.B. 64n4
Leach, E.L. 14n1, 40n4, 96n2, 118n2, 121n2

Leeuw, G. van der 27n5, 32n1, 33n4
Levenson, J. 40nn1,2, 42n2
Levi-Strauss, C. 22n3
Levine, B. 8, 76n1, 77nn1,2, 78-79, 97n1, 104, 105, 106, 127, 129n1, 130, 153, 183, 184
Lohfink, N. 42n1, 106n1, 126n1
Luckmann, T. 16nn1,3, 32n2, 33n2
Lynch, K. 27n4, 33n2, 218n1

Maass, F. 67n1
Malina, B.J. 30n1, 151n1
Mann, T.W. 71n1, 142
Maertens, J.T. 96n1
Mauss, M. 40n3, 122n1, 203n2
McCarthy, D.J. 135n1, 197n2
Meeks, W.A. 141-42n4
Merton, R.K. 27n5, 33nn2,3, 218n1
Mettinger, T.N.D. 68n2, 145nn1,2
Metzinger, A. 183nn1,3
Middleton, J. 78n2, 203n2
Milgrom, J. 8, 32-33n3, 46n3, 56n1, 56-57n2, 61n1, 76-80, 81nn1,2, 82n1, 83n2, 87, 96, 97n1, 98n1, 114n1, 121n3, 124nn2,3, 125n1, 126nn1,2, 127n4, 133nn1,2 134nn1,2, 137-38, 154n1, 164nn1,2, 167n2, 176-77, 183, 184, 195, 197n2, 198n1, 202, 203nn1,3, 204-205, 207n3, 208nn1,2, 210n1
Moberly, R.W.L. 141n3, 142nn2,4, 143n2, 146
Moerman, E. 151n1
Moore, S.F. 14n2, 14n3, 17n4, 18n1,n4, 19n2, 25n2, 26n2, 27nn1,3
Moore, W.E. 27n5, 33n2, 218nn1,3
Morgan, D.F. 216nn1,2
Morgenstern, J. 141nn3,4, 145n1
Myerhoff, B.G. 14n2, 17n4, 18nn1,4, 19n2, 25n2, 26n2, 27n1

Napier, B.D. 42n2
Newing, E.G. 46n1
Nilsson, M.P. 223n1
Noth, M. 8n3, 61n1, 63n1, 64n1, 66n3, 105n1, 106, 109n1, 118-19n4, 128n4, 141n3, 142n3, 143n3, 145n1, 153n2, 154nn1,2, 162n1, 164n2, 175n1, 195n2

Ohnuki-Tierney, E. 16n4
Otto, E. 66n3

Park, R.E. 20n4
Parsons, T. 23n1
Paschen, W. 132-33n3
Pedersen, J. 98n5, 191n1
Pepper, S.-C. 16n1, 33n2, 218n1
Peter, R. 96nn1,2,3
Pilch, J. 151-52n2
Plastaras, J. 141n2
Postal, S.K. 151n2
Prussner, F. 8n1

Rad, G. von 40, 132n3, 145n1
Rainey, A.F. 129n1
Rappaport, R. 9, 14n1, 14n2, 15n1,
   17nn1,4, 18n4, 19n1, 20n1, 21n1,
   22n1, 25n2, 26n1, 27n2, 28n2, 34n1,
   217, 218n4
Rendtorff, R. 66n2, 105n1, 106n2,
   125n2, 130, 146n1, 193n1, 195n2
Rocoeur, P. 15n2, 23n1, 33n4, 78n2,
   218n2, 226n1
Rigby, P. 10n1, 17n3
Ringgren, H. 125n2
Rogerson, J.W. 31n1, 37n1
Rost, L. 145n1
Rowley, H.H. 127n1

Sarna, N.M. 36n2
Sasson, M. 141n4, 146
Schechner, R. 20n4
Schmid, H.H. 40n1
Schmid, R. 130n4
Schmitt, R. 145n1,n2
Schneider, D. 19n2, 23n1
Schotz, P.D. 77n3, 176n4
Schramm, T. 66n3
Skorupski, J. 23n1
Smith, J.Z. 32n1, 40n1
Smith, P. 19n1, 27n4
Snaith, N.H. 97n4, 109n1, 128, 163n1,
   202n5, 203n1, 216n2, 219n1
Soler, J. 41n2, 220n1
Sorokin, P.A. 27nn4,5, 28n1, 32n2,
   33nn2,3, 218n1

Stamm, J.J. 77n3, 147n1
Steck, D.H. 147n1, 182n2, 218n5
Steinmueller, J.E. 183n3
Stuhlmueller, C. 96n2
Suhr, E. 141n4
Sullivan, H.P. 15nn1,2, 22n4, 27n1
Sullivan, L.E. 15n1

Talmon, S. 97n1, 98n5
Tawil, H. 97n1, 99
Thompson, L.T. 98n3
Tsevat, M. 221n1
Turner, T. 25n2, 27n1, 28n2
Turner, V. 9, 14n3, 15n1, 16n2, 16n3,
   18nn2,3,4, 19n2, 20-21, 22nn1,4, 24,
   27n2, 29n2, 29n4, 53-54, 90n1,
   91nn1,3, 92n1, 97n5, 98, 149, 166n3,
   197n2, 203n2, 218n4

Vaux, R. de 96n2, 121n4, 130n2,
   141n3, 176n4, 183
Vriezen, T.C. 83n2, 84n1

Wefing, S. 193n1, 195n1, 197n1, 206n1
Wellhausen, J. p.8
Wenham, G.J. 9, 41n4, 46n3, 61n1,
   96n2, 97n3, 109n1, 125nn1,3, 130n3,
   136n1, 137n2, 164nn1,2, 175n1,
   183n1, 208n1
Westermann, C. 40-41, 126n1, 145n1,
   181nn2,3, 220n1, 221
Wheelock, T.W. 15nn1,2
Wienfeld, M. 145n1
Wildberger, H. 147n1
Wilkinson, J. 153n3
Wold, D.J. 191n2, 192n2
Wolff, H.W. 135n1, 185n2, 221n1
Wright, D.P. 72n1, 83n1, 98n1, 164n1,
   165n1
Würthwein, E. 126n3
Wuthnow, R. 14n1, 20n4, 22n4

Zuesse, E.M. 15nn1,2, 20n1, 27n4,
   65n1, 79n2, 134n3, 151n1